60, 62, 63, 69, 70
79, 81, 82, 89

Politics and the Economy in Jordan

Jordan occupies centre stage in both Middle-Eastern and Arab politics, yet the Kingdom itself is comparatively under-researched. This volume contains contributions from some of Jordan's most respected academics in the fields of geography, economics and political science. A number of international specialists in Jordan have also made valuable contributions.

The book covers important aspects of the Jordanian economic and political scene that have not yet been written about in English. Aspects of Jordan's consumer society are examined, including the question of foreign aid support, the role of the private sector, and the demand for consumer durables. The economic vulnerability which an open consumer faces, so apparent recently in Jordan, is illustrated in the chapter on the balance of payments and inflation.

The contributors argue that Jordan has exhibited a certain economic resilience, despite economic and political problems, and that a national identity has been successfully fostered.

The editor, Rodney Wilson, is a Senior Lecturer in Economics at the University of Durham. He has researched and written extensively on Jordan's financial sector and on Jordan's foreign trade.

Routledge/SOAS Politics and Culture in the Middle East Series

Edited by Tony Allan, Centre for Near and Middle Eastern Studies, School of Oriental and African Studies

Egypt under Mubarak
Edited by Charles Tripp and Roger Owen

Turkish State, Turkish Society
Edited by Andrew Finkel and Nukhel Sirman

Forthcoming:

Modern Literature in the Middle East
Edited by Robin Ostle

Politics and the Economy in Jordan

Edited by
Rodney Wilson

Centre for Near and Middle Eastern Studies
School of Oriental and African Studies

London and New York

First published by Routledge 1991
11 New Fetter Lane, London EC4P 4EE

Simultaneously published in the USA and Canada
by Routledge
a division of Routledge, Chapman and Hall, Inc.
29 West 35th Street, New York, NY 10001

Typeset by Witwell Ltd, Southport
Printed in Great Britain by
Billings & Sons Ltd, Worcester

British Library Cataloguing in Publication Data

Politics and the economy in Jordan. – (Routledge/SOAS
  contemporary politics and culture in the Middle East
  series).
  1. Jordan. Politics   2. Jordan. Economic conditions
  I. Wilson, Rodney
  320.95695
  ISBN 0-415-05304-8

Library of Congress Cataloging-in-Publication Data

Politics and the economy in Jordan / [edited by] Rodney Wilson.
          p.   cm.
  Includes bibliographical references.
  ISBN 0-415-05304-8
  1. Jordan – Economic conditions.   2. Jordan – Politics and
  government.   I. Wilson, Rodney.
  HC415.26.P65   1990
  338.95695 – d c20   90-8155
                                                            CIP

Contents

Figures

Tables

Notes on contributors

Kamel Abu Jaber is a former Minister in the Government of Jordan. He is currently Professor of Politics in the University of Jordan, and has written widely on Jordanian affairs and on Jordan's regional relations.

Subrata Ghatak is a development economist who has worked for the World Bank and has taught in India and Canada. He was Senior Lecturer at the University of Leicester and is now Professor of Economics at the University of Florida, Gainsville.

Fawzi Khatib is a finance specialist, and Assistant Professor in Yarmouk University. He taught previously in the University of Algiers, and gained his Ph.D. in the University of Leicester.

Philip J. Robins specializes in the politics of the Middle East, especially Jordan, as a result of research for a Ph.D. at the University of Exeter. He is currently with the Royal Institute of International Affairs, in London.

Hassan A. K. Saleh is Professor of Geography in the University of Jordan. He specializes and writes extensively on the environmental resources of Jordan as well as on the physical geography of the Middle East generally.

Yezid Sayigh is a writer on Middle Eastern affairs. He is currently finalizing a Ph.D. at the University of Oxford on Jordanian politics.

Monther Share is Professor of Economics at Yarmouk University. He is a foreign trade specialist, currently working with the Ministry of Planning in Riyadh.

Zayd Sha'sha is a businessman and commentator on industrial and economic affairs in Jordan.

Aladdin Tileylioglu is Assistant Professor at Yarmouk University. He was formerly at the Middle East Technical University, Ankara, and is a macroeconomist with a particular interest in consumer behaviour.

Rodney Wilson is Reader in Economics at Durham University. He has researched and written extensively on Jordan's financial sector and on the Kingdom's foreign trade.

Saleh A. Al-Zu'bi is a former diplomat and currently a specialist in international relations in the Middle East. He is also Director of the Strategic Studies Centre in the University of Jordan.

Preface

The economy of Jordan and the evolution of its political institutions have always been overshadowed by special local circumstances and in particular by relations, occasionally traumatic, with Israel, which have had well-recorded military, demographic and economic impacts. The purpose of this book is to provide important insights into the Jordanian economic and political scene, which fill in the essential background against which current problems can be assessed. The aim has been to break new ground rather than to cover the familiar, and the contributions complement those contained in the earlier work on the economic development of Jordan edited by Bichara Khader and Adnan Badran, which was published by Croom Helm in 1987.

Clearly events have moved on during the last two years in both the economic and political spheres. The contributions by the economists from Yarmouk University shed considerable light on the underlying factors which have resulted in Jordan's current economic difficulties with serious foreign exchange shortages necessitating import restrictions, and continuing pressures on the dinar through the exchange rate. Further belt tightening seems likely in Jordan in the 1990s, and there are certain to be considerable social strains given the increasing numbers of new entrants into the job market and the shortage of employment opportunities. Jordan's highly educated and articulate school leavers and university graduates are one of the country's strengths, but they also have high aspirations, which will eventually be frustrated.

Jordan has, however, a long experience in successful crisis management, and there is reason for optimism that the economic challenges of the 1990s will be met despite the enormous difficulties. The entrepreneurial spirit and the adaptability of private enterprise is one encouraging feature, though the contribution by Zayd Sha'sha helps put the role of the private sector in perspective. If Fawzi Khatib's thesis concerning undersaving is correct, then the recent rises in interest rates may increase the supply of domestic funds for capital formation, though this will pose challenges for institutions such as the Jordan Islamic Bank.

Recent developments arising from the PLO acceptance of United Nations Resolutions on the Arab–Israeli conflict have raised prospects for peace, but Jordan's diplomats are certain to urge caution, given their long and difficult experience. Kamel Abu Jaber's and Saleh Zu'bi's contributions should be read when assessing the current Jordanian position. Though born out of conflict, the Kingdom of Jordan has established a firm national identity, as Yezid Sayigh shows, with its own loyalties and aspirations which are independent of those of its neighbours. From this position of confidence the state can cope with internal difficulties and give support to the parties involved in the search for a settlement to the Palestine issue, without undermining its own strength and identity as might have been the case in the past. The chapters on politics and international relations in this volume are certainly essential reading for all those interested in the peace process.

Meanwhile the Gulf crisis of 1990 has placed Jordan in a very exposed position in terms of its regional and international relations, and at the same time has highlighted the complexity of its internal politics. While the precise impact of these events was not clear while the book was in press, it was certain that Jordan's economy would be severely affected and at the same time its internal politics could also be affected in a major way.

Rodney Wilson

Acknowledgements

The publication was made possible through funds made available by the Research Committee of the School of Oriental and African Studies and the British Academy. We were also very grateful for the financial support provided by the British Council which assisted contributors from Jordan to travel to London. The study was strongly supported by staff of the Centre of Strategic Studies at the University of Jordan and we are particularly grateful to its Director, Salih Zubi, for all his assistance. The encouragement and guidance of Professor Adnan Bakhit, Dean of Research in the University of Jordan, is also very warmly recognized. We are especially grateful to all the contributors from Jordan who spared time for discussions and research and especially to those from the Economics Department, Yarmouk University from which essential financial assistance was forthcoming.

Editorial assistance and word-processing was contributed by a large number of people associated with the SOAS Centre of Near and Middle Eastern Studies, particularly Diana Gur, Bridget Harney and Alan Nicol, and the editor and contributors are very grateful indeed for the care given to the technical editing.

Rodney Wilson

Introduction
Rodney Wilson

Jordan is a remarkably resilient state, both economically and politically. Created out of conflict in a harsh arid environment, with its access to the sea cut off by the new state of Israel, the future of the country seemed highly uncertain in 1948. Yet forty years after, the achievements of the Kingdom have been remarkable. An oasis of political stability, King Hussein is the longest serving ruler in the Middle East, as well as in the Arab and Islamic worlds. The King, despite the small size of his realm, has managed to acquire the status of an international statesman, respected both in the West and by Arab leaders. Jordan plays a key role in Arab diplomacy, and is the only country to enjoy good relations with all Arab regimes, irrespective of their political colour. Amman was the sole Arab capital that could have hosted the crucial November 1987 Arab summit, and the King's mediation efforts bore fruit in mending the fences between Egypt and the majority of other Arab states.

Yet the Hashemite Kingdom has experienced many traumas in its short history. The entire West Bank, the most developed part of the country in the 1950s and 1960s, was lost to Israel in the 1967 War, together with the old city of Jerusalem, the historical centre of much of the region. Four years later, a violent civil war erupted between the Palestine Liberation Organization (PLO) and the Hashemite army, which backed the monarch. Yet unlike the Lebanese civil war, the decisive outcome of the struggle in Jordan was to enhance the stability of the country. The King was able to reassert his authority, but at the same time maintain a more liberal regime, with a degree of open discussion and debate, as well as press freedom, which could not be tolerated in neighbouring Syria or Iraq. This combination of firmness with disruptive forces and tolerance towards all citizens who identify with the state has proved remarkably popular. Palestinians from the West Bank, and many of those who were refugees from the lands within Israel's 1948 boundaries, have respect and often admiration for King Hussein

1

and his government, and are proud holders of Jordanian passports. No residents of East Jerusalem, for example, who were entitled to Israeli passports after the annexation of the old city in 1967, have opted to give up their Jordanian passports.

The Jordanian economy

The economic achievements of the Hashemite Kingdom have been considerable, as its citizens enjoy one of the highest standards of living in the Arab world. Growth rates during the 1970s and early 1980s were well in excess of 10 per cent per annum, and a modern infrastructure was established, with a good network of surfaced roads, an international airport near Amman, and excellent port facilities at Aqaba which serve Iraq as well as Jordan. At the same time health and social services were developed, with modern clinics and hospitals, and a school system established which has resulted in the best-educated population in the entire Arab world. Both the University of Jordan and Yarmouk University enjoy good academic reputations, with many of their staff having post-graduate qualifications from the United Kingdom and the United States.

The agricultural sector has been transformed, especially in the Jordan Valley, where it is on the Jordanian side that the desert has been made to bloom, rather than on the Israeli occupied side, which remains largely barren semi-scrub. The traditional agriculture has been modernized in the north of the country, with increased yields for tomatoes, citrus produce and olives. Production of wheat and barley has also risen, though it is insufficient to satisfy domestic demand. The major problem of the 1980s has been marketing, with overproduction rather than underproduction of certain items, notably tomatoes, aubergines and cucumbers. These used to be marketed in the Gulf, but these states now produce their own vegetables. Efforts have been made to diversify agriculture, and encourage crops where there is a shortage of local supply and a need for imports. Tomato production has been reduced, and the production of broccoli, garlic, leeks, fennel and celery has been increased. Jordan has now achieved self-sufficiency in these crops. Efforts are being made to increase cereal production, and boost fodder production for livestock to raise the proportion of domestic meat consumption produced locally. The Kingdom is self-sufficient in poultry, but red meat, especially mutton, will continue to be imported for the forseeable future.

The Kingdom's other primary products have been developed, notably phosphates and potash. These raw materials account for around one-third of all Jordan's export receipts, but prices are prone to severe instability in international markets. Jordan has, however, expanded phosphate production almost fourfold over the 1976–88 period, and it is the third largest producer in the world after the United States and Morocco. Given the pricing problems, much is marketed through countertrading arrangements with India, Romania, Yugoslavia and Indonesia, who acquire the raw phosphate for their fertilizer industries. Jordan has its own fertilizer industry, but export of processed phosphate is difficult as buyers also have their own industries to consider, and the Jordanian fertilizer industry has incurred heavy losses. Phosphate and potash by-products will be used for a newly established chemical industry due to come on-stream in 1990. Phosphoric acid will be one of the major products, which India is interested in buying.

Most manufacturing industry in Jordan is small scale, and primarily orientated towards the domestic market. The main acivities include the manufacturing of builders' supplies and household goods, especially furniture, using mostly imported wood. There is also a small food processing industry, most of its products being sold domestically, though a few are exported to Iraq and the Gulf. The local plastics and pharmaceuticals industries are more export orientated, Iraq being the main customer. Under Ba'athist socialism in Iraq, small manufacturing plants have been discouraged, and most heavy industries are in the state sector. Jordanian private entrepreneurs have capitalized on this to win a significant foothold in the Iraqi market for their own products, though the market has been depressed recently as a result of the Gulf War.

The service sector of the Jordanian economy is well developed with a well-organized banking system whose assets are almost as large as those of Syria, a much more populous country. Amman also has the second most important stock market in the Arab world after Kuwait. The Jordanian capital never inherited Beirut's financial entrepôt role as a banking centre after the Lebanese civil war as some had hoped. Rather the business went to London and other European centres directly, and the need to have an intermediary between the Gulf and Europe was made less important with the development of modern telecommunications. The tourist industry is the main service sector activity, but the number of visitors, most of whom come from other Arab countries, remains below 2 million. Around 300,000 Europeans visit Jordan annually, often combining business with trips to Petra and Jerash and Jordan's other antiquities. Too few Europeans come on repeat visits however, as the antiquities market is a once in a lifetime experience. Aqaba has developed to a modest extent as a 'sun and sand' resort, mainly for Arab tourists, but the food and quality of service are not up to Amman standards. Given the relatively high air fares to Jordan, most European visitors are from the more affluent but discerning classes of their societies, for whom short-comings matter.

External financial flows

Remittances and aid inflows from the Gulf have brought welcome foreign exchange earnings into Jordan, especially since 1974, and it is these that partly account for the growing prosperity of the Kingdom. Such financial inflows create distortions, however, and have contributed to Jordan taking on some of the characteristics of a leisure society, of high consumption but little production. Jordanian expatriates are increasingly returning home, partly as a result of the recession in the Gulf with the slump in oil prices. Rather than enter productive activity, many simply retire from active employment, and live on their accumulated savings. This partly reflects their difficulty in finding gainful employment in Jordan, but it is also a result of the acceptance of retirement after a working life, sometimes shorter than twenty years. Jordan's main resource is its people, and those who export themselves bring monetary benefits to the economy. Skills used and acquired in the Gulf are seldom used later for the benefit of Jordan, and in a sense the brain drain causes lasting damage, as many of the most talented migrate, and even when they bring their brains back, they seldom use them in a way which could aid economic development.

The aid inflows from the Gulf have similarly helped the government finance its expenditure, but the benefits have been monetary rather than developmental. These macro inflows, like the micro remittance flows, have maintained the Jordanian dinar at a high level, making domestic supplies expensive in relation to competing imports. This has hindered the expansion of the small business sector and local manufacturing, despite the favourable climate for free enterprise as a result of the absence of government regulation. Consequently, employment has expanded only slowly, and many of those leaving school and university in Jordan are unable to find employment. Many merely postpone entry into the job market by pursuing education to higher and higher levels. This only raises expectations and increases frustration, and it strains family relationships, as older sons and daughters are forced to live at home, and lack the resources to establish independent households.

The decline in remittances and aid from the Gulf may therefore be a blessing in disguise, if the Jordanian economy can rise to the challenge. Official remittance figures show a decline of around 15 per cent from the 1984 peak, but this is an underestimate as it excludes remittances through moneychangers. The decline in government aid has been more dramatic, amounting to one-quarter over the 1985-6 period, with the level 40 per cent below the 1982 peak. This has not, however, affected the level of public and private investment on which future growth partly depends. Public capital expenditure actually rose by over 30 per cent between 1985 and 1986, as buoyant tax receipts more than compensated for the decline in external government assistance. The government has increased its borrowing requirement, but there has been no difficulty in placing domestically the additional government bonds and treasury bills, though interest rates have risen by more than 6 per cent since 1984.

Savings, investment and growth

Higher interest rates have attracted greater domestic saving into the commercial banks, so there does not appear to be any crowding out effect, with the higher level of government borrowing and taxation affecting private savings. Indeed commercial bank credits to the private sector have continued to increase by over 9 per cent over the 1985-6 period. Against this background, not surprisingly, gross national product has continued to increase, the growth being 3.6 per cent over the 1985-6 period, compared to a zero rate the previous year. The economy is far from being overheated, however, and inflation has fallen to virtually zero according to both the official cost of living index and the wholesale price index. However, this is due not so much to domestic demand conditions as to the appreciation of the exchange rate against the US dollar, which has reduced import prices.

With Jordan's population continuing to increase at over 2 per cent per annum, a growth rate of 3-4 per cent gives little scope for rising living standards. Such growth is the best that can be hoped for over the short term up to the mid-1990s, however, with prospects after that depending largely on external conditions, since Jordan is a very open economy. It seems unlikely that the high growth rates of the 1970s and early 1980s will return even in the longer run, although as population growth falls, living standards will eventually rise faster. The reason for the lower growth rate is not any deficiency in public or private investment, which is running at a high level as already indicated. Rather it is the foreign exchange constraint, as the supply of foreign exchange compliments domestic

5

saving in Jordan. The returns on investment are lower when foreign exchange is not available, as the investment mix itself changes.

This seems to be what is happening in Jordan. So-called dual gap analysis applies, with the foreign exchange restraint curtailing growth, despite favourable domestic demand and supply conditions. Most investment items are imported, as Jordan has no capital goods industry. Imports have, however, fallen dramatically over the 1985–6 period from over JD 1074 million to JD 850 million. This has been necessary to help the balance of trade position, with the deficit falling from JD 764 million to JD 594 million. The policy of boosting public expenditure selectively and borrowing makes sense in the Jordanian context. A budget deficit does not necessarily imply a worsening external deficit as the recent experience shows. At the same time public spending, while not necessarily boosting growth, helps reduce social tensions, and serves to create employment opportunities. As the private sector has benefited from rather than been damaged by the increasing public expenditure, there seems to be no need for excessive government spending restraint. All this is, of course, contrary to the conventional economic wisdom in the International Monetary Fund and the World Bank. The Hashemite Kingdom is fortunate, however, in having little debt with such bodies, and therefore is not caught in the policy straitjacket in which some of its neighbours, notably Egypt, find themselves.

The scope of the book

This book is the edited contents of a one day conference on the Politics and the Economy in Jordan held on 19 May 1987, at the School of Oriental and African Studies of London University. The conference was convened and organized by Professor Kamel Abu Jaber of the University of Jordan, Dr Tony Allan of the Middle Eastern Centre at SOAS and myself. The aim was to encourage chapters on topics which had not hitherto been treated in detail in the Jordanian context. At the same time it was intended to provide a forum where the results of theses that had not hitherto been published could be presented. The chapters were specialized rather than general, as there has already been much of a more conventional nature published on Jordan's economy, society and politics. In particular, the proceedings of the Louvain conference in Belgium on the Economic Development of Jordan was published by Croom Helm in 1986 (Bardan and Khader 1986). Some of the participants at the London conference, including myself, had attended the 1985 conference in Louvain. Rather than merely develop the themes of that earlier conference, the objective of the organizers of the London session was to break fresh ground. At the same time the plan was to attract a large number of Jordanian participants, both to attend the conference, and to present chapters on their own country. The sessions proved lively, and the debate highly constructive, with a reasonable feedback, even for the presenters of the most specialized chapters.

Resources for development

The conference was divided into five consecutive sessions, three on the economy, and two on the politics of Jordan, and the order of presentations has been followed in this book. The first session was on Jordan's resources, both domestic and foreign. Dr Hassan Saleh of the University of Jordan has contributed a chapter on water resources and food production in Jordan. Dr Saleh, who studied for his Ph.D. in Durham University, is head of the Geography Department in the University of Jordan. His chapter is concerned with Jordan's growing food import bill, which is greater than all export receipts combined. He examines how the food import bill can be reduced by increasing domestic food production in Jordan, especially of those items which are in heavy demand. Jordan, of course, suffers from a large water deficiency, but there remains scope for extending irrigation despite the progress already made, and for a more effective use of both water and soil resources on existing irrigated land. Jordanian agriculture is advanced by Third World standards, but lessons learnt in one part of the country are not always applied elsewhere. Dr Saleh's chapter provides a useful overview of the achievements and deficiencies.

Dr Fawzi Khatib, who graduated with a Ph.D. from Leicester University in 1987, has now joined the Department of Economics at Yarmouk University as an Assistant Professor. His chapter examines the link between foreign aid and economic development, and considers whether it is the savings or foreign exchange constraint which is critical in the Jordanian context. If it is the latter then aid can indeed contribute to development. The empirical evidence from Jordan is considered, using an econometrical model in log-linear form. The model, which appears to be robust when several simulation exercises are carried out, confirms that foreign aid has had a favourable effect on Jordan's economic development during the 1970s and 1980s. Given this result, the implications of falling foreign assistance must be considered as detrimental for Jordan.

Market demand and supply

Three of the chapters are on market conditions in Jordan, and the ability of local supply to satisfy demand for manufactured goods. Jordan is often regarded as a free enterprise economy, where the private sector plays a dominant role. As Zayd Sha'sha points out, however, the state has exercised a growing role in both the micro and macro economy, though there has not been the wholesale nationalization of businesses as in neighbouring Iraq and Syria under the Ba'athist socialists. Zayd Sha'sha is able to speak from experience as the head of the Chambers of Commerce and Industry, which acts both as a pressure group for private business, and as a channel of communication between the Jordanian government and industry.

Dr Alladin Tileylioglu has contributed a chapter on the demand for consumer durables in Jordan. Originally from the Middle Eastern Technical University in Ankara, he now works as an Associate Professor in the Economics Department in Yarmouk University. His chapter is largely concerned with the car market in Jordan. Jordan has no vehicle industry of its own, most cars being imported from Japan and the European Community. A stock adjustment model is used to analyse consumer behaviour, with relative prices and income as the main determinants of the stock. The effect of changes in interest rates and credit availability on the demand for cars is also considered. These monetary effects are found to be significant, as many vehicles in Jordan are purchased through bank borrowing.

Jordan's trade and balance of payments problems are considered by Dr Monther Share, also an Assistant Professor in the Economics Faculty of Yarmouk, and the deputy dean. Dr Share is currently on leave in Saudi Arabia where he is working with the Ministry of Planning in Riyadh. Jordan enjoys a balance of payments surplus because of capital inflows, but its balance of trade is in chronic deficit. Imports are therefore largely dependent on the flow of remittances and aid to finance their purchase, which makes Jordan highly vulnerable to external forces over which it has little control. Policy makers are faced with a choice between two second best alternatives. Imports could be allowed to continue at a high level, but this would continue to impose foreign exchange strains and would result in external reliance. Alternatively, imports and balance trade could be curtailed, but this would mean that growth would be sacrificed. Clearly there are no easy answers to Jordan's balance of payments problems, but at least Monther Share's useful chapter reviews the constraints.

Banking and finance

Two chapters deal with the question of financial intermediation. Subrata Ghatak of Leicester University, and his former postgraduate research student Fawzi Khatib, examined the relationship between inflation, financial intermediation and economic growth in Jordan. The concept of 'financial repression', which has recently received much attention in the literature on economic development, was applied in the Jordanian context. Most financial repression models concentrate on the impact of interest rate ceilings on savings, investment and economic growth, the hypothesis being that low interest deters savings, and reduces the supply of loanable funds to finance development. In Jordan, inflation has reduced the real rate of interest, and made savings less attractive. A regression model reveals a negative relationship between inflation and time and savings deposits. At the same time the relationship between the growth of such deposits and investment is found to be positive. The conclusion must therefore be that inflation is damaging to financial intermediation, and therefore to investment, on which future growth depends.

My own chapter concerned with Islamic Banking in Jordan, as I wrote about the ordinary commercial banks for the earlier book on the Economic Development of Jordan (Bardan and Khader 1986). The subject of Islamic finance has received increasing attention in recent years, both from Moslem scholars, and from those in the West with an interest in Islamic affairs. Much of the writing is of a theoretical nature however, and it is only very recently that the results of empirical investigations have started to appear. This research is intended as a modest contribution to this empirical work. The Jordanian experience is of particular interest, as the financial structure of the Kingdom is run on Western lines, with a few private commercial banks dominating, and the Central Bank playing a conventional regulatory role. Given this type of financial framework, there are several issues in Islamic banking that it is pertinent to consider. First, to what extent do Islamic banks need to compete with the conventional commercial banks? Second, do Islamic banks attract new depositors, who have not hitherto saved with banks, or do they merely draw depositors away from the other banks? Third, how does the use of funds differ, since Islamic banks cannot provide interest-yielding loans? Finally, in a free enterprise economy such as Jordan, how attractive are Islamic companies, including banks, to investors, compared with ordinary joint stock companies?

Special legislation was passed in 1978 to allow the Jordan Islamic

Bank to operate. This institution is a public company with its shares quoted on the Amman Financial Market. It is associated with the Al Baraka group of Saudi Arabia, which holds a minor stake in the equity. Deposits have grown rapidly, with almost JD 100 million held in joint investment accounts on which depositors earn 90 per cent of the declared profit for distribution each year. One year's notice is required for withdrawals to earn such a return, which amounts to 5 per cent. Around JD 25 million is held in trust (current) accounts on which no return is earned. Specified investment accounts, for which depositors specify how their funds should be invested, are also growing in popularity, over JD 13 million being held in this type of 'income unit trust'. The Jordan Islamic Bank has branches throughout the Kingdom from Irbid to Aqaba, and there are 65,000 depositors. It has become a major Jordanian financial institution. Depositors are given first priority as far as advances are concerned. Funds are advanced for trade credit on a repurchasing and leasing basis, and the bank also invests in its clients' businesses on a profit-sharing basis. Almost 28.5 per cent of funds are advanced to small manufacturing establishments, a higher proportion than is the case with other Jordanian banks.

There have been few problems with bankruptcy amongst clients, who include the more devout sectors of the small business and merchant community with a reputation for honesty in their dealings. The Jordan Islamic Bank has managed to continue its expansion despite the difficult economic climate in Jordan in the mid-1980s and future prospects appear encouraging. A major housing project in Amman has been financed by the Bank, which includes a mosque and a primary school for the children of the devout.

Jordan's politics

Two of the chapters relate to political matters in Jordan. Yezid Sayigh's chapter is to some extent philosophical in approach, as it addresses the fundamental question of identity in the Jordanian context.

Jordan has enjoyed remarkable internal stability since the early 1970s, despite a turbulent past. The Kingdom has overcome the material and political consequences of losing the West Bank in 1967 and those of the civil war in 1970–1. In fact, by resolving the issue of power, the two events accelerated the process of state formation in Jordan. Since then, the legitimacy of the Hashemite throne has been widely accepted, and it has interacted with its environment more confidently. Assisting this change has been a mutual recognition by rival Arab governments of the impracticality of overthrowing each other by military force. The consolidation of the regional system and the injection of oil wealth since 1973 have also contributed to Jordan's national security, while increasing the incentives for internal stability. This is in marked contrast to the formative years of the Emirate of Transjordan and to the interwar period of 1948–67, when the existence of Jordan itself and of the monarchy was challenged in turn by the indigenous Jordanians, the Palestinians and neighbouring Arab states.

A decade and a half of stability does not mean that the threat to Jordan's cohesion has entirely disappeared, however. The Palestinian issue remains at the heart of Jordanian security problems. This is due to geography, to competition over the West Bank, but above all to the fact that over half of Jordan's people are of Palestinian origin. This means that the throne must retain a stake in the Palestinian issue to avoid estrangement with its Palestinian subjects, although such a course has the potential to place Jordan in conflict with Israel, the PLO and other Arabs. Major shifts in the regional balance of forces or in the Jordanian economy may also excerbate internal tensions, including Transjordanian–Palestinian antipathy. Thus, there are endemic, systemic threats to both Jordanian entity and identity as envisaged by the Hashemite monarchy. None the less, socioeconomic development and political evolution have strengthened state–citizen bonds and reinforced defence against external pressure. The division of roles between Jordan and the PLO, despite areas of ambiguity, and effective acceptance of Israel's permanence and of a loss of the West Bank have all also allowed Jordan's leadership to concentrate on developing the East Bank as the home of the modern Jordanian state. Now, in the early 1990s, the Jordanian entity is well consolidated, although the specifically Jordanian identity on which it is based is still in transition. Whether the political and economic trials looming in the coming decade will slow the process or accelerate it remains to be seen.

Philip Robins's chapter is more specific in nature, dealing with the electoral law passed in Jordan in 1986. The law is examined in the context of the recall of the Jordanian parliament in January 1984. The former electoral law is considered in detail, and its effect on by-elections over the 1984–6 period assessed. The new law is then compared to the old law. This reveals changing political objectives, which reflect the changing political power structure in Jordan.

International relations

The chapters on politics by these two young researchers, based on their theses, are followed by two final contributions from well-established academics at the University of Jordan. Professor Kamel Abu Jaber looks at Jordan's position in a troubled region, focusing in particular on the never-ending Arab–Israeli conflict and the even more bloody Iran–Iraq war. Jordan was, of course, directly affected by the Arab–Israeli conflict through the loss of territory, and the refugee influx. The Jordanian government has been placed in a difficult situation over the years by Israeli intransigence, and suspicions run deep in Amman concerning further Israeli expansionist plans. The pessimism concerning the Arab–Israeli conflict is compounded by worries over the Iran–Iraq war and its regional implications. Jordan has supported its Arab neighbour, Iraq, both morally and logistically by opening its supply routes from Aqaba to Iraqi conveys. Without this support, it is doubtful if the Iraqi war effort could have continued.

Salih Zubi of the Strategic Studies Centre of the University of Jordan looks at Jordan's foreign policy in its international as well as regional setting. Jordan benefits from having a king whose status as an international statesman is widely recognized, and whose political experience is longer than that of any other Arab ruler. The King has excellent personal relations with many Western leaders including the UK Prime Minister, Margaret Thatcher, but at the same time pursues an independent, non-aligned foreign policy. This is recognized in the Communist world where there is as much respect for Jordan as there is for Syria, despite the fact that the Soviet Union has a treaty of friendship with Syria, but not Jordan. The King has been concerned not to close doors, but to allow as much freedom of manoeuvre as possible in an ever-changing political situation. Hence when President Sadat visited Jerusalem, and normalized relations with Israel, there was no question of Jordan following his lead. At the same time, however, Jordan did not want to cut off relations with Egypt, even though there was disapproval of Sadat's policy. It is this cautious strategy of leaving open all options that has helped King Hussein survive in the turmoil of Middle Eastern politics. Adaptability has brought stability. It is the long-term domestic stability which has contributed more than any other factor to Jordan's economic prosperity and development, a fact that is widely appreciated in the Kingdom itself.

Reference

Bardan, A. and Khader, B. (eds) (1986), *The Economic Development of Jordan*, Croom Helm, London.

Part one

Resources and foreign aid

Chapter one

Water resources and food production in Jordan

Hassan A. K. Saleh

When discussing the economy of Jordan, one cannot ignore water and food. Water resources are considered a national asset and essential to satisfy the demand for food. Scarcity of water is the most serious of several constraints that limit development of food production. Therefore, Jordan depends largely on rainfall for its water and food resources.

This chapter will include an evaluation of the present state of water and food in Jordan, and the role of man in exploiting and managing these important resources. The government, in cooperation with the private sector, has taken numerous measures aimed at developing these resources. Despite this effort, it has not yet been possible to achieve a reasonable degree of food self-sufficiency.

In the last few years Jordan has witnessed substantial social and economic changes which have made a major contribution to the expansion of domestic demand for foodstuffs. This has led to an ever-increasing reliance on food imports, which increased from an annual average of JD 41 million for the period 1973–5, to JD 179.9 million for the period 1981–5.

This chapter is divided into three parts. The first part deals with the land and the people of Jordan and is a basis for the following two parts. The second part discusses the present state of ground and surface water resources, with reference to the water balance and water use in irrigation. The third part analyses food production and its sufficiency, with reference to the factors affecting food supplies. A regression model was used to analyse these factors, in addition to other simple statistical methods which were used to compute variation and correlation coefficients, as well as self-sufficiency ratios.

Land and people

The physical background

Topography

Jordan can be divided into three physiographic regions which are from west to east as follows: the Jordan valley, the highlands and the desert plateaux (Figure 1.1). The rift valley comprises the low lying Jordan Valley, the Dead Sea and the Wadi Araba. The Jordan River descends from below sea level at the Dead Sea. The valley through which the Jordan flows into the Dead Sea is about 105 km long and from 5 to 25 km wide. The river drains the water of Lake Tiberias, the Yarmouk and the few other streams and wadis from the side of plateau into the Dead Sea (Saleh 1971, p. 1; Hashemite Kingdom of Jordan 1973, p. 2).

The highlands east of the rift extend as a backbone of Jordan from the Yarmouk river in the north to Aqaba in the south. Several wadis and some twelve perennial streams cut across this upland area, dissecting it into many well-defined hills and plateaux. Four main blocks, however, are readily distinguishable, divided by the Yarmouk, Zarqa, Mujib, Balqa, Moab and Edom. Their height is about 1,200 m on average above sea level.

The desert plateau, lying east of the highlands, is by no means uniform. It rises about 600 m on average above sea level. Its undulating land is dissected by dry wadis descending from the highlands eastward, and draining inland into the depressions of Al Jafr, Al Azraq and Wadi Sirhan. Prominent landmarks in the desert result from past volcanic activity and from the exposure by erosion of durable volcanic intrusions known as inselbergs (Saleh 1975, pp. 19–20; Buheiry 1972, pp. 54–5).

Soil and vegetation

The different types of soil in Jordan are illustrated in Figure 1.2. In highland Jordan, limestone is usually weathered into calcareous or silt clay. This is an important soil-forming material, and in the wetter areas it assumes a typically reddish brown colour. It is usually heavy and only rarely contains the debris of the original limestone. Most of the food agricultural soils of the Jordanian plateau belong to these red Mediterranean soils (Aresvik 1976, pp. 22–3).

Yellow Mediterranean soils and regosols are also found in some parts of the highlands, in the scarps and in the Rift Valley. The sirrozems, on the other hand, are the grey desert soils covering about half of Jordan. Alluvial soils are found in the Jordan flood

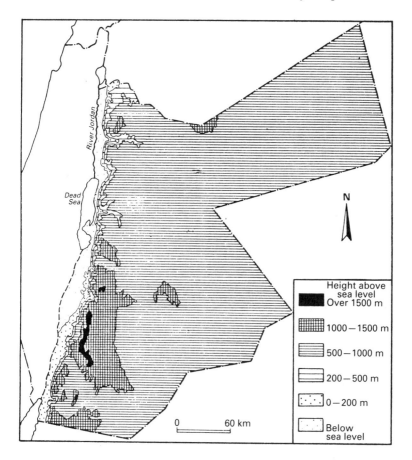

Figure 1.1 Relief features

plain and in the bottoms of the valleys (Fisher *et al.* 1968, pp. 16–20). Most of the soils are rich in mineral components and poor in organic matter. Alluvial and red Mediterranean soils are the best of all soils in Jordan. When deep, these soils form excellent cropland. Their natural fertility is relatively high. On the whole, the problem of erosion and salinity is an obstacle to cultivation, and it often causes low productivity.

The flora of Jordan fall into three phytogeographical regions: the Mediterranean, the Irano-Turanian and the Saharo-Sindian. These three floral regions correspond to the three vegetational zones of

19

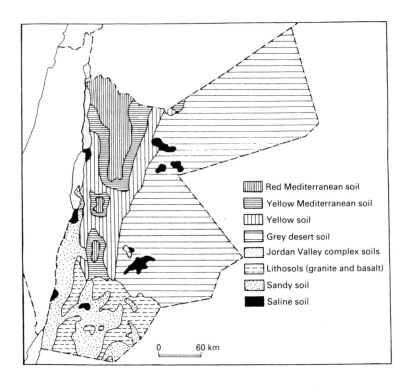

The legend reads:

- Red Mediterranean soil
- Yellow Mediterranean soil
- Yellow soil
- Grey desert soil
- Jordan Valley complex soils
- Lithosols (granite and basalt)
- Sandy soil
- Saline soil

0   60 km

Figure 1.2   The soils

forest, steppe and desert. The Mediterranean forest is scattered on the highlands, encircled by steppe grasses. The different types of vegetation are shown in Figure 1.3. The dominant species of the forest are pines and different varieties of oak and bushes, whereas that of the steppe is *artemisia herba-alba* and those of the desert are drought-resistant halophytic species (Eig 1951, pp. 112–14; Zohary 1962, p. 73).

Rainfall

The total area of Jordan is 92,544 km². Of this area, only 9 per cent receives more than 200 mm of rainfall and can be considered productive agricultural land. The area of marginal land (200–300 mm) is about 5.3 million dunums (1 dunum = 0.1 hectare), or 5.7 per cent of the total area of Jordan. That of semi-arid land (300–500 mm) is about 1.7 dunums, or 1.8 per cent, and that of

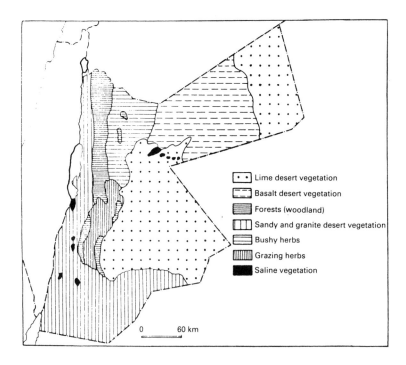

Figure legend:
- ⋅⋅ Lime desert vegetation
- ▭ Basalt desert vegetation
- ▤ Forests (woodland)
- ▥ Sandy and granite desert vegetation
- ▤ Bushy herbs
- ▦ Grazing herbs
- ■ Saline vegetation

0   60 km

Figure 1.3 Vegetation

semi-humid land (500 mm and more) is about 1 million dunums, or 1.1 per cent of the total area (Duwayri 1985, p. 126).

It can be concluded that about two-thirds of the total area of Jordan receives less than 50 mm annually, this quantity representing more than one-fifth of the total rainwater. On the other extreme, 1 per cent of the total area receives more than 500 mm annually, this quantity representing about 8 per cent of the total rainwater falling in Jordan (see Table 1.1 and Figure 1.4).

The average rainfall quantity in Jordan is approximately 6,885 million m³, plus about 2,000 million m³ that fall on catchment areas outside Jordan. A large amount (about 75 per cent of the total rainfall) is lost through evaporation. It is estimated that about 15 per cent of the total rainfall flows down rivers and streams. About 10 per cent of the total rainfall percolates underground to replenish subterranean water, part of which will rise to the surface in the form of springs. Renewable water resources, surface and subterranean,

Table 1.1   Annual average rainfall for various areas of Jordan

Rainfall (mm)	Area (km²)	Quantity of rain water (million m³)	% of area	% of rain water
Less than 50	59,327	1,483.2	64.1	21.6
50–100	13,851	1,038.8	15.0	15.1
100–150	7,293	911.6	8.0	13.2
150–200	4,102	717.9	4.4	10.4
200–250	2,145	482.6	2.3	7.0
250–300	1,803	495.8	2.0	7.2
300–400	1,781	625.8	1.9	9.1
400–500	1,253	563.9	1.3	8.2
500–600	777	427.3	0.8	6.2
More than 600	212	137.8	0.2	2.0
Total	92,544	6,884.7	100	100

Source: Natural Resources Authority 1974

are currently estimated at 1,200 million m³. Of this quantity, irrigated agriculture has used less than half (about 520 million m³) in 1985 (Ministry of Planning 1986, p. 497; Hashemite Kingdom of Jordan 1978, p. 7).

Because of rainfall variation, annual changes in agricultural output have been very great. Wheat production in a good year may be four or five times that in a bad year (Mazur 1979, p. 147). The correlation between annual rainfall and both field crop areas and production is high. The north-western parts of Jordan receive the highest quantities of annual rainfall with the lowest coefficients of variation in rainfall and field crop production. In contrast, the south-eastern parts of Jordan receive lowest quantities of annual rainfall with highest coefficients of variation in rainfall and field crop production (Saleh 1975, p. 40) (Figure 1.5).

Not only is production of field crops affected by spatial variation of rainfall, but it is also affected by irregular distribution of rainfall during the course of the year. With the exception of the dry summers, rain falls during three periods of the year: in autumn (the early rain of October and November), in winter (the seasonal rain of December–February) and in spring (the later rain of March–May). In order to have a successful growing season, rain must fall during these three periods in sufficient quantities. If early rain is low in quantity or late, the field crops will be unable to grow. Moreover, late rain determines the extent of agricultural output, and extreme insufficiency may result in failure of both winter and summer crops.

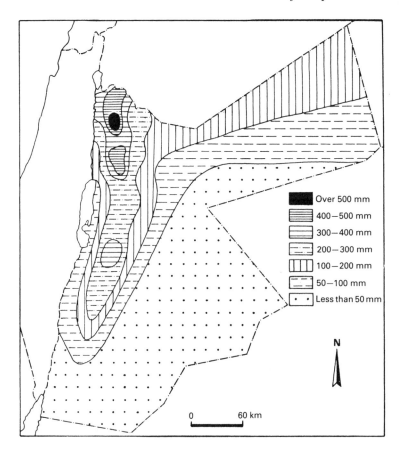

Figure 1.4 Annual rainfall distribution, 1952–74

Successive dry years are disastrous for farmers. On average, rainfall is distributed as follows: October 2.6 per cent, November 7.7 per cent, December 20.7 per cent, January 23.5 per cent, February 19.7 per cent, March, 17.6 per cent, April 6.4 per cent and May 1.8 per cent (Saleh 1985, p. 31). The region of sufficient rainfall for cropping in a normal year forms a long, narrow belt extending from the north-west corner at the Syrian border down to a point between Petra and Ma'an. This belt also contains most of the towns and the bulk of population (Nyrop 1980, p. 121).

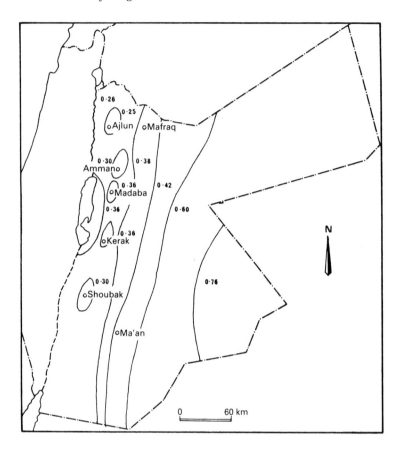

Figure 1.5 Variation coefficients of rainfall

The demographic background

Population growth

The size of the total population of the East Bank increased from 680,000 in 1952 to 2.67 million in 1985. The annual population growth rate increased from 3.1 per cent during the period 1952–60 to 4.8 per cent during the period 1961–76. The rate decreased to 3.9 per cent per annum during the period 1980–5. The high population growth rate is due to a high natural increase rate (3.4 per cent) and net migration. The natural increase is caused by a very high crude birth rate (4.5 per cent) and relatively low, and still declining, crude death rates (1.1 per cent) (Ministry of Planning 1986, p. 95).

Improved public health and medical care have raised the reproductive capacity of couples, permitting them, increasingly, to translate the high demand for children into actual fertility. They also resulted in a relatively high expectation of life at birth which, in 1985, was 67 years for males, and 71 years for females (Tabbarah 1981, p. 12; ECWA 1985, p. 72). The health resources of Jordan have improved considerably over the last thirty years. The numbers of hospital beds, clinics, health centres and health manpower per capita have increased markedly. In 1961, for example, the physician–population ratio was estimated to be eighteen physicians per 10,000 inhabitants; in 1985 the ratio had increased to 113 physicians per 10,000 inhabitants (Ministry of Planning 1986, p. 107).

During the last thirty years or so, migration has played an extremely important role in the demography of Jordan. Due to the many military conflicts in the area, large numbers of Palestinians have been displaced and made refugees. As a result of the large influx of refugees and displaced persons and the substantial movements from rural areas, the urban centres of Jordan have experienced rapid growth (Samha 1980, p. 48).

Population distribution

In 1985, the population of the East Bank was estimated at 2.7 million. The average density was 29.1 per km^2, but it differs from one governorate to another due to various factors. Over 80 per cent of the population lives in the north-western and middle parts of Jordan with the vast majority of inhabitants concentrated in the governorates of Amman, Irbid and Zarqa, which account for 83.8 per cent of the total population (Department of Statistics 1985, p. 2; ECWA 1979, p. 4).

It is worth mentioning that Amman and Zarqa governorates have 55.9 per cent of total population and 27 per cent of total arable land. But Irbid and Mafraq governorates have 27.9 per cent of the total population and 50 per cent of the total arable land, and Karak governorate has 4.3 per cent of the total population and 14.5 per cent of the total arable land. The governorates of Balqa, Ma'an and Tafila resemble the governorates of Amman and Zarqa in having population pressure on agricultural resources. Balqa has 6.9 per cent of the total population and 3.4 per cent of total arable land. Ma'an and Tafila governorates have 3.5 per cent and 1.5 per cent of total population respectively, but they have together 4.6 per cent of total arable land.

Jordan is one of the countries that have undergone rapid urbanization during the last thirty years. Both compulsory and voluntary internal migration have led to the rapid growth of some cities such as Amman, Zarqa and Irbid. The percentage of urban population has increased from 44 per cent of the total population in 1961 to 74 per cent in 1985. Three-quarters of the population of the Amman and Zarqa governorates are concentrated in the metropolitan region of Amman–Zarqa.

Population structure

With respect to its age–sex structure, Jordan is not much different from neighbouring Arab states. The male to female ratio was 105 per cent in 1985. A sizeable proportion of Jordan's population (50 per cent in 1985) is under 15 years of age. The group aged between 15 and 59 accounted for 46 per cent of the total, while those of 60 years of age and above accounted for 4 per cent of the total population (Ministry of Planning 1986, p. 96). One of the most important characteristics of the Jordanian labour force is the very low crude participation rate. For the last twenty years the participation rate has remained almost constant at 20 per cent. Several factors account for this state of affairs including the large proportion of people under 15 years of age, low female participation rates, and the continued outflow of manpower, especially of the younger generation, to other countries.

The size of the Jordanian work force was estimated at 502,000 in 1985. Its growth rate during the period 1961–85 was estimated at 3.5 per cent per annum. The outflow of Jordanian workers to other countries has continued at an average rate of 9,000 workers a year, while increased domestic demand for labour has led to the importation of manpower from other Arab and non-Arab countries. In 1985, the number of foreign workers was estimated at 143,000 or about 28.4 per cent of the total labour force in Jordan. Non-Jordanian workers are mainly employed in services, construction and agriculture.

Jordanians who work abroad were estimated at 339,000 in 1985. Unemployment has witnessed a considerable fluctuation during the last twenty-five years. It was 7.1 per cent in 1961, but it increased to 14 per cent after the occupation of the West Bank. In 1973, it was 8 per cent, but it decreased in 1976 to 2 per cent. It was estimated at 8 per cent in 1985.

The local labour market has witnessed considerable changes due to socioeconomic developments during the period 1961–85. The relative size of the labour force engaged in agriculture has declined

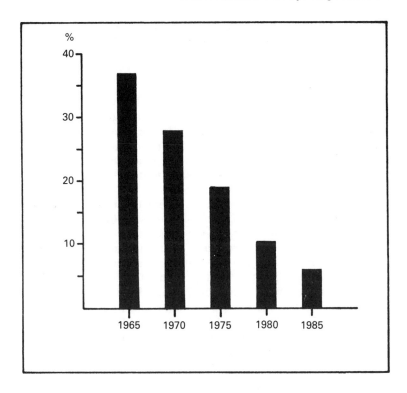

Figure 1.6 Percentage of workforce engaged in agriculture

by 33.5 per cent of the total in 1961 to 11.5 per cent in 1979, and 7.8 per cent in 1985. The absolute numbers grew over the 1961–79 period from 73,000 to 74,000 but since then there has been a decline to 39,000 (Ministry of Planning 1986, pp. 100–3) (Figure 1.6).

Water resources

Water in Jordan is one of the main components of the natural resource base. Not only does water aid food production but it is an indispensable part of the socioeconomic system. Any shortage of water supply has a negative effect on the general development effort. Jordan suffers from limited water resources due to its dry climate and relatively scarce and fluctuating rainfall. Average annual rainfall ranges from approximately 600 mm to under 50 mm. In addition, evaporation rates are very high.

Water balance

Water balance data for Jordan show a uniform drought pattern over the country, and this indicates that a water deficit is the dominant factor. Generally, there are two seasons in Jordan. The winter crop season usually occurs between November and April. In this season the rainfall can exceed potential evapotranspiration. The excess in rainfall is reserved as soil moisture storage to be used by crops in the following months.

Computation of the water balance during the winter crop season showed that highlands have seasonal water surpluses of more than 300 mm in an average year. At the same time, some parts of the Jordan Valley and the desert region have seasonal water deficits of more than 300 mm (Figure 1.7). During the summer season, soil moisture is negligible, this lasting from May to October, when water deficits cover all parts of Jordan. High values of water deficits are most marked in the Jordan Valley, particularly in its southern parts, where totals of 800 mm are exceeded. The magnitude of water deficits gives an indication of the irrigation needs for many crops (Saleh 1972b, pp. 37-8) (Figure 1.8).

The soil moisture content varies throughout the year under the influence of the precipitation amount, and to some extent also according to drainage and runoff. The soil moisture capacity is as high as 250 mm in the northern parts of the highlands, and as low as 75 mm in both southern parts of Jordan and desert plateaux (Kawasma 1983, pp. 73-6). It is convenient to use the soil moisture index, which is the result of dividing soil moisture storage by soil moisture capacity. The changes in the moisture index during the year reveal that a sharp rise is recorded from November–December to the peak of February–March. After March a continuous decrease occurs from April to October. Consequently, Jordan can be divided into three agroclimatic regions as follows:

1 *The Highlands*: The climatic water balance shows a water surplus during the seasonal rainfall period, and a low water deficit during the remainder of the year. Rainfed agriculture is dominant in this region, but it should be supported by irrigation if necessary, especially in the dry years.
2 *The Jordan Valley*: It suffers from water deficit most of the year, especially towards the south. Agriculture should be supported by substantial irrigation most of the year.

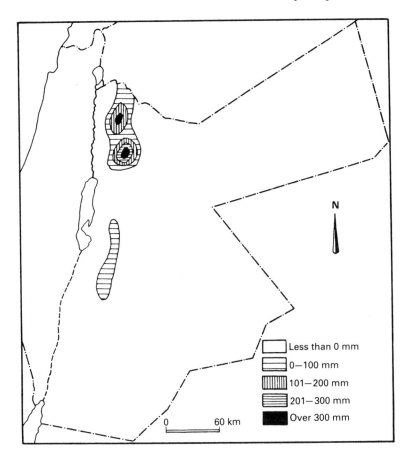

Figure 1.7 Water balance during the winter crop season

3 *The Desert Plateaux*: The desert of Jordan suffers severely from water deficit throughout the year. Agriculture should be supported by perennial irrigation (Mas'ad 1987, pp. 20–1).

Finally, Jordan is characterized by high seasonal water requirements and deficient actual moisture consumption for most of its rainfed agriculture, especially for wheat.

Groundwater

Groundwater is one source of water supply that has increasing importance to socioeconomic development (Abdo 1986, p. 2). The

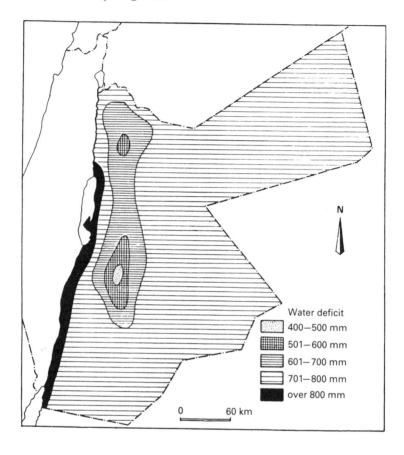

Figure 1.8 Deficits during the dry summer

mean annual rainfall over thirty years (1944–74) is 8,885 million m³, from which 1,220 million m³ only is exploitable. Seventy per cent of this exploitable water drains westward, the rest can only be developed by the drilling of wells to penetrate aquifers at variable depths (Kilani 1986, p. 143).

The National Water Plan for Jordan prepared by a German consulting firm and based on information and studies available to the Natural Resources Authority (NRA), estimated the average annual volume of water resources at 1,100 million m³, of which 220 million m³ are groundwater (Natural Resources Authority 1977). According to studies conducted in 1975, the volume of groundwater

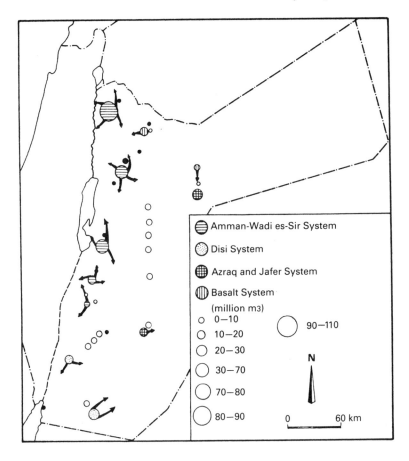

Figure 1.9   Systems of aquifer recharge

originating from rainfall and rivers was estimated at 250 million m³, while the volume of groundwater formed over the ages was estimated at 16,000 million m³ (Natural Resources Authority 1978).

Some aquifer systems have been recognized in Jordan, and they provide water for small springs and wells (Figure 1.9). The total recharge to the Amman–Wadi Sir system, which is the most important in Jordan, is estimated at 336 million m³ per annum. The salinity of the well waters of this system range from 300 to 1,860 ppm, making it acceptable for most uses.

A basalt aquifer system extends across the north-eastern parts of Jordan, with total recharge estimated at 37 million m³ per annum.

The amount of total dissolved solids (TDS) in its waters ranges from 200 to 530 ppm, again acceptable for all purposes.

The Rijam system of both the Azraq and the Jafr basins, receives a total recharge estimated at 27 million m³ per annum. Concentration of TDS ranges from 350 to 1,500 ppm in the southern half of the Azraq basin, and from 500 to 1,100 ppm in the Jafr basin.

The Hummar system contains a large quantity of groundwater which has accumulated since ancient times (150 million m³). Concentration of TDS in the waters of this aquifer system ranges from 230 to 525 ppm. These waters are suitable for domestic purposes, irrigation and many industrial uses.

The direct recharge is relatively small in the Kurnub–Zarqa aquifer system. Runoff provides some indirect recharge for these aquifers. The group sediments give rise to numerous small springs. Chemical composition of the waters shows that TDS values range from 300 to 2,800 ppm. The waters are suitable for domestic purposes and many industrial uses.

The total spring recharge from the Na'ur system is of the order of 4.5 million m³ per annum. This aquifer system is unlikely to be exploited for large-scale development of groundwater for irrigated agriculture or for industry.

The Disi aquifer system takes its indirect recharge mainly from Saudi Arabia where it is estimated at 6.7 million m³ per annum. There is another 10 million m³ of direct recharge flowing from Ras el Naqab as a result of rainstorms and runoff.

The sediments system exists at the bottom of the valleys, especially at the bottom of the Jordan Valley and Wadi Araba. It takes its recharge mainly from floods of rivers and streams. Salinity of its waters differ from one place to another, according to the annual recharge amount and to the existence of saline deposits between alluvium. This system has been exploited at the time of writing in Wadi Araba, and in the Jordan Valley (FAO 1974, pp. 12–14).

The above-mentioned aquifer systems are scattered inside groundwater basins (Figure 1.10). Most of the exploited aquifers are not deep at the time of writing, but plans have been put forward to exploit deep aquifers all over the country in the future. Jordan is divided into the following three major groundwater basins:

1 *The Dead Sea Basin*: This includes the basins of Yarmouk, Zarqa, the Jordan Valley and Dhuleil in the north, and the basins of Mujib – southern Ghors – northern Wadi Araba in the south.
2 *Desert Basins*: These include the Azraq, Hamad, Jafr, Disi and Wadi Sirhan basins.

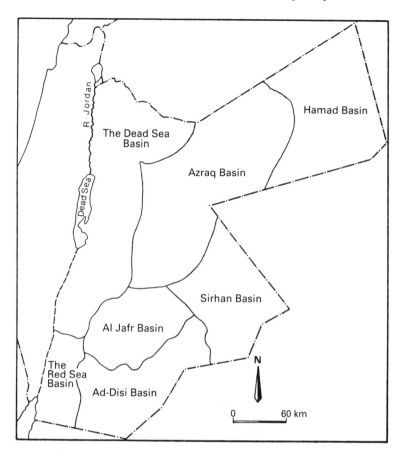

Figure 1.10 Major groundwater basins

3 *The Red Sea Basin*: This includes the southern Wadi Araba and
  Wadi el Yutm basins (Hirzalla 1985, p. 15).

The results of well water samples, which were chemically analysed,
revealed that about two-thirds of the wells in Jordan belong to the
third class C3S1, according to the American system. About a
quarter of the wells belong to the second class C2S1, whereas a
tenth of the wells belong to the fourth class C4S1 or C4S2 (Saleh
1977, p. 129).

The intensive pumping of groundwater, in the desert and in some

33

parts of the Jordan valley, has caused the depletion of stored water, and the deterioration of the water quality. TDS of well waters in the Jordan Valley range from 500 ppm to 250 ppm; in the southern Ghors they range from 800 ppm to 3,000 ppm; in the Jafr they range from 500 ppm to 3,500 ppm; in the Sadi Sirhan–Hamad they range from 100 ppm to 2,500 ppm (Hirzalla 1985, p.18).

It can be seen from Table 1.2 that overpumping of well waters for desert soil irrigation in the Wadi Dhuleil area during the last twenty years has caused a remarkable rise of water salinity. This phenomenon exists also in some other areas in the desert and in the middle and southern Ghors. Undoubtedly, saline irrigation waters have caused deterioration in the soils and weakened their productivity.

Table 1.2   Chemical analysis of water during the pumping tests of some wells in the Wadi Dhulei area in 1965 and 1985

Number of well	TDS (ppm) 1965	TDS (ppm) 1985
DP 16	294	2,246
DP 18	291	3,232
DP 21	285	2,240
DP 24	301	2,067
DP 25	346	1,945
DP 26	320	2,816

Source: Kilani 1986, p. 155

The results of the spring water samples showed that half of the springs vary in their discharge due to variation in rainfall. Only 5 per cent of springs showed constant discharges. About forty of the stream wadis showed small seasonal variations in their discharge because of their dependence on springs as sources of water.

The quality of spring waters in Jordan is generally good. About 70 per cent of springs had TDS values of less than 500 ppm, 16 per cent of them had TDS ranging from 500 to 1,000 ppm, and 10 per cent of them had high salinities because their TDS values were more than 1,500 ppm (Saleh 1977, pp. 137–8).

Surface water

The mean annual base discharge of all streams and wadis of Jordan is estimated at 447 million m³. Of this, approximately 218 million m³ is from the Yarmouk river. It can be seen from Table 1.3 that the average annual streamflow is estimated at 788 million m³, of which 447 million m³ is base streamflow and 348 million m³ is flood streamflow. A considerable part of these flows come from ground-

Table 1.3 Surface water resources in Jordan

Basin	Mean annual discharge (million m³)		
	Base	Flood	Total
Yarmouk basin	218	182	400
Zarqa basin	47	48	95
Azraq basin	10	12	22
Jordan Valley and Side wadis	70	14	84
Dead Sea basin	60	40	100
Southern Ghors and Wadi Araba	37	8	45
Wadi Araba Highlands	—	—	3
Disi–Mudawara–Yutm Wadi	—	1.4	1.4
Jafr–Shidiya	5	10	15
Hamad–Sirhan	—	23	23
Total	447	348.4	788.4

Source: Hirzalla 1985, p. 20

water discharge rather than from direct rainfall runoff during the annual rainy season between November and May. No consideration was given to the flows in the Jordan River. It is to be noted that the Yarmouk basin is the most important in terms of discharge volume compared with other catchment basins. Moreover, the discharge volume of catchment basins tends to increase towards the north and decrease towards the south. The volume of surface water in Jordan is small relative to its total area.

The characteristics of rainfall are reflected in the annual volume of flood stream discharges, which differs from one stream to another. The flucutation of flood streamflow requires the erection of dams on the streams and wadis to store water, which can be exploited during the dry summer seasons for irrigation as well as supplying aquifers with additional recharge. Dams can also protect the irrigated agriculture under them from flood hazards.

The Government of Jordan has erected for this purpose thirteen storage dams on some streams and wadis, with storage capacity estimated at 90 million m³ (see Table 1.4 and Figure 1.11). It has planned to erect more dams with storage capacity estimated at 320 million m³. The King Talal dam is the largest of all existing dams in Jordan. It was planned to raise the storage capacity of this dam from 56 to 90 million m³ during the development plan (1981–90). After completion of the works, stored water will be used for augmenting the irrigation of approximately 160,000 dunums of Ghor lands.

The Al Arab dam comes next after the King Talal dam with regard to water capacity. It has storage capacity of 20 million m³

Table 1.4 Distribution of existing dams

Name of dam	Dam capacity	Water uses
King Talal	56.0	Irrigation
Kafrein	4.8	Irrigation
Shueib	2.3	Irrigation
Ziqlab	4.3	Irrigation
Al Arab	20.0	Irrigation
Al Luhfi	0.7	Irrigation, animal drinking
Al Aqib	1.4	Groundwater recharge
Al Bowaida	0.7	Irrigation, animal drinking
Um el Jimal	1.8	Irrigation, animal drinking
Al Ghadir Al Abyad	0.7	Irrigation, animal drinking
Al Sirhan	1.7	Irrigation, animal drinking
Al Sultani	1.2	Irrigation, animal drinking
Al Qatrana	4.2	Irrigation, animal drinking

Source: Natural Resources Authority 1974

from the Wadi Al Arab floods and the Yarmouk River. Water from the dam is currently utilized in irrigating 12,500 dunums of northern Ghor lands, and in supplying the East Ghor Canal in the dry months with approximately 10 million m³ of water per annum. It is worth mentioning that irrigation is the main use of all dams built on the streams and wadis. The first five dams were constructed on tributaries of the Jordan River which have perennial waters. In contrast, the remainder of dams were built on dry wadis running in the desert, and depended on floods to store their waters.

The present development plan (1986–90) includes some suggested dam projects under study or construction. The Al Maqarim dam project aims at storing 486 million m³ of Yarmouk River flood water, and using it for irrigation, drinking and industrial purposes. Four dam projects are proposed in the Jordan Valley for the purpose of storing water during winter in appropriate locations for use in irrigation. The Al Mallaha dam is the most important of all these dams. This project aims at storing about 45 million m³ of flood water during the winter from the East Ghor Canal in order to irrigate approximately 60.000 dunums of the southern parts of the Jordan Valley.

The Kifranja and Al Yabis projects aim at constructing rockfill dams with a storage capacity of 14 million m³. They will store the flood waters of each of these wadis, and pump 10 million m³ from the East Ghor Canal, to meet local needs and make up for the shortage in irrigation water in the area. The project for increasing the height of Kafrein dam aims at raising the storage capacity of the present Kafrein dam from 3.8 million m³ to 6.3 million m³.

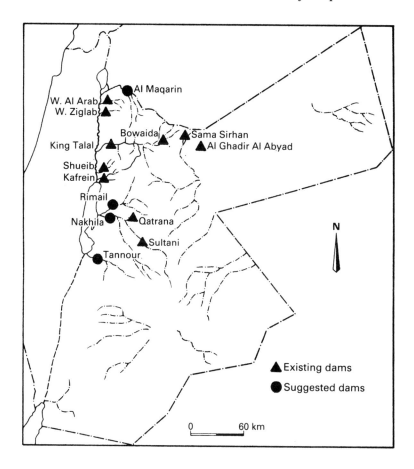

Figure 1.11 Dam locations

Three dam projects are proposed for some wadis running to the Dead Sea. The Al Tannour dam project aims at constructing a rockfill dam on Wadi al Hasa for storing 12 million m³ of flood water to be used for irrigation new lands in the southern Ghors. The Al Rimail dam project aims at constructing a dam on Wadi Al Wala to store 40 million m³ of water for irrigation and drinking purposes. The Al Nikhila dam project aims at constructing a dam on Wadi Al Mujib with a storage capacity of 7 million m³ of water to be used for irrigation purposes.

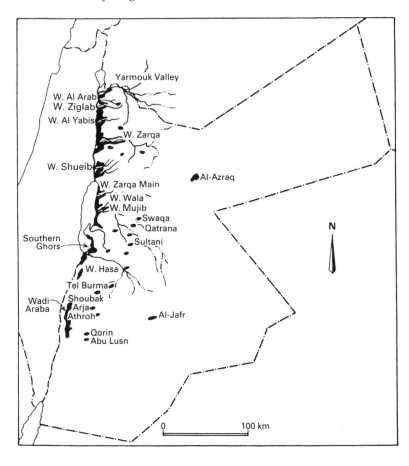

Figure 1.12   Areas of irrigated agriculture

Water use in irrigation

Irrigation was used for thousands of years in the area that became Jordan. It is the main determinant of agriculture in the Jordan Valley, the Wadi Araba and the desert (see Figure 1.12). In order to exploit water resources in irrigation, they should be assessed in terms of quantity as well as quality.

British consulting firms estimated the total surface and ground water that is suitable for consumption and could be economically utilized at 627 million m³ annually. In 1980, water consumption in

Jordan was estimated at 434 million m³, of which 353 million m³ was consumed in irrigation. Water consumption increased to 520 million m³ in 1985, of which 409 million m³ was consumed in irrigation. Irrigated agriculture in the Ghor area and Wadi Araba consumed 309 million m³, distributed on approximately 270,000 dunums. In the highlands and desert, there were about 90,000 dunums of irrigated agriculture that consumed 100 million m³ in 1985 (Ministry of Planning 1986, p. 497).

The average annual water consumption for irrigated agriculture in the Ghor areas was assumed to be approximately 1,000 m³ per dunum, corresponding to a cropping density of up to 128 per cent. It was estimated that quantities of water to be developed to cover the needs of consumption would increase from 520 million m³ in 1985 to 705 million m³ in 1990, to 820 million m³ in 1995 and to 934 million m³ in 2000. The share of irrigated agriculture from this anticipated water consumption would be 553 million m³ in 1990, 624 million m³ in 1995 and 687 million m³ in 2000 (Ministry of Planning 1986, p. 497).

The use of modern methods and techniques in irrigated agriculture, such as spray and drip irrigation, has been adopted to reduce the amount of water used. Innovations have been introduced to increase productivity which may contribute to solving the problem of food production. It is necessary to know the real needs of crops for water by using the required amounts of water in the best way and at the appropriate time. The optimum use of water has raised irrigation efficiency to over 75 per cent in the Jordan Valley.

The quality of irrigation water is one of the most important factors affecting plant growth. Water suitability for irrigation is a function of total salt concentrations, kinds of ions, types of soil colloid, varieties of plant to be grown, soil management and time (Shammout 1969, pp. 3-5).

The quality of irrigation water differs from one source to another, and from one time to another, according to the characteristics of surface and groundwater. The Jordan River water is low in quality because of its salinity (Saleh 1972b, p. 45), while the Zarqa River water is affected by organic pollution as well as by increasing salinity. The figures of Zarqa Agricultural Department indicated that about seventy-two wells in the Zarqa Valley, as well as a large number of fountains, have been polluted. Moreover, about 22,000 dunums of irrigated agriculture in the Zarqa Valley (Ruseifa, Awajan, Zarqa and Sukhnah areas) have become barren through water pollution. Analysis of samples taken from the King Talal dam water during the period from 15 July to 15 November 1985 showed that the water of the lake behind the dam was polluted with different organic materials (Titi 1986, pp. 23–32).

Moreover, numerous exploited wells in the middle Ghors, Wadi Dhuleil and Al Jafr have suffered from salinity hazards, through overpumping. In Jordan, the electrical conductivity (EC) of water used for irrigation is usually between 200 and 2,000 micromhos per cm. Many private agricultural enterprises failed because the EC of irrigation water was too high. The presence of sodium, boron or bicarbonate produces harmful effects on plants when present in high concentrations in the irrigation water.

The remainder of surface and ground water provision in Jordan is dependent on irrigation. The East Ghor Canal Project has diverted high-quality water by gravity from the Yarmouk River into an 88 km canal in the East Jordan Valley. The system also receives high-quality water from seven small perennial streams that flow westward to the Jordan River.

It is worth mentioning that irrigated agriculture represents approximately 8 per cent of the cultivated land, but it produces more than 40 per cent of total agricultural production, and about 70 per cent of the gross value of agricultural production. Moreover, it provides 85 per cent of agricultural exports (Duwayri 1985, p. 127; Nyrop 1980, pp. 121–6; Howayej 1985, p. 124).

Food production and its determinants

Present trends

In spite of the fluctuations of food and agricultural production, there was an overall upward trend during the period 1974–85 (see Table 1.5 and Figures 1.13 and 1.14). Fluctuations can be caused by variations in rainfall and other climatic conditions. Apart from climate, factors such as prices, employment, income and demand may also influence the fluctuations, but their effects are difficult to isolate from those of climate alone.

It is important to emphasize the role of food and agricultural production in the economic development process. The value of domestic agricultural product has risen from JD 24.6 million, at current prices, during the period 1973–5, to JD 49.2 million during the period 1976–80, then to JD 90.7 million during the period 1981–4, and to an estimated JD 112 million in 1985. Nevertheless, its contribution to GDP declined from about 9 per cent during the Three-Year Plan, to 8.6 per cent during the first Five-Year Plan, and to 7.9 per cent during the second Five-Year Plan (Ministry of Planning 1986, p. 53).

Table 1.5   Indices of food and agricultural production in Jordan (1979–81 = 100)

Item (production)	1974	1977	1981	1982	1983	1984	1985
Food	92	76	111	109	122	121	126
Livestock	65	75	111	111	111	149	138
Agriculture	92	76	111	110	124	121	124
Crops	107	78	108	112	141	110	127
Cereals	374	72	77	83	192	71	163

Source: FAO 1985a, pp. 78–86

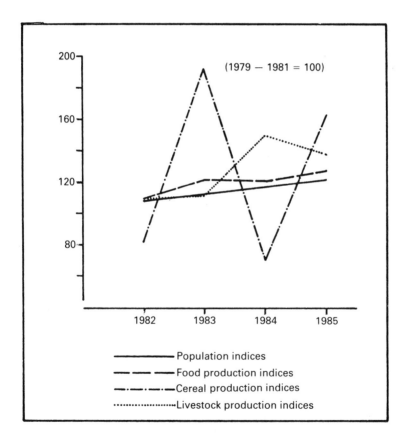

(1979 − 1981 = 100)

——— Population indices
— — — Food production indices
—·—·—·— Cereal production indices
················· Livestock production indices

Figure 1.13   Population and food production growth rates

41

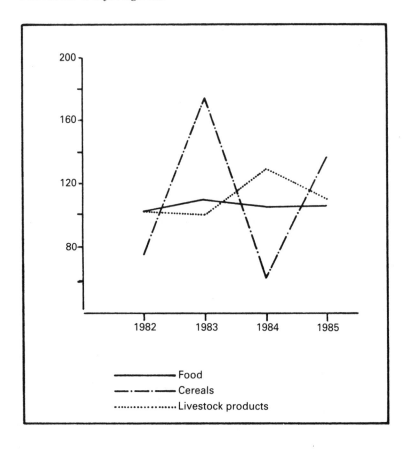

Figure 1.14   Per capita food production indices (1979–81 = 100)

The value added in the agricultural, forestry and fishing sector has increased (in constant 1980 prices) from JD 69.4 million in 1980 to JD 97.5 million in 1985, an annual growth rate during the period 1980–5 estimated at 7 per cent (Ministry of Planning 1986, p. 53). The growth of value added in agriculture can be attributed to cooperation between government and private sector.

Government has contributed to building infrastructure, particularly irrigation systems, extension services, financial credits and conservation procedures. The private sector has invested in agriculture, partly in response to these government measures.

It should be noted that there is a trend towards planting more fruit and olive trees. This is being encouraged by the government through the Highland Agricultural Development Project, which is being financed by the World Food Programme of the Food and Agriculture Organization. The main objective of this project is to develop and protect agriculture in the highlands through the introduction of improved land-use systems under which land can be used in accordance with its suitability (Duwayri 1985, p. 127).

Irrigated agriculture has contributed to increasing the income of farmers through the development of production. Efforts have been exerted to introduce advanced technology, especially in irrigation and agriculture under plastics, as well as a continuous upgrading of irrigation, fertilization and disease control techniques.

With the exception of cereal and field crop production which decreased between the first and second Five-Year Plans by 9.5 per cent it should be noted from Table 1.6 that all of the food production items increased by different percentages. Vegetable production was the highest of all, as it increased by 124 per cent. This is due to the fact that farmers have tended to reduce the area cultivated with field crops and to expand the area cultivated with vegetables and fruit. The figures indicate that the average cultivated area with vegetables has increased from 300,000 dunums for the period 1976–80 to 990,889 dunums in 1985, or an increase of more than 200 per cent. On the other hand, more than three-quarters (77 per cent) of the vegetable acreage is irrigated at the time of writing, as this is concentrated on the Ghors (Ministry of Planning 1981; Department of Statistics 1985, pp. 90–1).

Olives and citrus production have increased by 87.5 per cent and 65 per cent respectively. This is a result of expansion of their areas,

Table 1.6 Average food production for the period 1976–85 (thousands of tons)

Product	Average production		Change %
	1976–80	*1981–5*	
Cereal and field crops	109	99	9.5
Vegetables	276	628	124.0
Fruits excluding citrus	46	41	10.9
Citrus	20	33	65.0
Olives	24	45	87.5
Dairy products	39	49	20.4
Red meat	7	9.5	27.4
Broiler meat	25	37	48.0
Eggs (millions)	280	402	43.5

Source: Ministry of Planning 1986, p. 536

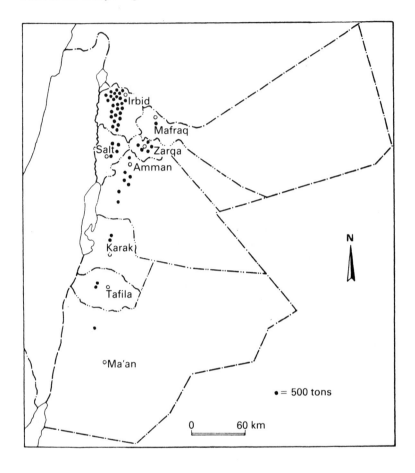

Figure 1.15 Distribution of olive production

with olives as the dominant crop in the highlands (see Figure 1.15), and citrus the dominant fruit in the Ghors.

Factors affecting food supplies

To shed some light on the factors affecting food supplies, a regression model was used (Table 1.7). Food production during the period 1970–80 was the dependent variable (Y), and nine independent variables (X_1–X_9) were selected.

Table 1.7 Results of stepwise regression of Y on X_1–X_9

Independent variable (X)		R (%)	R^2 (%)	Change in value of R^2	Level of significance
X_2	Cereal yield	0.76	0.57	0.57	99
X_7	Value of manure imports	0.73	0.89	0.31	99
X_1	Cereal cultivated area	0.09	0.91	0.02	99
X_6	Livestock numbers	0.29	0.92	0.01	99
X_8	Value of farm machinery imports	0.43	0.93	0.004	99
X_9	Value of pesticides imports	0.73	0.93	0.003	95
X_3	Value of per capita income	0.65	0.93	0.001	95
X_5	Numbers of engaged tractors	0.58	0.96	0.03	None
X_4	Percentage engaged in agriculture	0.24	0.99	0.03	99

The correlation (R) can be classified into three categories:

1 high variable correlations with food production, which include cereal yield (R = 0.76), the value of manure and pesticide imports (R = 0.73), and the value of the per capita income (R = 0.65);
2 medium variable correlations which include the number of engaged tractors (R = 0.58) and the value of the farm machinery imports (R = 0.43);
3 low variable correlations which are livestock numbers (R = 0.29), percentage engaged in agriculture (R = 0.24), and the area cultivated with cereals (R = 0.09).

Interpretation of all independent variables is estimated at 0.99 of the total dispersion of food production (Y), and these are significant at the 99 per cent level. The cereal crop variable (X_2) is an expression of climate, soil, topography, farmers' characteristics and agricultural methods. Owing to the importance of X_2 as a major factor affecting food production, it was possible to interpret 57 per cent of total dispersion of Y, and it was significant at the 99 per cent level (Figure 1.16).

The value of manure is an expression of the use of manure on the farms, especially the irrigated farms. This variable (X_7) is placed second rank in importance. As a major factor affecting food production, it was able to interpret 31 per cent of the total dispersion of Y, and it was significant at the 99 per cent level.

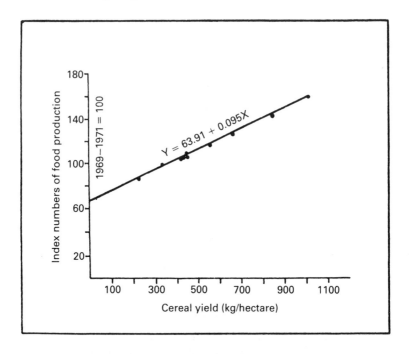

Figure 1.16 Relationship between cereal yield and food production

The percentage of persons engaged in agriculture is an indicator of the role of the labour force in food production. This variable (X_4) interpreted 3 per cent of the total dispersion of Y, and it was significant at the 99 per cent level. With the exception of X_5 which interpreted 3 per cent of the total dispersion of Y without significance, the remainder of the variables were weak in their interpretation of total dispersion of Y, but most of them are significant at the 99 per cent level.

Sufficiency of food production

The degree of self-sufficiency measures the ratio of domestic food production to domestic food consumption. It has been mentioned already that cereal yield interpreted a high percentage of food production (Y) dispersion at a high level of significance (99 per cent). The major determinants of food consumption are family size, family composition, family income, or increase in both population and per capita income level. Other factors of importance are price changes or income elasticity of demand, urban or rural residence, occupation, social status and a number of sociological, cultural, psychological and environmental conditions.

Jordan has experienced a high annual population growth rate during the last two decades, in addition to large changes in the per capita income level, which increased from JD 536.1 million in 1980 (at market price) to JD 603.7 million in 1983. But it began to decline from JD 594 million in 1984 to JD 556.9 million in 1985 (Ministry of Planning 1986, p. 49), influenced by the region-wide economic recession. The impact of urbanization on food consumption and demand is equally important. The urban population represents about three-quarters of the total population of Jordan (FAO 1973, pp. 1–16).

The figures in Table 1.8 indicate that expenditure on food is strongly related to the size of the population and per capita income level. In 1980, Amman governorate had the highest expenditure on food. This is mainly because it contained 56 per cent of the total population, in addition to enjoying high values of per capita income level which has encouraged the people to spend a significant part of their income on food (54.4 per cent of total expenditure). Amman governorate, including the biggest urban centre in Jordan (Amman city), spent nearly half the total Jordanian expenditure on cereals, more than half of the total on meat, and two-thirds of the total on vegetables, fruit, eggs and dairy products.

Irbid governorate was second after the governorate of Amman in population and food expenditure. It contained 28 per cent of the total population of Jordan and spent 28.8 per cent of total food expenditure in Jordan. Balqa, Karak and Ma'an governorates ranked third, fourth and fifth, respectively, in both population and food expenditure.

Table 1.8 Geographical distribution of expenditure on food commodities in 1980 (JD millions)

Commodity	Amman	Irbid	Balqa	Karak	Ma'an	Jordan
Cereals	22.7	15.8	4.0	2.7	1.6	47.0
Meat	57.2	27.6	6.7	7.4	3.1	102.1
Vegetables and fruit	40.7	16.8	5.2	4.4	2.3	69.5
Eggs and dairy products	41.4	24.5	4.8	3.7	2.2	76.4
Other	33.7	19.7	5.7	4.4	1.8	65.4
Total	195.7	104.4	26.4	22.8	11.0	360.4

Source: Department of Statistics 1985

Table 1.9 Sufficiency ratios for cereal and field crops for the period 1983–5

Items	Production (1,000 tons)			Consumption (1,000 tons)			Sufficiency ratio (%)		
	1983	1984	1985	1983	1984	1985	1983	1984	1985
Cereals	151	62	130	689.7	853.6	779.1	21.9	7.3	16.7
Wheat	116	50	100	423.5	475.0	417.9	27.4	10.5	23.9
Barley	34	12	30	51.4	191.8	104.9	66.1	6.3	28.6
Rice	0	0	0	34.4	55.2	51.0	0.0	0.0	0.0
Pulses	16	5	8	31.9	17.6	23.2	50.1	28.4	34.5

Sources: FAO 1985a, b

Sufficiency of cereal and field crops

Sufficiency ratios of cereals in general and of wheat in particular have been exposed to remarkable fluctuations and instability. The sufficiency ratio computed for cereals, for the period 1970–82 (see Table 1.9 and Figure 1.17), averaged about 22 per cent, and its variation coefficient was 60 per cent. Jordan produced more than one-fifth of its cereals consumption, while its wheat production was one-third of its consumption on average. The wheat sufficiency ratio ranged from 68 per cent in 1974, a wet year, to 5 per cent in 1979, a dry year.

It can be concluded that even in the short period 1983–5, the sufficiency ratio from cereal and field crops has fluctuated as a result of the incidence of dryness in 1984 (see Figure 1.18). The average ratio for cereals was 15.3 per cent, while it was 20.6 per cent for wheat, 30.3 per cent for barley and 37.6 per cent for pulses. It is noteworthy that Jordan produced about one-fifth of its consumption from wheat, whereas the country did not produce any of the rice consumed. Consequently, wheat and rice imports were estimated at 439,000 and 47,000 tons respectively, on average.

Sufficiency of vegetables and fruits

With the exception of onions, water melons, garlic, sweet melons and potatoes, which are not produced in sufficient quantity for local needs, the remainder of the vegetables have a surplus production (see Table 1.10 and Figure 1.19). The average sufficiency ratio of vegetables for the period 1971–7 was estimated at 162 per cent. The vegetable crops differ from each other with respect to sufficiency. For example, the average ratio for string beans was 236 per cent, for aubergines 220 per cent, for cabbage and cauliflower 200

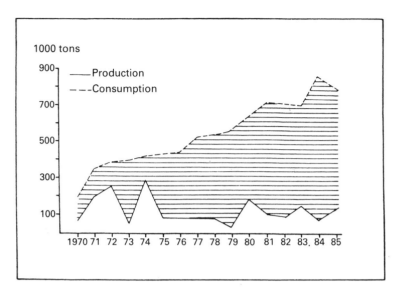

Figure 1.17 Sufficiency for cereals, 1970–85

per cent, for tomatoes 187 per cent, and for each of summer squash and broad beans 167 per cent (Khashman 1978, p. 344). Since 77.6 per cent of the vegetable area was irrigated on average for the period 1974–82, the variation coefficient for vegetable production ranged between 28 per cent (tomatoes) and 51 per cent (cucumbers).

The sufficiency ratio of fruit and olive production was 46 per cent on average for the 1970s. Deficiency of fruit production differs from one crop to another. The ratio for grapes was 82 per cent, bananas 70 per cent, olives 53 per cent, citrus 40 per cent, apples 10 per cent and other crops 22 per cent (Saleh 1985, pp. 74–5).

With the exception of citrus and bananas cultivated under irrigation in the Ghors, most fruit and olives grow in the highlands as rainfed crops. The variation coefficient for fruit and olive production is higher than that for vegetable production. It ranges, on average, for the period 1974–82 between 31 per cent (grapes) and 197 per cent (figs) (Saleh 1985, p. 67).

It can be noted that the sufficiency ratio for vegetable production generally, and tomatoes in particular, has declined because the government encouraged the farmers, especially in the Ghors, to execute the new suggested cropping pattern which reduce the marketing bottlenecks. Implementation of this policy aims at 153 per cent and 197 per cent for total vegetable production and tomato production respectively.

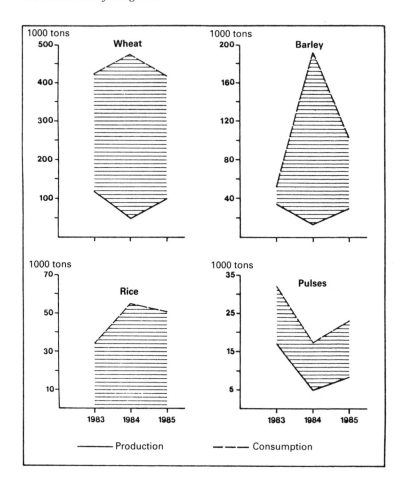

Figure 1.18 Sufficiency for cereals and field crops, 1983–5

On the other hand, the increase of the sufficiency ratio for fruit production generally and organges particularly is because their consumption declined by percentages higher than that of production. The average of their sufficiency ratio was estimated at 49 per cent and 56 per cent respectively. This means that fruit production in Jordan represents about half of consumption (Figure 1.20).

Table 1.10 Sufficiency ratios for vegetable and fruit production for the period 1983–5

Items	Production (1,000 tons)			Consumption (1,000 tons)			Sufficiency ratio (%)		
	1983	1984	1985	1983	1984	1985	1983	1984	1985
Vegetables	590	454	525	300	345	400	197	132	131
Tomatoes	212	209	220	97	101	133	219	208	166
Fruit	124	78	110	281	218	162	44	36	68
Oranges	31	13	25	62	37	30	50	35	83

Sources: FAO 1985a, b

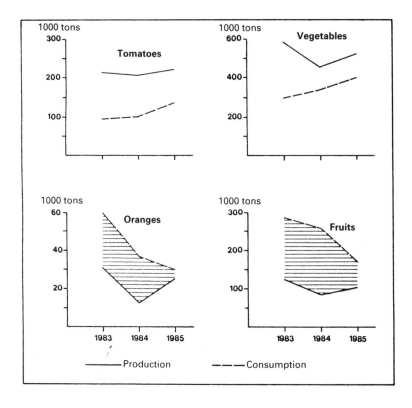

Figure 1.19 Sufficiency for vegetables and fruit, 1983–5

Table 1.11 Sufficiency ratios for livestock products for the period 1983–5

Items	Production (1,000 tons)			Consumption (1,000 tons)			Sufficiency ratio (%)		
	1983	1984	1985	1983	1984	1985	1983	1984	1985
Red meat	10.0	9.9	12.0	30.0	35.0	35.0	33.3	28.2	34.2
White meat	37.0	38.0	39.0	42.0	44.0	45.0	88.0	86.3	86.6
Milk	61.0	62.0	63.0	73.9	76.5	76.6	82.6	81.1	82.2
Fish	0.1	0.1	0.15	1.5	2.9	3.5	6.5	4.0	4.2
Eggs	25.4	26.0	26.0	20.9	24.4	20.1	121.5	106.4	129.3

Sources: FAO 1985a,b

Sufficiency of livestock products

Sufficiency ratios for livestock products for 1983–5 are shown in Table 1.11. Sufficiency ratios for red meat production ranged from 36.8 per cent (1981) to 71.6 per cent (1971) (Figure 1.20). The variation coefficient for this ratio was 22 per cent for the period 1970–81. The ratio for white meat (poultry) range from 81.6 per cent (1982) to 96.6 per cent (1973) (Figure 1.21). The variation coefficient for this ratio was 5 per cent for the period 1970–82. The average sufficiency ratio for milk and fish production was 45 per cent and 5 per cent respectively for the period 1970–81 (Figure 1.22). For egg production, it was 80 per cent for the period 1971–82 (Figure 1.23). This ratio ranged between 36 per cent (1972) and 120 per cent (1982). The variation coefficient for egg production was 35 per cent for the same period (Saleh 1985, pp. 75–97).

The average sufficiency ratio for red meat was 31.9 per cent for the period 1983–5. The ratio for white meat was 86.9 per cent on average, whereas it was 82 per cent for milk. Jordan suffers from a high deficiency in its production of fish, where the ratio was 5 per cent only. On the other hand there was a remarkable surplus in the production of eggs, where the ratio was 119 per cent.

Food trade balance

The average value of food imports represents 27 per cent of the total value of Jordan's imports from 1968 to 1976. This percentage declined to 17 per cent, on average, for the period 1978–82. The value of foodstuff and live animal imports increased overall by 119 per cent between 1978 and 1982; the value of live animal imports increased by 223 per cent, rice by 144 per cent, sugar by 130 per cent, and flour and wheat by 114 per cent.

The average value of foodstuffs and live animal imports was

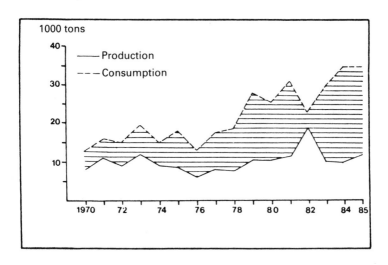

Figure 1.20   Sufficiency for red meat, 1970–85

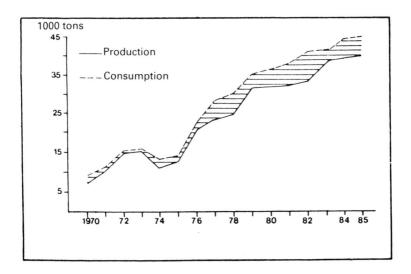

Figure 1.21   Sufficiency for white meat, 1970–85

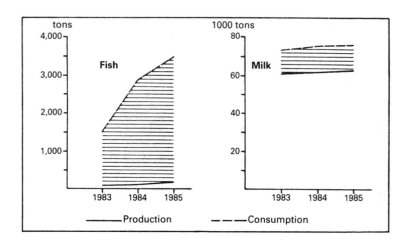

Figure 1.22 Sufficiency for fish and milk, 1983–5

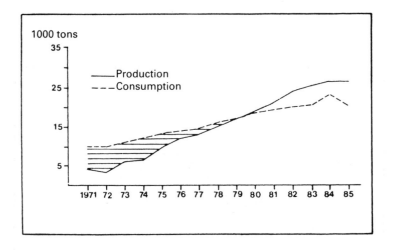

Figure 1.23 Sufficiency for eggs, 1970–85

estimated at JD 135 million for the period 1978–82, and its variation coefficient was 28 per cent. The average value of exports was estimated at JD 26.9 million for the same period, its variation coefficient being 32 per cent. Therefore, the deficiency in food trade balance was JD 108.1 million on average.

Table 1.12 The value of food trade balance for the period 1980–3 (thousands of JD)

Item	1980	1981	1982	1983
Food and live animal imports	118,789	167,930	191,924	180,366
Food and live animal exports	23,495	33,035	39,144	36,277
Trade balance	−95,294	−134,895	−152,780	−144,089

Source: Central Bank of Jordan 1987, pp. 56–8

The deficiency in the trade balance for food and live animals peaked in 1982 at JD 153 million and declined in 1983 to JD 144 million (see Table 1.12). It is probable that the decline has continued up to 1987 as a result of recession, and this implies real hardship for many consumers.

Conclusion

The direct relationship between resources and food production appears to be obvious in Jordan. The water resources, which are rain, surface and groundwater, play an important role in food production through their influence on crop yields. This is emphasized by the fact that irrigated agriculture represents approximately 8 per cent of the cultivated land, but it produces more than 40 per cent of the total agricultural production, about 70 per cent of the gross value of agricultural production, and about 85 per cent of agricultural exports.

Cereal yield variables, which are an expression of climate, soils, topography, farmers' characteristics and agricultural methods, account for 57 per cent of total dispersion of the food production which is the dependent variable Y. Since the productivity of agricultural land is still low, the annual food production growth rate will remain low when compared with the high annual population and per capita income growth rates. Consequently, food production cannot meet food demand, and a food gap appears as an indicator of this deficiency. The annual growth rate of the value added in the agricultural sector has been estimated at 7 per cent for the period 1980–5. Nevertheless, it is less than the annual increase in the rate of the food demand, which has been estimated at 7.8 per cent for the same period.

The figures for the self-sufficiency ratio for food production have indicated that there is a remarkable deficit in the production of cereals and field crops, fruits and olives, meat, dairy products, fish and some kinds of vegetables. On the other hand, there is a surplus in the production of most kinds of vegetables and in the production of eggs. There are some commodities which are not produced, such as rice, sugar, tea, coffee, cocoa and spices.

Jordan is heavily dependent on food imports which are a real burden on its national economy. For the import of food and live animals, spending was JD 192 million in 1982, and JD 180 million in 1983. The deficiency in the trade balance for food and live animals was estimated at JD 153 million in 1982, and JD 144 million in 1983. The cost of the imported food amounted to 16 per cent of the total Jordanian imports in 1983. Moreover, it amounted to more than 112 per cent of total exports, and it consumed about 17 per cent of the GDP.

Any solution of the food problem requires action on more than one front. This is because it is strongly related to natural, economic and human resources. Therefore, it cannot be tackled separately from other socioeconomic problems. The development of food production must be treated as a system which is related to and interacts with other socioeconomic systems. There is a strong mutual relationship between the components of the food system on the one hand, and other socioeconomic systems on the other. This determines the development of the following resources.

1 *Land and water.* It is necessary to conduct surveys of land and water each decade. This valuation of land and water enables the implementation of a conservation policy and the classification of land and water for optimum uses. The ultimate aim is to raise the agricultural land capability by increasing irrigable land to the maximum extent with available water resources, while developing water resources through replenishing surface and ground storage.
2 *Forestry, pastures and fisheries.* It is important to develop these natural resources through a conservation policy which aims at protecting them. This policy can lead to a halting of resource deterioration and bring about utilization to the best economic advantage.
3 *Agriculture, industry, transportation and marketing.* These are useful in increasing productivity of crops through the introduction of modern production techniques, applying research findings and developing extension services. Integrated rural development can be taken as a system in which some sectors react during the development process, and where infrastructure can be developed to serve rural agroindustries.

4 *Agricultural population*. Farmers must be educated through a system of integrated rural development. The human capital element is vital.

Finally, all these objectives need more coordination between the local authorities, in addition to cooperation between Jordan and its financial backers abroad, such as the Arab development funds which can allocate some of their investments into food projects.

References

Abdo, G. M. (1986), 'Aquifer management using optimisation techniques', in K. H. Prosl and E. Salameh (eds), *Proceedings of the International Congress about Groundwater in Semi Arid and Arid Regions*, Vol. 1, WRSC–University of Jordan, pp. 1–20.

Aresvik, O. (1976), *The Agricultural Development of Jordan*, Praeger, New York.

Buheiry, S. (1972), *Geography of Arabian Deserts* (in Arabic), Amman.

Central Bank of Jordan (1987), *Monthly Statistical Bulletin*, Vol. 23, No. 1, Amman.

Department of Statistics (1985), *The Annual Statistical Bulletin for Jordan*, Amman.

Duwayri, M. (1985), 'Farm systems in rain-fed areas', in A. B. Zahlan (ed.), *The Agricultural Sector of Jordan: Policy and System Studies*, Ithaca Press, London, pp. 125–58.

ECWA (1979), *The Population Situation in the ECWA Region: Jordan*, Economic Commission for Western Asia, Beirut.

—— (1985), *Statistical Bulletin of ECWA 1983*, Economic Commission for Western Asia, Baghdad.

Eig, A. (1951), *A Geobotanical Survey of Transjordan*, Research Council, Jerusalem.

FAO (1973), 'The impact of urbanisation on food demand', *Monthly Bulletin of Agricultural Economics and Statistics*, Vol. 22, No. 9, pp. 1–16.

—— (1974), *Development and Use of Groundwater Resources of East Jordan*, terminal report, Food and Agriculture Organization, Rome.

—— (1985a), *Production Yearbook*, Vol. 39, Food and Agriculture Organization, Rome.

—— (1985b), *Trade Yearbook*, Vol. 39, Food and Agriculture Organization, Rome.

Fisher, W. B. *et al.* (1968), *Soil and Land Potential Survey of the Highlands of North West Jordan*, Durham.

Hashemite Kingdom of Jordan (1973), *Jordan: Land and People*, Amman.

—— (1978), *Integrated Regional Development Study of the Northern Jordan*, Vol. II, Japan International Cooperation Agency, Amman.

Hirzalla, B. (1985), 'Water resources of Jordan', unpublished paper read at the conference of water resources held in Kuwait in 1985.

Howayej, B. (1985), 'Farm systems in irrigated areas', in A. B. Zahlan (ed.), *The Agricultural Sector of Jordan*, Ithaca Press, London, pp. 89-125.

Kawasma, Y. (1983), *Climatic Water Balance in Jordan: Characteristics and Application*, State University of Ghent, Ghent.

Khashman, A. (1978), 'The problem of food in Jordan', unpublished MA thesis submitted to Cairo University (in Arabic).

Kilani, A. (1986), 'Hydrogeological investigation for flood water storage and utilisation', in K. H. Prosl and E. Salameh (eds), *Proceedings of the International Congress about Groundwater in Semi-arid and Arid Regions*, Vol. I, University of Jordan, Amman, pp. 143-71.

Mas'ad, A. (1987), 'Environmental hydrology of Jordan', *Annals of the Faculty of Arts*, University of Kuwait, Vol. VIII, pp. 5-113.

Mazur, M. P. (1979), *Economic Growth and Development in Jordan*, Croom Helm, London.

Ministry of Planning (1981), *Five-Year Plan for Economic and Social Development, 1981-1985*, Vol. I, Economy, Amman.

—— (1986), *Five-Year Plan for Economic and Social Development, 1986-1990*, Vol. I, Economy, Amman (in Arabic).

Natural Resources Authority (1974), *Water Studies in Jordan*, Amman.

—— (1977), *National Water Master Plan of Jordan*, Vols 1-3, Amman.

—— (1978), *Proceedings of the National Water Symposium*, 19-22 March, Amman.

Nyrop, R. F. (1980), *Jordan, a Country Study*, American University, Washington, DC.

Saleh, H. (1971), 'Problems of water erosion in the East Jordan Valley', *Faculty of Arts Journal*, University of Jordan, May, pp. 1-12.

—— (1972a), 'The geographical basis of the Arab–Israeli dispute on the water of River Jordan', *Faculty of Arts Journal*, University of Jordan, Vol. 3, No. 1, pp. 28-50 (in Arabic).

—— (1972b), 'An estimation of the water balance in Jordan', *Faculty of Arts Journal*, University of Jordan, Vol. 3, No. 2, pp. 33-42.

—— (1975), *Food Production in Jordan*, Institute of Arab Research and Studies, Cairo (in Arabic).

—— (1977), 'Groundwater resources in Jordan', *Bulletin of Arab Research and Studies*, Vol. 8, No. 8, pp. 95-146 (in Arabic).

—— (1985), *Food Resources of Jordan*, Dar Ash-Shuruq, Amman (in Arabic).

Samha, M. (1980), 'Migration of refugees and non-refugees to Amman 1948-1977', *Population Bulletin of ECWA*, No. 19, Baghdad, pp. 47-67.

Shammout, S. (1969), 'Hypothesis for the estimation of water suitability for irrigation', *Quarterly Journal of the Natural Resources Authority*, Vol. 1, No. 1, pp. 3-5.

Tabbarah, R. (1981), 'Population, human resources and development in the Arab World', *Population Bulletin of ECWA*, No. 20, pp. 5-38.

Titi, S. (1986), 'Pollution of surface-water resources in Jordan and the role of environmental education in handling it', unpublished Ph.D. thesis submitted to Columbia Pacific University under the supervision of H. Saleh.

Zohary, M. (1962), *Plant Life of Palestine*, The Roland Press, New York.

Chapter two

Foreign aid and economic development in Jordan: an empirical investigation

Fawzi Khatib

Introduction

Jordan is a small country with meagre resources and high rate of growth of population (4.8 per cent in 1980, Zaghal 1983). The problem of economic development of Jordan was further aggravated following the forcible immigration of the Palestinians into Jordan as a result of the Israeli occupation of Palestine in 1948 and the West Bank in 1967. Historically, foreign aid has played a vital role in the economic development of many developed and developing countries and Jordan is no exception.

However, the relationship between foreign aid and economic development is still a controversial issue. In this chapter the relationship between foreign aid and economic development in Jordan is examined. In the first section, the different theories and views on foreign aid are reviewed and their relevance to Jordan is examined. In the second section, the magnitude and effects of foreign aid to Jordan are highlighted, while an econometric model concerning the relationship between foreign aid and economic growth in Jordan is formulated in the third section. In the fourth section, the statistical results are presented and analysed. Finally, the simulation exercises and the policy implication of the model are examined in the concluding section.

Foreign aid and economic growth: a review of the literature

As stated earlier, the relationship between foreign aid and economic development has become an important issue for investigation. Different schools have studied the impact of foreign assistance on economic development in contrasting ways. The positive association between foreign assistance and economic development was emphasized by the dual gap approach. This school (see, for example, Rosenstein-Rodan 1961; Fei and Paauw 1965; Chenery and Bruno 1962; McKinnon 1966; and Chenery and Strout 1966) argues that the major bottlenecks that limit growth in less developed countries (LDCs) are the saving and the foreign exchange constraints. The former constraint is a shortage of domestic savings to match investment opportunities, while the latter constraint is the shortage of foreign exchange to finance needed imports of capital and intermediate goods. Therefore, foreign aid represents an addition to the supply of resources available to a country, and serves as a method of breaking the bottlenecks which should increase economic growth.

Chenery and Strout (1966), in their much-cited work in the literature of dual gap analysis, stress the inherent inflexibilities in the LDCs and argue that an LDC can neither increase its exports nor reduce imports without causing underutilization in the economy.[1] In their basic model designed for Pakistan, they distinguished between three phases as far as foreign requirements are concerned.

A typical LDC, according to Chenery and Strout, often starts in a skill-limited phase (called phase 1) with an apparent lack of skills required to undertake investment programmes. Phase 2 normally begins when investment reaches the level required to sustain the target rate of growth. At this stage the foreign aid requirement is determined by the saving limitation.[2] In phase 3, the balance of payments limit will be effective and foreign aid is required to fill the trade gap (between import requirements and export earnings). The total requirements of external capital to complete the transition to self-sustained growth can be determined as the sum of the capital requirements for each phase that the economy goes through.

However, not everybody will accept this argument without question. The negative association between foreign aid and economic development was emphasized by Griffin and Enos (1970) and others (see, for example, Rahman 1968; Weisskopf 1972; Gorgens 1976; Bornschier *et al.* 1978; and Bauer and Yamey 1982). This school believes that foreign assistance makes little contribution, if any, to economic development. However, these findings were challenged by Gupta (1970) who applied Rahman's equation to the same countries included in Chenery and Strout's study and found a complementarity between foreign assistance and domestic savings.[3]

A similar result was also reported by Papanek (1973). He found that foreign aid has a more significant effect on growth rate.[4] It is worth mentioning that whether foreign aid has a positive or negative impact on economic growth is really a matter for empirical investigation. In the next sections, the relationship between foreign aid and economic development in Jordan will be examined from an econometric point of view and within a macroeconomic context.

Foreign aid and economic growth in Jordan

Before we examine the scope and magnitude of foreign aid to Jordan, a brief review of the main features of the Jordanian economy might be helpful.

As previously mentioned, Jordan depended on foreign aid since the early years of independence. In the early 1950s, Jordan's economic prospects were universally regarded as dismal. The Kingdom possessed few natural resources, no industry and a shortage of paved roads. Agriculture relied almost entirely on a sparse and uneven pattern of rainfall. In 1955, a mission from the World Bank visited Jordan and concluded that an annual growth rate of 4 per cent would be difficult to attain. In practice however, Jordan attained economic growth rates which were quite remarkable. Between 1955 and 1966, GNP in Jordan grew by 14.1 per cent per annum in current prices. Despite the severe but temporary setback to the economy during the late 1960s and the beginning of the 1970s,[5] the real rate of growth of GNP averaged 6 per cent per annum (in real terms) during the period 1963–85. It is worth noting that during the same period, GDP increased more than thirteenfold (Khatib n.d.).

As far as the sectoral contribution in GDP is concerned, the value added in agriculture represented about 11 per cent of GDP during the same period. The completion of the East Ghor Canal resulted in Jordan's agricultural growth shifting from rainfed dry farming to the more dependable and lucrative production of irrigation fruits and vegetable crops.

Although initially handicapped by the lack of natural resources and inadequate transport facilities, Jordan's industry began to grow rapidly during the early 1960s. The relative share of manufacturing and mining in GDP averaged 13.9 per cent during the 1963–85 period. The trend in industrial growth was interrupted by the 1967 war and the isolation from the West Bank markets and resources, and by the tariffs policy imposed by Israel on West Bank imports from the East Bank.

As far as the international sector is concerned, Jordan depends largely on imports to satisfy its consumption and investment needs. In fact, Jordan's balance of payments is characterized by a chronic trade deficit that dates back to the early 1950s. Table 2.1 shows that during the period 1963–85, the balance of trade had been in chronic deficit. The deficit increased steadily from JD 41.24 million in 1963,

Table 2.1   Jordan's foreign trade sector (1963–84, JD millions)

	Imports	Exports	Balance of trade	Imports/ GDP	Exports/ GDP
1963	47.80	6.56	−41.24	37.03	5.08
1964	50.30	7.00	−43.30	33.76	4.00
1965	56.00	7.70	−48.30	33.41	4.59
1966	68.20	8.70	−59.50	40.00	5.10
1967	55.00	10.00	−45.00	41.92	7.62
1968	57.50	12.20	−45.30	36.84	7.82
1969	67.70	11.90	−55.80	36.91	6.49
1970	65.90	9.30	−56.60	37.79	5.33
1971	76.60	8.80	−67.80	41.14	4.73
1972	95.30	12.60	−82.70	45.99	6.08
1973	108.20	14.00	−94.20	49.56	6.41
1974	156.50	39.40	−117.10	63.28	15.93
1975	234.00	40.10	−193.90	74.98	12.85
1976	339.50	49.50	−290.00	80.53	11.74
1977	454.40	60.20	−394.20	88.37	11.71
1978	458.80	64.10	−394.70	72.57	10.14
1979	589.50	82.50	−507.00	78.29	10.96
1980	716.00	120.00	−596.00	73.14	12.26
1981	1,047.50	169.03	−878.47	90.61	14.62
1982	1,142.50	185.60	−956.90	86.34	14.03
1983	1,103.30	160.10	−943.20	76.97	11.17
1984	1,071.30	261.00	−810.30	70.34	17.14
1985	1,074.44	255.35	−819.09	68.29	16.23
Average	397.23	69.37	−327.85	59.05	9.68

Source: The Central Bank of Jordan, *Annual Reports*, and author's calculation

to JD 117.1 million in 1974, JD 596 million in 1980, JD 956.9 and JD 819.1 million in 1982 and 1985 respectively.[6]

The ratio of exports to GDP was only 9.4 per cent on average (Table 2.1), but the ratio of imports to GDP was 58.6 per cent over the entire 1963–85 period. Exports consist mainly of phosphates and some vegetables. The share of capital goods and raw materials represented 44 per cent of total imports in 1964, then increased to 60 per cent in 1975 and finally reached 68 per cent in 1983.

It is worth noting that the trade deficit was partly offset by an increasing surplus in the balance of services. This consisted of remittances of Jordanians working abroad, receipts and aid. Jordan's impressive record of growth during the 1970s was due in large measure to the sevenfold increase in oil prices which resulted in large amounts of remittances and generous aid from Arab oil exporting countries.

Between 1963 and 1985 capital inflows (mainly aid and remittances) represented 45.5 per cent of GDP. Total capital inflows

Table 2.2 The relative importance of foreign inflow (1963–84, JD millions)

	Aid[1] (1)	Rem[2] (2)	(1+2)/BoT[3]	(1+2)/GDP
1963	22.50	8.52	75.22	24.03
1964	28.25	11.60	92.03	26.74
1965	41.63	12.90	112.90	32.54
1966	46.52	15.20	103.73	36.20
1967	51.58	11.30	139.73	47.93
1968	53.10	10.30	139.96	40.61
1969	45.80	14.00	107.17	32.61
1970	39.10	12.60	91.34	29.64
1971	35.50	13.20	71.83	26.15
1972	65.96	13.80	96.44	38.49
1973	61.10	23.20	89.49	38.62
1974	84.40	32.00	99.40	47.07
1975	138.00	63.90	104.13	64.69
1976	122.00	140.80	90.62	62.33
1977	167.00	145.90	79.38	60.85
1978	102.00	148.80	63.54	39.67
1979	318.10	168.30	95.94	64.59
1980	390.00	206.30	100.05	60.91
1981	416.30	344.90	86.65	65.84
1982	350.00	372.20	75.47	54.58
1983	295.00	414.80	75.25	49.52
1984	282.56	362.10	79.86	42.49
1985	317.54	275.90	72.45	37.72
Average	156.60	127.60	94.00	45.46

Notes:
1 Unrequited transfers to private and central government
2 Net remittances
3 Balance of trade

Source: The Central Bank of Jordan, *Annual Reports*, and author's calculation

exceeded the balance of trade deficit in seven years during this period and averaged 94 per cent of the trade deficit.

As far as the trend in remittances is concerned, Table 2.2 shows that total remittances, as officially recorded, increased more than fiftyfold during the period in question. The growth of the volume of remittances was very substantial, especially during the period between 1979 and 1982. A primary cause of the rapid growth in remittances was the increase in employment and earnings of Jordanian workers in the oil-producing countries after the oil price revolution of 1973 (Saket 1983).

Table 2.3   Foreign aid to Jordan: major donors (percentages)

Years	UK	USA	Arab countries
1956–66	14.20	45.0	—
1967–72	9.44	52.9	6.43
1973–85	3.70	8.5	85.10

Sources: For the first two periods, see Saket 1976, Tables 3.C, 3.D and 3.I. For the third period see Khatib n.d.

Total foreign aid received by Jordan has increased more than nineteenfold during the same period (1963–85). Table 2.3 shows the relative importance of foreign aid from the major donors.

Between 1950 and 1967, most of Jordanian's foreign aid receipts came mainly from the United Kingdom and the United States in the form of 'Budget Support'. Prior to 1950, Britain was the sole donor of aid but its proportion to total aid declined to an average of 11 per cent in 1960 and about 6.2 per cent for the period 1960–72 (Saket 1976). In 1985, foreign aid from the UK was estimated to be less than 1 per cent of total aid.

The United States was the most important source of aid during the period 1957–66 (45 per cent of total aid), when Jordan received JD 189 million (85 per cent in the form of budget support) in grants and about JD 19.4 million in the form of technical assistance (Saket 1976, p. 114). Although the importance of US aid declined significantly after 1967, this aid still represented about 10 per cent of total aid received by Jordan.

The flow of aid from Arab oil countries started after the 'Khartoum Agreement' in 1967 when Kuwait, Libya and Saudi Arabia agreed to provide an annual grant of JD 37.7 million to Jordan. Between 1967 and 1985, aid received from Arab oil countries represented about 82.4 per cent of total aid received by Jordan.

Finally, it is worth mentioning that foreign aid represented the main source of finance for the government deficit. The foreign aid receipts of central government accounted for more than 55 per cent of total government revenues in some years, including 1970 and 1980.

Having examined the scope and magnitude of foreign aid to Jordan, the next section will investigate empirically the impact of foreign aid on the economic growth of Jordan from a macro-economic point of view. In this section, an econometric model is formulated and the statistical results are analysed.

The econometric model

This section presents an econometric model to illustrate the impact of foreign aid on economic development. The policy implication of the model may be helpful to decision makers in Jordan. As discussed earlier, foreign assistance to Jordan was mainly received in the form of budget support. Foreign aid was used to finance government consumption as well as investment (see Table 2.2).

A strong correlation is expected between government expenditures and aid. A similar relationship is also expected between imports and aid since imports bills were partly financed through foreign assistance. Therefore, the focus will be on the behaviour of the public sector and imports and their implications for the overall absorptive capacity of the economy. The model consists of six behavioural equations for private consumption (PC), government consumption (GC), private investment (PI), government investment (GI) and imports (M). Also, there are four identities for total consumption (TC), gross investment (TI), disposable income (YD) and national income (Y).

Private consumption is expected to depend on disposable income (YD), and remittances (RE), while public consumption depends on national income (Y) and foreign assistance (FA). In the private investment function, both GDP and remittances of Jordanians abroad (RE) are expected to affect the behaviour of this sector.

In formulating the government investment equation, we anticipate a positive relationship between government domestic revenues (GR), foreign aid (FA) and public expenditure on investment (GI). Given the partial adjustment mechanism, a lagged one year dependent variable could also be suggested. The inclusion of this variable could be explained by the delay in decision making and interruption in project implementation as a result of unforseen factors (such as delays in receiving aid).

Imports are expected to be a function of GDP, remittances (RE) and the volume of foreign aid (FA). The terms of trade (TR) (defined as export unit value/import unit value) is also tested in the import function.

The model covers the period between 1963 and 1985. All data are in nominal terms, deflated by the cost-of-living index, the only deflator available for the entire period. The structural equations of the model are formulated in log function and the complete model is estimated by Ordinary Least Squares (OLS). Because of the recursive nature of the model, OLS seems appropriate, as it yields unbiased estimates.[7] In order to correct for serial correlation the Cochrane–Orcane technique is applied and the value of ρ is estimated and tested for the degree of significance.

Definition of variables

The endogenous variables

PC	Private consumption expenditure
GC	Government consumption expenditure
PI	Private investment
GI	Government investment
M	Imports
Yd	Disposable income
Y	Gross National Product
GDP	Gross Domestic Product
GR	Government domestic revenues (taxes and non-taxes)

The predetermined variables

FA	Foreign aid (unrequited transfers)
FA_{t-1}	Foreign aid lagged one year
RE	Jordanian remittances from abroad
M_{t-1}	Imports lagged one year
GI_{t-1}	Government investment lagged one year
IS	Changes in stock
FI	Net factor income from abroad
X	Exports
TR	Terms of trade

The identities

$$TC = PC + GC + IS$$
$$TI = PI + GI$$
$$Yd = Y - Taxes$$
$$Y \ (GNP) = TC + TI + FI + (X - M)$$

The behavioural equations (in log function)

$$PC = a_0 + a_1 Yd + a_2 RE + U_1$$
$$GC = b_0 + b_1 Y + b_2 FA_{t-1} + U_2$$
$$PI = c_0 + c_1 GDP + c_2 RE + U_3$$
$$GI = e_0 + e_1 GR + e_2 FA + e_3 GI_{t-1} + U_4$$
$$M = f_0 + f_1 GDP + I_2 RE + I_3 FA + U_5$$

Estimation of the model

The statistical results of the model, the log-linear estimates of the behavioural equations, are as follows:

$$\log PC = -.045 + .986 \log Yd \qquad (2.1)$$
$$(31.61)$$

$R^2 = .98$ DW = .98   F = 999.31   SEE = .052

$$\log GC = 1.43 + .38 \log Y + .214 \log FA_{t-1} \qquad (2.2)$$
$$(3.07) \quad (3.01) \quad (1.91)$$

$R^2 = .76$ DW = 2.41   F = 31.97   SEE = .653

$$\log PI = -10.63 + 2.37 \log GDP + 1.25 \log RE \qquad (2.3)$$
$$(-2.71) \quad (2.85) \quad (2.96)$$

$R^2 = .82$ DW = 1.98   F = 32.40   SEE = .554

$$\log GI = -.96 + .34 \log GR + .38 \log FA + .46 \log GI^{t-1} \quad (2.4)$$
$$*(-1.65) \quad *(1.49) \quad (2.34) \quad (2.40)$$

$R^2 = .91$ DW = .054   F = 63.90   SEE = .201

$$\log M = -.31 + .55 \log GDP + .4 \log RE + .16 \log FA^{t-1} \quad (2.5)$$
$$(3.43) \quad (6.54) \quad (2.59)$$

$R^2 = .95$ DW = 2.08   F = 121.36   SEE = 0.75
               $\rho = .5$ t = 2.4

* Significant at 10 per cent level only.

Other variables (such as RE in the PC equation, GI in the PI equation and TR in the M equation) were tested but found unsatisfactory and then were dropped from the model.

As Equations 2.1 to 2.5 show, the statistical fit is good as judged from the coefficient of determination adjusted for degree of freedom R^2. All variables are significant at the 1 per cent and 5 per cent levels (except the ER which is significant at the 10 per cent level only). The DW and Durbin's h statistics are at the level where the null hypothesis of auto-correlations is rejected at the 1 per cent level.

The foreign aid variable (FA) is found to be positive and highly significant in affecting public expenditures and import equations. The overall impact of foreign assistance has a favourable effect on economic development and the growth of GNP in Jordan as previously predicted.

Forecasting performance of the model

The performance of the model is examined using various criteria. The root mean square error, mean absolute error, regression coefficient of actual on predicted values, correlation coefficient and

Theil's inequality coefficient are all applied. In testing for the validity and stability of the model, the well-known Chow and Farley–Hinich (F–H) tests are employed.[9] The estimated model is simulated under different periods to detect for the degree of sensitivity of the model's parameters to these changes. The actual and simulated figures indicate that the model is stable and tracks the historical time path of the variables fairly well. The simulation results are presented in the Appendix to this chapter.

In applying Chow and F–H tests, two periods were distinguished: 1963–75 and 1974–85. It is not surprising that the first period was rather more sensitive to changes than the second. This could be related to the unsettled situation which the country witnessed during the 1967–71 period.

In general, we can conclude that in both tests the stability of the model is proved to be valid. However, the error measures of both tests are presented in Tables 2.4, 2.5 and 2.6.

Policy implication of the model

To evaluate the impact of aid on the economy of Jordan, simulation exercises were carried out under different scenarios. Table 2.7 summarizes our statistical findings. However, the complete simulation exercises for each scenario are tabulated in the Appendix.

Table 2.4   Chow test (1963–85)

	RMSE[1]	MAE[2]	RC[3]	CO[4]	Theil[5]
PC	.05304	.0409	.9968	.9906	.0001
GC	.12112	.0938	1.0000	.8823	.0006
PI	.54420	.4340	.7895	.9005	.0221
GI	.18160	.1499	1.0000	.9584	.0018
M	.11620	.0927	1.0005	.9837	.0005
TC	.13810	.1051	.9905	.9728	.0001
TI	.48530	.3955	.8477	.9748	.0039
GNP	.44990	.3551	.9171	.9943	.0004

Notes:
1 Root-mean-square error
2 Mean absolute error
3 Regression coefficient of actual on predicted variable
4 Correlation coefficient
5 Theil's inequality coefficient

Source: Farley and Hinich 1970

Table 2.5 Farley–Hinich test – simulation exercise using 1963–85 coefficients for 1963–75

	RMSE[1]	MAE[2]	RC[3]	CO[4]	Theil[5]
PC	.0364	.0301	1.0560	.9702	.0001
GC	.1348	.1019	1.0000	.5669	.0008
PI	.6901	.6014	.5224	.1116	.0634
GI	.2054	.1819	1.0781	.8832	.0031
M	.1239	.1017	1.0296	.8952	.0006
TC	.1401	.1036	.9067	.6357	.0002
TI	.5899	.4937	.4187	.4928	.0008
GNP	.5778	.4811	.7310	.9013	.0010

Notes:
1 Root-mean-square error
2 Mean absolute error
3 Regression coefficient of actual on predicted variable
4 Correlation coefficient
5 Theil's inequality coefficient

Source: Farley and Hinich 1970

Table 2.6 Farley–Hinich test – simulation exercise using 1963–85 coefficients for 1974–85

	RMSE[1]	MAE[2]	RC[3]	CO[4]	Theil[5]
PC	.0644	.0512	1.010	.9701	.0001
GC	.1000	.0814	.7003	.7609	.0004
PI	.3529	.2840	1.015	.8933	.0067
GI	.1664	.1293	.5784	.8104	.0012
M	.1202	.0944	.7462	.9706	.0004
TC	.1296	.09815	.9214	.9408	.0001
TI	.3356	.2931	.9096	.9346	.0001
GNP	.2871	.2489	.8915	.9837	.0005

Notes:
1 Root-mean-square error
2 Mean absolute error
3 Regression coefficient of actual on predicted variable
4 Correlation coefficient
5 Theil's inequality coefficient

Conclusion

The positive correlation between foreign assistance and economic growth has been confirmed in the case of Jordan. The statistical

Table 2.7 Summary of the simulation exercises (impact of FA reduction on economic variables)

	Scenario 1 FA reduced by 25% (%)	Scenario 2 FA reduced by 50% (%)	Scenario 3 FA reduced by 75% (%)
GC	-1.46	-3.37	-6.49
GI	-3.14	-6.76	-13.04
M	-1.84	-3.67	- 6.62
TC	-.004	-2.22	-.0003
TI	-4.57	-6.53	- 9.92
GNP	-1.46	-2.25	- 3.42

results of our econometric model indicate that foreign aid has had a favourable effect on economic development and growth in Jordan. The policy implication of these findings is that more foreign aid would raise the economic growth rate of Jordan. However, it is worth noting that the flow of aid from Arab countries was erratic and governed by the volatile circumstances that affect pan-Arab politics. Also, there is no need to emphasize that, for political reasons, donor sources may abruptly decrease the amount of aid or may even completely cut off aid. This, in fact, has been the experience of Jordan. In 1971, for example, Kuwait suspended aid flows to Jordan, and Libya cut off aid altogether (and the economic growth rate was affected). For this reason, an attempt has been made to simulate the impact of any potential reduction in the volume of foreign aid on the development process in Jordan. Three different assumptions are made. The statistical results of these simulations indicate how much the real growth could be affected (see Table 2.7). If foreign aid is reduced by half of its actual level, then the real growth rate of GNP will decline by 2.1 per cent. If the worst comes to the worst and foreign aid is cut to 75 per cent of its actual level, an assumption which seems to be very pessimistic, the Jordanian economy could still achieve positive rates of growth, but only just.

The policy implication of this empirical study is that Jordan needs to seek ways and means of both augmenting domestic resources and utilizing the available resources more effectively until the need for aid declines or ceases completely.

Appendix: Simulation exercises to evaluate the impact of aid on the Jordanian economy

Table 2A.1 Simulation exercise: scenario 1 (FA reduced by 25%)

	Actual PC	Sim. PC	Actual GC	Sim. GC	Actual PI	Sim. PI	Actual GI	Sim. GI	Actual M	Sim. M	Actual TC	Sim. TC	Actual TI	Sim. TI	Actual GNP	Sim. GNP
1965	5.61	5.64	4.42	4.46	3.22	2.48	3.09	3.07	4.70	4.64	9.85	10.10	6.30	5.55	17.40	16.97
1966	5.67	5.67	4.27	4.47	3.51	2.54	2.99	3.15	4.88	4.72	9.95	10.14	6.50	5.70	17.76	17.31
1967	5.30	5.37	4.44	4.47	3.01	1.78	3.26	3.29	4.66	4.79	9.73	9.77	6.26	5.07	17.37	16.08
1968	5.46	5.50	4.64	4.54	1.92	2.04	3.77	4.40	4.67	4.72	10.37	10.04	6.68	5.45	17.18	16.83
1969	5.63	5.63	4.74	4.58	3.12	2.47	3.72	3.62	4.79	4.75	10.37	10.22	6.84	6.09	18.69	17.83
1970	5.55	5.52	4.59	4.50	2.77	2.12	3.27	3.48	4.71	4.72	10.14	10.02	6.04	5.60	17.27	16.70
1971	5.55	5.53	4.56	4.46	2.57	2.14	3.57	3.22	4.80	4.63	10.11	9.99	6.15	5.36	17.14	16.39
1972	5.58	5.56	4.62	4.44	2.07	2.24	3.83	3.61	4.96	4.84	10.20	10.00	5.91	5.85	17.11	16.97
1973	5.50	5.52	4.67	4.55	2.13	2.29	4.00	3.70	4.97	4.87	10.17	10.07	6.13	5.98	17.68	17.54
1974	5.41	5.47	4.70	4.51	3.12	2.25	3.88	3.85	5.17	4.90	10.11	9.98	7.00	6.09	19.31	18.55
1975	5.69	5.65	4.62	4.60	2.17	2.79	4.37	3.99	5.46	5.18	10.30	10.26	6.54	6.78	19.24	19.70
1976	5.79	5.94	4.94	4.79	4.19	3.58	4.23	4.25	5.72	5.44	10.73	10.74	8.43	7.83	22.08	21.77
1977	5.91	5.94	4.83	4.76	3.76	3.68	4.72	4.29	5.88	5.63	10.75	10.71	8.48	7.97	21.95	21.65
1978	6.01	6.06	4.93	4.83	3.99	3.97	4.69	4.30	5.81	5.64	10.95	10.89	8.68	8.27	22.35	22.05
1979	6.14	6.09	5.02	4.73	4.16	4.07	4.82	4.68	5.93	5.85	11.15	10.81	8.99	8.75	22.86	22.37
1980	6.17	6.26	4.95	4.99	4.59	4.51	4.88	4.80	6.03	6.02	11.11	11.25	9.47	9.31	23.60	23.59
1981	6.30	6.36	5.00	5.06	5.08	4.79	4.89	4.87	6.30	6.11	11.30	11.42	9.96	9.67	24.57	24.57
1982	6.38	6.41	5.06	5.07	5.12	4.95	4.80	4.82	6.31	6.24	11.44	11.48	9.92	9.76	24.67	24.63
1983	6.44	6.41	5.09	5.03	4.76	5.01	4.76	4.70	6.24	6.20	11.53	11.45	9.52	9.70	24.20	24.35
1984	6.43	6.44	5.14	4.98	4.67	5.06	4.71	4.66	6.18	6.15	11.57	11.42	9.37	9.72	24.61	24.84
1985	6.28	6.23	5.03	4.89	4.03	4.53	4.65	4.56	6.00	6.01	11.30	11.13	8.68	9.10	23.19	23.42
Mean	5.85	5.87	4.77	4.70	3.52	3.30	4.14	4.01	5.44	5.34	10.61	10.56	7.66	7.31	20.49	20.19
% change				-1.49				-3.14		-1.84		-.004		-4.57		-1.46

Table 2A.2 Simulation exercise: scenario 2 (FA reduced by 50%)

	Actual PC	Sim. PC	Actual GC	Sim. GC	Actual PI	Sim. PI	Actual GI	Sim. GI	Actual M	Sim. M	Actual TC	Sim. TC	Actual TI	Sim. TI	Actual GNP	Sim. GNP
1965	5.61	5.64	4.24	4.38	3.22	2.48	3.09	2.92	4.70	4.54	9.85	10.02	6.30	5.40	17.40	16.82
1966	5.67	5.67	4.27	4.38	3.51	2.54	2.99	3.00	4.88	4.63	9.95	10.05	6.50	5.54	17.76	17.16
1967	5.30	5.37	4.44	4.31	3.01	1.78	3.26	3.13	4.66	4.70	9.73	9.68	6.26	4.91	17.37	15.93
1968	5.46	5.50	4.64	4.45	1.92	2.04	3.77	3.25	4.67	4.63	10.10	9.95	5.68	5.29	17.18	16.68
1969	5.63	5.63	4.74	4.50	2.77	2.47	3.72	3.47	4.79	4.66	10.37	10.13	6.84	5.93	18.69	17.68
1970	5.55	5.52	4.59	4.42	2.57	2.12	3.27	3.32	4.71	4.62	10.14	9.94	6.04	5.44	17.27	16.55
1971	5.55	5.53	4.56	4.37	2.07	2.14	3.57	3.06	4.80	4.54	10.11	9.90	6.15	5.20	17.14	16.24
1972	5.58	5.56	4.62	4.35	2.13	2.24	3.83	3.45	4.96	4.74	10.20	9.91	5.91	5.69	17.11	16.82
1973	5.50	5.52	4.67	4.47	3.12	2.29	4.00	3.54	4.97	4.78	10.17	9.98	6.13	5.83	17.68	17.39
1974	5.41	5.47	4.70	4.42	2.17	2.25	3.88	3.69	5.17	4.80	10.11	9.89	7.00	5.94	19.31	18.40
1975	5.69	5.65	4.62	4.52	4.19	2.79	4.37	3.83	5.46	5.09	10.30	10.17	6.54	6.62	19.24	19.56
1976	5.79	5.94	4.94	4.71	3.76	3.58	4.23	4.10	5.72	5.35	10.73	10.65	8.43	7.67	22.08	21.62
1977	5.91	5.95	4.83	4.67	3.99	3.68	4.72	4.13	5.88	5.54	10.75	10.62	8.48	7.82	21.95	21.50
1978	6.01	6.06	4.93	4.74	4.16	3.97	4.69	4.15	5.81	5.55	10.95	10.80	8.68	8.11	22.35	21.90
1979	6.14	6.09	5.02	4.64	4.59	4.07	4.82	4.53	5.93	5.75	11.15	10.73	8.99	8.60	22.86	22.22
1980	6.17	6.26	4.95	4.90	5.08	4.51	4.88	4.65	6.03	5.92	11.11	11.16	9.47	9.15	23.60	23.44
1981	6.30	6.36	5.00	4.97	5.12	4.79	4.89	4.72	6.30	6.02	11.30	11.33	9.96	9.51	24.57	24.42
1982	6.38	6.41	5.06	4.98	4.76	4.95	4.80	4.66	6.31	6.15	11.44	11.39	9.92	9.61	24.67	24.48
1983	6.44	6.41	5.09	4.95	4.67	5.01	4.76	4.54	6.24	6.10	11.53	11.36	9.52	9.55	24.20	24.20
1984	6.43	6.44	5.14	4.89	4.67	5.06	4.71	4.50	6.18	6.05	11.57	11.33	9.37	9.57	24.61	24.69
1985	6.28	6.23	5.03	4.81	4.03	4.53	4.65	4.41	6.00	5.91	11.30	11.04	8.68	8.94	23.19	23.28
Mean	5.85	5.87	4.77	4.61	3.52	3.30	4.14	3.86	5.44	5.24	10.16	10.48	7.66	7.16	20.49	20.05
% change				-3.35				-6.76		-3.67		-1.24		-6.53		-2.15

Table 2A.3 Simulation exercise: scenario 3 (FA reduced by 75%)

	Actual PC	Sim. PC	Actual GC	Sim. GC	Actual PI	Sim. PI	Actual GI	Sim. GI	Actual M	Sim. M	Actual TC	Sim. TC	Actual TI	Sim. TI	Actual GNP	Sim. GNP
1965	5.61	5.64	4.24	4.23	3.22	2.48	3.09	2.66	4.70	4.38	9.85	9.87	6.30	5.14	17.40	16.57
1966	5.67	5.67	4.27	4.24	3.51	3.54	2.99	2.74	4.88	4.47	9.95	9.90	6.50	5.28	17.76	16.91
1967	5.30	5.37	4.44	4.16	3.01	1.78	3.26	2.87	4.66	4.54	9.73	9.53	6.26	4.65	17.37	15.68
1968	5.46	5.50	4.64	4.30	1.92	2.04	3.77	2.99	4.67	4.47	10.10	9.81	5.68	5.03	17.18	16.43
1969	5.63	5.63	4.74	4.35	3.12	2.47	3.72	3.21	4.79	4.50	10.37	9.98	6.84	5.67	18.69	17.43
1970	5.55	5.52	4.59	4.27	2.77	2.12	3.27	3.06	4.71	4.46	10.14	9.79	6.04	5.18	17.27	16.30
1971	5.55	5.53	4.56	4.22	2.57	2.14	3.57	2.80	4.80	4.38	10.11	9.75	6.15	4.94	17.14	15.99
1972	5.58	5.56	4.62	4.21	2.07	2.24	3.83	3.19	4.96	4.58	10.20	9.76	5.91	5.43	17.11	16.57
1973	5.50	5.52	4.67	4.32	2.13	2.29	4.00	3.28	4.97	4.62	10.17	9.83	6.13	5.57	17.68	17.14
1974	5.41	5.47	4.70	4.27	3.12	2.25	3.88	3.43	5.17	4.64	10.11	9.74	7.00	5.67	19.31	18.15
1975	5.69	5.65	4.62	4.37	2.17	2.79	4.37	3.57	5.46	4.93	10.30	10.02	6.54	6.36	19.24	19.30
1976	5.79	5.94	4.94	4.56	4.19	3.58	4.23	3.83	5.72	5.19	10.73	10.50	8.43	7.41	22.08	21.37
1977	5.91	5.95	4.83	4.53	3.76	3.68	4.72	3.87	5.88	5.38	10.75	10.47	8.48	7.55	21.95	21.25
1978	6.01	6.06	4.93	4.59	3.99	3.97	4.69	3.88	5.81	5.39	10.95	10.65	8.68	7.85	22.35	21.65
1979	6.14	6.09	5.02	4.49	4.16	4.09	4.82	4.26	5.93	5.59	11.15	10.58	8.99	8.33	22.86	21.97
1980	6.17	6.26	4.95	4.76	4.59	4.51	4.88	4.39	6.03	5.76	11.11	11.02	9.47	8.89	23.60	23.19
1981	6.30	6.36	5.00	4.82	5.08	4.79	4.89	4.46	6.30	5.86	11.30	11.18	9.96	9.25	24.57	24.17
1982	6.38	6.41	5.06	4.83	5.12	4.95	4.80	4.40	6.31	5.99	11.44	11.24	9.92	9.35	24.67	24.23
1983	6.44	6.41	5.09	4.80	4.76	5.01	4.76	4.28	6.24	5.94	11.53	11.21	9.52	9.28	24.20	23.95
1984	6.43	6.44	5.14	4.75	4.67	5.06	4.71	4.24	6.18	5.90	11.57	11.18	9.37	9.30	24.61	24.44
1985	6.28	6.23	5.03	4.66	4.03	4.53	4.65	4.15	6.00	5.75	11.30	10.89	8.68	8.68	23.19	23.02
Mean	5.85	5.87	4.77	4.46	3.52	3.30	4.14	3.60	5.44	5.08	10.16	10.13	7.66	6.90	20.49	19.79
% change				-6.49				-13.04		-6.62		-.0003		-9.92		-3.42

Notes

1 Rapid increase in exports requires the development of new export products which is limited by productive capacity and institutional factors (Chenery and Strout 1966, p. 689).
2 In both phases, the role of foreign aid is to fill the gap between investments and savings.
3 By testing the association between domestic savings and foreign aid. However, this relationship was examined in the case of Jordan and gave the result:

$$S/Y = 0.05 - 0.26 \quad F/Y = R^2 = 0.1 \quad D - W = 0.43 \quad t = -1$$

The F/Y variable is not significant. Accordingly, we could not confirm any complimentarity or substitution between domestic savings and foreign aid in Jordan.
4 A mixed result was obtained by Gorgens (1976), Bornschier *et al.* (1978), and Fei and Ranis (1968).
5 This period witnessed the Arab–Israeli War in 1967 and the civil war in 1970.
6 One JD = £ sterling 1.95 in March 1987.
7 A block identification test was carried out and indicated the absence of simultaneous bias among variables and, accordingly, the OLS is suggested.
8 For more details see Chow 1969, Farley and Hinich 1970.

References

Bauer, P. and Yamey, B. (1982), 'The political economy of foreign aid', *Lloyds Bank Review*, January, p. 61.
Bornschier, B., Chase Dunn, C. and Robinson, R. (1978), 'Cross-national evidence of the effects of foreign investment and aid on economic growth and inequality: a survey of findings and a re-analysis', *American Journal of Sociology*, Vol. 84, No. 3.
Chenery, H. and Bruno, M. (1962), 'Development alternatives in an open economy: the case of Israel', *The Economic Journal*, Vol. 72.
Chenery, H. and Strout, A. (1966), 'Foreign assistance and economic development', *The American Economic Review*, September.
Chow, G. C. (1969), 'Test of equality between sets of coefficients in two linear regressions', *Econometrica*, Vol. 25.
Farley, I. and Kinich, M. (1970), 'A test for shifting slope coefficient in a linear model', *Journal of The American Association*, Vol. 65.
Fei, J. and Paauw, D. (1965), 'Foreign assistance and self help: a reappraisal of development finance', *The Review of Economics and Statistics*, August.
Fei, J. and Ranis, G. (1968), 'Foreign assistance and economic development: a comment', *The American Economic Review*, September, 1968.
Gorgens, E. (1976), 'Development aid – an obstacle to economic growth in developing countries?', *German Economic Review*, Vol. 14.

Griffin, K. and Enos, J. (1970), 'Foreign assistance: objectives and consequences', *Economic Development and Cultural Change*, April 1970.

Gupta, K. (1970), 'Foreign capital and domestic savings: a test of Haavelmo's Hypothesis with cross-country data: a comment', *The Review of Economics and Statistics*, Vol. 52, No. 2, May 1970.

Khatib, F., n.d., 'Foreign aid and economic development in Jordan: an empirical investigation', Unpublished Paper of the University of Lancaster, Lancaster.

McKinnon, R. (1966), 'Foreign exchange constraints in economic development and efficient aid allocation: a rejoinder', *The Economic Journal*, March 1966, p. 170.

Papanek, G. F. (1973), 'Aid, foreign private investment: savings and growth in less developed countries', *Journal of Political Economy*, Vol. 81, No. 1, January–February 1973.

Rahman, M. (1968), 'Foreign capital and domestic savings: a test of Haavelmo's Hypotheses with cross country data', *The Review of Economics and Statistics*, Notes Vol. 50, p. 137.

Rosenstein-Rodan, P. N. (1961), 'International aid for underdeveloped countries', *The Review of Economics and Statistics*, No. 2, p. 107.

Saket, B. (1976), 'Foreign aid to Jordan (1924/25–1972/73), its magnitude, composition and effect', Ph.D. thesis, University of Keele, England.

—— (1983), 'Economic use of remittances – the case of Jordan', Amman, March.

Weisskopf, T. (1972), 'The impact of foreign capital inflow on domestic savings in underdeveloped countries', *Journal of International Economics*, Vol. 2, p. 25.

Zagal, A. (1983), *Social Changes in Jordan*, Yarmouk University, Jordan.

Part two

The economy

Chapter three

The role of the private sector in Jordan's economy
Zayd J. Sha'sha

Introduction

Jordan has a mixed economy, with both government and private sector playing important roles. Originally, virtually all economic activity was in private hands, but since the 1950s the government has played an increasing role.

Though this change occurred in an area known for revolutionary change and reorganizational violence, it did not happen that way in Jordan. Instead, it came through a slow and informal process of reacting and/or coexisting with local, regional and international economic and political factors. No laws or directives exist covering this phenomenon. It all resulted from executive decisions taken on a case-by-case basis leading to a comprehensive partnership between government and market. To a great extent the interference of government in the business life of Jordan came by invitation of the private sector.

An adequate legal framework for the formal organization of the private sector has existed since 1949, and organizations to represent and protect private sector activities have been active ever since the inception of the state. Such entities were never against governmental interference. Nevertheless, during some periods in the late 1970s and more so in the early 1980s, they passively complained about the extent to which this role had reached.

Responding to the complaints of the private sector, King Hussein reinstated, in his Letter of Appointment of the present cabinet, the basic lines of economic thinking in the country. Jordan will always basically be a private enterprise economy. Currently, it is the Government of Jordan which is pushing the private sector to assert itself more independently. Though the reaction is not yet as anticipated, the general mood of the country favours free enterprise.

Understanding the role of the private sector in Jordan necessitates reviewing the evolution of the relationship between it and the state. This involves examining the following points:

1 the leadership of economic activities affecting the orientation of economic activities of the country;
2 the significance of the private sector's role compared to public sector activities;
3 the ability of the private sector to affect and influence administrative attitudes and initiate and/or modify existing laws to stay in line with the dynamic nature of the market and its needs, and equally important, its ability to keep clear the line of demarcation between government activities and trading activities and avoid mutual trespassing;
4 the ability of the private sector to affect local political elections and eventually have a say in the general economic policy of the country.

Since adequate statistics are not available to satisfy the quantitative part of the evaluation, this review will be limited to the historical aspect of the subject. The graveness of the matter is that the institutions which are supposed to form the private sector do not have among their files the data needed for such assessment.

For the purposes of this article, the private sector will be defined to mean (1) individuals or non-government commercial entities which are basically profit-oriented and (2) companies which are at least 51 per cent owned by non-government institutions. If the ownership of a certain entity is private but the management is under the control of delegated civil servants, then such institutions are excluded from this definition.

Historical development

To understand the developments leading to the present situation, it is appropriate to divide the sectoral development in Jordan into stages, each of which coincides with one of the stages of the development of the country.

The first of these stages starts with the arrival of Prince Abdullah Ibn al Hussein, the founder of the Hashemite Kingdom of Jordan, and lasts until 1967. Though this stage could be further divided into two parts, it is preferable, for the sake of brevity, to keep it as one. In the early part, ending in 1951, the foundations for building modern Jordan were laid down. The country was then small and underdeveloped. It was the period when the priority was to stabilize the authority of the government. In this period the power of the private sector best maintained itself by its ability to convince the government to postpone the declaration of the income tax law. It also had a clear impact on decisions leading to changes of government. It was in this period that the law for the formation of chambers of commerce was passed (law no. 41, 1949). This stage ended with the occupation of the West Bank of Jordan by Israel in the 1967 war. The second part of this period (1951-67) was characterized by the quiet and normal evolution of the country. Intersectoral relations were clear, and the private sector was the leader. Except for one case, all economic activities were privately initiated, and government intervention came through the invitation and insistence of the private sector.

The second stage was the planned economic development era which started in 1973 and which is still in force. Unlike the previous period, this stage is characterized by forced growth. The nature of the development sought and the size of the projects launched were far beyond the ability of the private sector to initiate. Whereas in the previous stage the decision to initiate economic activity was determined by local market needs, in the 1970s the planners had to identify foreign market opportunities in order to encourage exports.

This period also witnessed the creation of government Investment Institution Funds either in the form of Civil Service pension funds, Social Security or major employers' pension funds. These institutions assumed a major part in the economic development of the country by initiating the large investment projects specified in the Development Plans. This phenomenon has led to a drastic reduction in the relative weight of the individual investor.

Ironically, this period also witnessed more participation of the private sector in the national planning process. It saw the direct involvement of elected bodies representing the private sector in the formulation and review of laws pertaining to various aspects of life in Jordan. It also saw their membership in national committees set up for the design and follow-up of the national economic development plans for the country. Such a role was sought by the government for the private sector, rather than being initiated as a result of business lobbying.

Demographic changes forced on the country by the political events during the last forty years have left clear marks on the nature of the business community. This is reflected in the mobility and flexibility of the Jordanian private sector. The stability of the country, and the ability of Jordan's political and social systems to absorb the human influxes resulting from regional conflicts, added to the enrichment of the potential of the private sector.

Regional political upheavals and developments in the area had an impact on the 'general mood' existing between government and private sector. It was necessary to play down the private sector during some periods because of the need to coexist with socialist Arab neighbours. Private business in the Middle East experienced a wide range of attitude from governments, ranging from disregard to a desire to nationalize. Yet Jordan has been consistent in its respect for free enterprise and its commitment to the private sector.

Organizational structure of the private sector

Even though the legislation setting the parameters and form for organizing the private sector into well-defined bodies appeared in 1949, the informal organizational steps in that direction started earlier. Together these materialized in that early 1950s through the formation of the Amman Chamber of Commerce.

Currently, the private sector can organize itself into legally recognized interest groups by virtue of law no. 41 of 1949, the Law of Chambers of Commerce and Industry, which defines the function, the role and the party to whom such 'Chambers' report in their 'advisory capacity'.

This law allows the start-up of a chamber of commerce or industry in any governorate in which there are more than twenty qualified applicants. It leaves the final approval to the discretion of the Minister of Economy (later named the Minister of Industry and Trade) and vests the authority of defining financial costs and benefits in the Cabinet. The following is a selected list of such organizations.

The Chambers of Commerce

Because trading is, and has always been, the major private sector activity in the country, chambers of commerce are the largest bodies in this field. And since the governorate of Amman, the capital, constitutes no less than 40 per cent of the population of the country, the Amman Chamber of Commerce is the largest and oldest elected private sector body in Jordan. Consequently, it is the leader among similar local institutions. Currently, every governorate in Jordan has its own chamber of commerce, and together they constitute the primary lobby group for free commerce in the country.

The Chamber of Industry of Amman

This was founded in Amman in 1964 when the industrial establishments' number became relatively sizeable. Before that date all such non-trading units were members in the Chamber of Commerce.

Members include all major industrial concerns within the governate of Amman, and for these enterprises membership is compulsory. Other industrial entities outside the capital have the option of either joining their local chamber of commerce or the Chamber of Industry of Amman.

In 1987 the membership of the Chamber of Industry of Amman exceeded 4,000. However, the voting members do not exceed 20 per cent of that figure, since a minimum level of capital/employment is needed to qualify members for voting. Because of this irregularity in the election rights, and in an attempt to create better communication channels among the members and the Board of Directors, a sectoral representation advisory system was formalized recently.

The Union of Farmers

As its name implies, this body is meant to specialize in matters pertaining to the agricultural sector of Jordan. It is governed by the same law as the Chambers of Commerce and Agriculture. However, due to its relatively recent formation, it has not yet made an impact on the national economy comparable to the chambers of commerce.

The Bankers' Association

This is a type of club which promotes the exchange of experience and knowledge among its members. Established in 1979, it has been active in presenting bankers' opinions to the government. It should be noted that banks are also members of the Chamber of Commerce. Currently, the vice chairman of the Amman Chamber of Commerce is a member of the Bankers' Association.

Union of Construction Contractors

A recently formed association which includes among its members different types of construction contractors. Thus far, its impact has been minimal.

Jordanian Businessmen's Association

This association was initiated as a means to promote relations with the private sector in Egypt after the resumption of political and economic relations after the boycott resulting from the Camp David agreement which Egypt signed. The necessity of creating the association resulted from the decision of the General Federation of Arab Chambers of Commerce to boycott all Egyptian official entities as a result of the Camp David agreements and any Arab chamber dealing with them. This body is the only one in Jordan where all branches of activity are represented; therefore, it can be regarded as a national economic forum.

The Federation of Jordanian Chambers of Commerce, Agriculture and Industry

Under the umbrella of Arab unity, a Pan-Arab Federation for Chambers of Commerce, Agriculture and Industry was formed in the early 1950s. All private sector institutions in the countries which are members of the Arab League are members in this organization which has been trying for many years to improve commercial relations between Arab countries. The Jordanian chapter includes Chambers of Commerce but does not include the Chamber of Industry. This organization now acts as the national Chamber of Commerce.

How the partnership between government and the private sector developed

The gradual increase in the role of government in the non-government side of Jordan (whether directly or through government organizations), came at different periods for different reasons and in different forms. It is this non-uniformity of approach which indicates that originally the public sector did not intend to play the role it is currently assuming. The close link between government and business has led to the present partnership reflecting itself in the 'move to help' situation. As examples of how this situation developed, it is useful to consider the experience of a few sectors. Even though the others are not identical in conditions, the motive, mode and result are similar.

Commerce

Commerce or trading was the backbone of the economy of Transjordan and continues to be the same in modern Jordan. Until the early 1970s, the private sector had a totally free hand in importing and distributing all legal commodities. No restrictions ever existed on sources or quantities, nor did interference exist except by market forces.

Price developments, especially the sudden jump in international commodity prices in the mid-1970s, caused hardship for many Jordanians. At the same time with the inflow of funds from the Gulf, which benefited only some Jordanians, domestic inflation increased. The government therefore decided to intervene itself in the market for foodstuffs. This was done by initiating a Ministry of

Supplies whose job was to guarantee the continuous availability of 'essential' commodities such as sugar, wheat and rice in the market and at prices affordable to the average citizen. The government organized the market and prohibited the private sector from importing the same goods. This initiated the shrinkage of the role of the private sector.

The list of 'essentials', because it was not defined by the decree forming the Ministry of Supplies, developed in size subject to the interpretation of different ministers. It currently includes meat, wheat, sugar, rice and (though for totally different reasons) cigarettes. Non-essential food items are open for import by the private sector; however, such goods are to be priced by the Ministry of Supplies and are subject to the Health and Standards Bureau. Currently, no less than thirty basic food and grocery generic items are subject to price controls. Some non-food items are also included, and some are priced by the government. Automative spare parts are an example of the latter.

Later, in response to the inflationary period of the 1970s, the Jordanian government devised multiple effect institutions called 'consumer associations' for both the civil and military sectors. Such institutions are supposed to offer their members, who are substantial in number, goods at negligible margins of profit. This service improves the real income of the beneficiaries on the one hand and acts as a general market price suppressor on the other hand.

As it stands, the private sector can operate in the local trade of all commodities, serving as a distribution outlet for importers. The Ministry of Supplies also operates in this capacity, and therefore retail trading is mixed. Consumer societies trade side by side with the private sector.

Fully-fledged commercial operations including import and export of goods as well as local marketing are open to the private sector in any commodity that does not fall under the 'essentials' category. The triangular business is becoming a Jordanian phenomenon, and the government has helped by starting Free Zones and passing the necessary legislation to allow these to operate.

Industry

Until 1967, except for a few cases, the private sector was the initiator of activities in industry. This of course came as a result of the natural evolution in local and regional demand translated by the trader into a local manufacturing (in full or in part) facility. The exception to this was the initiation of the cement industry in 1951 by the government. The motive was the need for the product, but the size of investment then was enormous compared to the finance available from the average trader. The cement industry was therefore organized on a joint venture basis, with the state providing 51 per cent of the capital, but local, private investors given the majority of seats on the board of directors.

In the rest of the cases where government funds formed part of the equity of an industry activity, it was in response to the need of these factories to overcome shortages of funds affecting the continuity of employment.

The second stage of development witnessed a new era in manufacturing. The continuous call for the national development made both sectors get more actively involved in the industrialization process of the country. The type of major projects suggested to make Jordan an exporter of processed raw materials required finance well above what the private sector could secure. Projects like potash production, fertilizers and cement cost hundreds of millions of dinars, figures well in excess of previous investments in Jordan. For this reason the private sector had to give way to the government. State funding was crucial for the new ventures which needed legally secured periodical cash inflows from secure sources such as social security contributions. They needed also to call on the government to arrange for state guaranteed borrowings.

The private sector, meanwhile, concentrated on medium-sized and small industries where total project cost did not, on average, exceed 5-6 million, and could be financed by personal or corporate equities and by guarantees.

Another reason for government interference was the policy adopted in the early 1950s which lasted until the mid-1960s and which granted monopolistic concessions for the creation of locally strategic industries which the local market could not sustain if any competition was allowed. Such projects included cement and petroleum refining. In such cases, the government either participated directly in the equity and management or retained the right to price the products or both. It should be mentioned here that this approach had a positive effect on the development of the industrial sector. These concessions encouraged Jordanians to participate in the development process with a minimum return on investment guaranteed by the government.

At present, most industrial fields, especially the ones recommended in the development plans, are open to the private sector. Special industrial finance at rates cheaper than the market and for periods extended to fifteen years are available through specialized financial institutions. Jordan also has been encouraging the private investor to operate in most fields by granting long-term exemptions from income taxes and by providing fully serviced available sites.

Agriculture

Until 1967, the efforts in agriculture were concentrated on the development of the West Bank as the main agriculture and touristic part of the country. A major part of government spending on these two sectors during the period 1951–67 went to the West Bank. The war of 1967 left the country with a relatively meagre agricultural activity requiring a restart in the eastern part of the Jordan valley.

The role of the private sector in this field has been and still is of major importance. Government had in the first stage concentrated on cheap agriculture financing and advisory services. The actual farming activity, financed directly or through supplies of requirements, transport and marketing locally and in export markets, has been a private sector responsibility.

The lack of regional planning and the weak technical skills of the Jordanian farmers led to concentration on traditional crops such as tomatoes and aubergines. This led to a periodical excessive oversupply, especially since 1975 when export markets began their own similar production. Such oversupply became a national problem in the late 1970s leading to government interference in the buying of surplus tomato crops at 'compensation' prices. Later on the government started its own tomato paste manufacturing plants as one way of reducing its loss in the buying of these surpluses.

This was the start of events leading to the formation of the Governmental Agricultural Marketing Company targeted at opening new markets for Jordanian produce and also as an instrument for organizing the sector's activity.

The private sector has increased agricultural productivity by introducing new technology in irrigation. This has increased output in tomato and lettuce production. Currently, it is the private sector which is assuming the responsibility of starting desert farming with the blessing of the government.

Transport

The transport sector has always been a private activity. Overland transport has been the main activity and was especially crucial for petroleum supplies until the late 1950s when the pipelines were built.

As a result of the growth of trade in the region with Jordan being a politically stable oasis, transit business into neighbouring Arab countries through the Port of Aqaba flourished, and overland transport acquired further importance. The Jordanian transport community expanded its activity into owning and/or managing the truck fleets in the Gulf area.

Until recently the state continued to organize this sector. However, in the past few years neighbouring Arab countries, in an attempt to secure the consignment of their goods coming through Aqaba, established joint venture companies with the government of Jordan creating land transport companies which started to operate commercially.

Shipping is a new activity with heavier government weight than in the overland sector. The state does not have a monopoly, and the private sector is still an operator in this field.

Banking

Even before any government regulations concerning this sector, banking was already well established. The government is mainly involved in the commercial banking sector through the activities of the central bank. Specialized lending institutions in agriculture, industry, housing and community development are the governmental contribution to the banking system.

Other factors affecting the role of the state

The increase in the role of the government sector did not come about solely for the above reasons. Among the other factors leading to the increasing share of the public sector in the economic field were the shift of interest of the private individual to the speculative profits realized in the local stock market. Since the mid-1970s, tax free profits realized from the sale of shares and bonds became a national fever causing a major chunk of individuals' investment to shift from dividend earning and long-term real growth shares to fast earning activity. This phenomenon manifested itself in an oversubscription of issue shares that changed hands before any actual work in the project was realized.

The appeal of real estate trading activity for the same period also led to a reduction in investors' interest in industrial or long term finance. The inflow of petromoney into Jordan reflected itself in construction and real estate trading leading to inflationary profits. Since land trading was not subject to taxes, it became a major part of national activity. This blocked substantial amounts of liquidity, thus depriving the productive sectors of their chance of growth.

While the private sector was occupied with these side activities, the public sector was proceeding with its investment programme. The result was a further gain in the relative weight of the public sector in the Jordanian economy.

Another factor leading to the present situation was the concentration of efforts on operating in the petromarkets. This led the majority of Jordanians to treat their country as a leisure or 'retirement market'. Though this was financially rewarding for both private individuals and the country, it made encroachment by the public sector an easy matter. The private sector was the 'host' for most of the cases where the government intervened.

The present situation

The unique feature of Jordan is that the government interference in the economy was not intended to lessen the private sector or to compete with it. It was more a case of complementarity imposed on the country by unanticipated circumstances. The private sector was expected to perform and was not hindered except by its own interests and desires. The situation remains the same.

It is worth noting, however, that the private sector in Jordan is not made up of specialized operators because of the limited market size. People are sometimes traders, industrialists and farmers all at the same time. This leads to a compromising attitude toward issues related to the structural objectives of the economy.

Currently, the government is encouraging the private sector to resume its role in leading the economy. Even more important is the fact that government enterprises are in the process of being prepared for privatization.

Irrespective of how the temporary image of the country might appear, Jordan is a country endowed with wise and stable leadership that has been consistent in advocating and supporting free economy principles. This fact is one of the major underlying reasons why the private sector has always been receptive to the participation of the public sector in the market.

Chapter four

The demand for motorcars in Jordan

Aladdin Tileylioglu

The objective of this chapter is to examine the main determinants of the demand for motorcars in Jordan. A stock adjustment model that views consumers as attempting to adjust actual to desired stocks of automobiles is employed to analyse consumer behaviour. The empirical analysis is presented in two parts. The first part aims to investigate the effects of income, relative prices and credit availability on the demand for motorcars where the stock of automobiles and the annual purchases are alternately used as the dependent variables. In the second part, an attempt is made to examine the influence of monetary variables on the demand for automobiles where consumer expenditures on motorcars are taken as the dependent variable and treated as investment (Hamburger 1967, p. 1,131). To measure monetary variables, interest rates, the aggregate money supply and the rate of change in money supply are taken.

In the first section a brief account of Jordan's economy is given as a background for the study. This is followed by an analysis of the market for new and second-hand automobiles in Jordan. The model is then outlined and the main hypotheses are discussed. The empirical estimation of the model is presented and finally the results are summarized and discussed.

Jordan's economy and the automobile

Jordan's economy is largely characterized by a lack of financial and natural resources. Yet Jordan has achieved a steady and very high economic growth between 1975 and 1981 during the oil boom in the Middle East. Since then a steady decrease in the growth rate has been observed which may be attributed to the decline in the economies of oil-producing countries of the Middle East. Jordan's dependence on aid from these countries and its reliance on workers' remittances which come from the same source may have contributed to this decline.

Jordan also has a very high consumption rate. Total consumption has most of the time exceeded GDP reflecting negative or very small saving. The high consumption rate has been the result of a very large inflow of remittances during the same period.

Parallel to this development, large increases in the demand for consumer durables have been witnessed. There has also been a rapid growth in the stock of automobiles (Table 4.1). The number of motorcars reached 186,000 in 1986. This means that on average there are nearly eight cars for every hundred persons in Jordan.

There is no motorcar production in Jordan. Neither is there any restriction on the import of automobiles by type, size or make. As a result of this the stock of cars consists of a large number of different makes. The only important restriction related to motorcars is that cars which are over five years old may not be imported to Jordan. This restriction was introduced to prevent Jordan from being a dumping ground, particularly for cars brought into the country by people working in the Gulf region. Despite this restriction, cars exceeding the five-year limit may still enter the country and be used. Such cars may be imported under the 'Temporary Import Law' and used by foreigners who have permits to reside and work in Jordan.

The large variety of makes and types of cars imported may put a heavy burden on the country by increasing the cost of importing the necessary parts and accessories needed to maintain the stock of automobiles. These parts have to be imported in small quantities from a large number of different countries, eventually increasing the running cost for consumers.

Cars are not officially classified by type, make or size in the Jordan import statistics. Still an analysis of the market for automobiles clearly reveals that the majority of cars in use have engine sizes of below 2,000 cc. The reasons for this is not only the relatively high petrol prices and expensive parts that increase the cost of running a large car, but also the very high customs duty imposed on car imports. Custom duty on automobiles ranges from 100 per cent to 200 per cent of their import prices, depending on the engine size, the age of the car and the extras it contains (Table 4.2). Air-conditioning, sun-roofs, tinted glass, stereo radio/cassettes and metallic colour are some of the extras that increase the duty paid on cars. Examination of Table 4.2 shows that the customs duty increases by 30 per cent when a car has over 2,000 cc engine size. The market for automobiles is also characterized by the large number of Mercedes cars, most of which have over 2,000 cc engines. As in many other countries the Mercedes is a sign of

Table 4.1 Growth in stock of automobiles

Year	Stock of motorcars	New purchases of motorcars	Average prices of motorcars (JD)	Expenditure on motorcar (JD)	Consumer credits (JD thousands)
1970	10,050	1,868	567.5	1,060,039	4,142
1971	10,366	2,251	1,086.7	2,446,236	3,278
1972	11,173	1,684	2,128.5	3,584,490	3,894
1973	12,802	3,186	1,194.8	3,806,779	4,555
1974	16,101	4,352	1,603.9	6,980,395	5,815
1975	21,306	5,913	1,995.2	11,797,636	7,402
1976	28,615	11,394	2,004.0	22,763,669	11,365
1977	39,613	22,427	1,652.0	37,048,019	13,075
1978	50,905	15,732	3,482.0	54,777,532	21,212
1979	61,828	17,023	4,401.8	74,931,944	29,662
1980	75,998	14,170	6,536.5	92,622,873	38,717
1981	89,598	13,600	8,316.1	113,100,068	60,834
1982	105,475	15,881	8,557.9	135,899,053	69,596
1983	118,935	13,456	11,669.6	156,956,445	108,096
1984	130,109	17,174	10,184.3	174,864,344	121,459

Sources: First three columns from Ministry of Finance, Custom Department; fourth and fifth columns from Central Bank of Jordan Statistical Yearbook, various issues

Table 4.2 Custom duty on cars by size of engine and age

Year	Engine size (cc)			
	< 2,000	2,001–2,500	2,501–3,000	> 3,001
	(%)	(%)	(%)	(%)
1986	100	130	150	200
1985	85	115	135	185
1984	75	105	120	175
1983	65	95	115	165
1982	60	90	110	160

Source: Ministry of Finance

prestige in Jordan. The availability of hire purchase facilities from dealers and consumers credits with easy terms from banks are incentives for people who wish to enjoy the prestige of driving such cars.

New automobiles are generally imported and sold by authorized dealers, some of which have very efficient after-sale services. The high custom duty imposed on car imports and relatively high markup on their prices, makes automobiles very expensive, particularly compared with neighbouring Gulf countries where no tax is levied on cars.

As indicated above, attractive hire purchase facilities are offered to customers which include a down payment of approximately one-quarter of the total price of a car with monthly instalments of up to four years for the outstanding balance. The rate of interest plus other expenses applied to the outstanding balance, in general, does not exceed the current interest rate plus other expenses charged by banks on consumer credits.

Trade-in facilities are also offered by new car dealers, but these are not extensively used by clients. Car owners prefer selling their cars privately to trading them in for new ones.

There is no law restricting individuals from importing and selling automobiles. This makes it very attractive for Jordanians working abroad, particularly the 300,000 working in the Gulf region, to travel by car from the country where they work, spend their holiday with their family and relatives in Jordan and sell them before they fly back to their place of work. This has been a very popular practice as workers recover most of their travel expenses. However, these people generally bring second-hand cars and they do not constitute a threat to dealers in the market for new automobiles.

It is very difficult to determine the magnitude of the second-hand car market in Jordan. No information is available concerning the sales of licensed dealers or private individuals. More activity is observed in the second-hand automobile market particularly during the weeks prior to the two religious festivals of 'Eid-Ramadan' and 'Eid-Al-Adha'. At this time many Jordanians working abroad are holidaying in Jordan, selling their cars privately or through a second-hand car dealer before returning to their work.

An important feature of the second-hand car market in Jordan is the limited information available to buyers concerning the product quality and the accompanying risk. There are no trade regulations that require private sellers or dealers to provide a warranty of mechanical condition to buyers. The only assurance about quality is a test drive and an independent inspection of mechanical soundness of the vehicle which is made on demand and paid for by the prospective buyers.

To protect prospective buyers from such risk a law or regulation could be introduced that requires a dealer to inspect the car and certify it for a specified level of mechanical condition. Naturally, such practice increases the price by the inspection cost plus the expected repair costs by the dealer, both of which should not exceed the resultant increase in valuation of the car. This cost increase eventually increases the price to be paid by the prospective buyer.

The effect of introducing such regulation into the second-hand car market would be to increse the flow of cars to the dealers. Most buyers would prefer to buy from dealers an inspected and certified car for a higher price, rather than buy an automobile of uncertain quality. Of course, this assumes that the dealers do satisfy the conditions for such inspection and certification. As a result, total sales volume in the second-hand motorcar market might be expected to increase.

The model

Our model of the demand for automobiles is a stock adjustment model in which consumers are viewed as having a desired stock of cars to which they adjust gradually. The formulation of the demand function is similar to Burstein (1960), Chow (1960), Hamburger (1967), and Stone and Rowe (1957).

Let new purchases of motorcars during year t be ΔM_t, the desired stock of automobiles at the end of year t be M^*_t and the total stock at the end of the year t − 1 be M_t. If we first assume that the existing stock of cars adjusts to its desired level instantaneously, then purchases of motorcars during year t equals the difference between the desired stock at the end of year t, and the depreciated stock of motorcars at the end of year t – 1. Formally:

$$\Delta M_t = M^*_t - kM_{t-1} \tag{4.1}$$

Where k is a fraction of the stock of cars that takes into account annual depreciation and scrappage. Second we assume the desired stock to be a function of a set of economic variables such as the price of automobiles relative to prices of all other goods purchased by consumers, PM, disposable income expressed in constant prices, YD, and credit availability, CA. Then annual purchases of automobiles may be expressed as follows:

$$\Delta M_t = M^*_t (PM_t, YD_t, CA_t, U_t) - kM_{t-1} \tag{4.2}$$

Where U is a random element, that shows the effect of all variables other than PM, YD and CA on the demand for the desired stock.

The demand for automobiles may be viewed as consisting of two parts, annual purchases which are made to fill the gap between the old stock remaining from a previous year and the total desired stock, and annual purchases for replacement of the old stock. Accordingly, M may be written as

$$\Delta M_t = (M^*_t - M_{t-1}) + (1 - k)M_{t-1} \tag{4.3}$$

The first term on the right-hand side is the demand for desired change in the stock and the second is the demand for replacement of old stock.

There is no reason to expect the existing stock to adjust instantaneously to its desired level. The individual consumer would respond to changes in prices and income and as a result he may not change his stock of motorcars at once (Chow 1960, p. 154). If only a fraction β of the desired change in ownership is assumed to take place in one year then (4.3) becomes:

$$\Delta M_t = \beta(M^*_t - M_{t-1}) + (1 - k) M_{t-1} \tag{4.4}$$

Substituting (4.2) into (4.4) yields

$$\Delta M_t = \beta[M^*_t(PM_t, YD_t, CA_t, U_t) - M_{t-1}] \tag{4.5}$$

where β represents the adjustment coefficient which is $0 < \beta < 1$. It measures the average speed at which consumers adjust to their desired stock levels of cars during the current period. The adjustment is instantaneous when $\beta = 1$ and partial when $\beta < 1$.

If we assume that a non-linear relationship exists between the demand for automobiles and its determinants, then our estimating equation will take the following form:

$$\ln M_t = a_0 + a_1 \ln PM_t + a_2 \ln YD_t + a_3 \ln CA_t + a_4 \ln M_{t-1} + u_t \qquad (4.6)$$

Where u is the stochastic disturbance term, and all the variables are as defined in the Appendix.

The demand for motorcars is expected to vary positively with all types of income and inversely with the relative prices of automobiles. A positive relationship is also expected between motorcar demand and credit availability. Total consumer credit is taken as a proxy for credit availability and also for the positive effect of the hire purchase facilities available for car buyers. To account for the prices of all other consumer goods, the consumer price index is included and a positive relationship is expected between automobile demand and this variable.

To examine the influence of monetary variables on the demand for motorcars, we have taken consumer expenditures on motorcars as the dependent variable. The expected relationship between this variable and the rate of interest on government securities is negative. This variable is taken as measure of the yields available on financial assets. The rate of interest on time and saving deposits is also taken as a measure of yields on saving accounts. We also expect an inverse relationship between this variable and consumer expenditures on motorcars. The money supply which is defined as demand deposits plus currency in the hands of the public and the rate of change in money supply are included in the analysis to provide an explanation for the influence of money on consumer behaviour. A positive relationship is expected between these variables and the dependent variable.

Empirical results

Ordinary least squares regression is used in estimating the demand function for motorcars in Jordan. The analyses is based on annual time-series data covering the period 1970–84. The results are presented in two different tables. In Table 4.3 the regression results for the stock of motorcars are given with income, motorcar prices and credit availability as the explanatory variables. Initially an attempt is made to explain both the stock of automobiles and purchases of new automobiles. The results for the former are presented below, while it was not possible to obtain acceptable results that can be reported in the study for the latter.

Table 4.3 presents a set of regression results for the stock of automobiles. All of the regression equations have R^2 equal to 0.99, implying that explanatory variables explain nearly all the variations in the dependent variable. The calculated t ratios for the regression coefficients (shown under each coefficient in brackets) are above the acceptable level in most cases. The Durbin-Watson (DW) statistics in 1a, 1b, and 1f suggest that there is positive serial correlation in the residuals while in 1c inclusion of the credit availability coefficient increased the DW to 2.51 to suggest negative serial correlation in the residuals. In 1d and 1e the test is inconclusive. No attempt is made to re-estimate the model with the assumption that the residuals follow a pattern of first-order serial correlation.

An analysis of the coefficients shows that the price of motorcars variable exhibits some instability. Its coefficient has the negative sign as expected *a priori* in 1a, 1b and 1c and it is nearly twice its standard error in 1a, highly significant in 1c, and insignificant in 1b. It is significant but has the wrong sign in 1d, which may be due to inclusion of the lagged dependent variable or exclusion of the variable for price of all other goods from the equation. Real income and real disposable income are used alternately to account for the effect of income on the demand for automobiles. Both variables were found to effect automobile demand positively as expected *a priori*.

Coefficients of real income in 1a, 1e and 1f are highly significant. The coefficient of disposable income is large and highly significant in 1e and significant at the 10 per cent level and much smaller in magnitude in 1b and 1d. The inclusion of the consumer credit variable showed that the demand for automobiles was highly sensitive to changes in credit availability. The greater the available credit for consumers the greater the demand for motorcars and vice versa. The coefficient of the lagged dependent variable was very significant and had the expected positive sign, so were coefficients of prices of other goods variables.

The estimated adjustment coefficient is obtained from the coefficient of the lagged dependent variable which is an estimate of $(1 - k)$ (Chow 1960, p. 161). The variable k is estimated by dividing the old stock at the end of the year with total stock at the beginning of the year. It was found to be very close to 0.80. According to equation 1d the adjustment coefficient is 0.53. The price elasticity of demand for stock is −0.19 and the income elasticity is 0.66 (1c). Disposable income is used in this equation. In equation 1a where

Table 4.3 Regression results for stock of motorcars in Jordan, 1970–84

Equation number	Dependent variable	Intercept	PM_t	YG_t	YD_t	CA_t	POG_t	M_{t-1}	R^2	DW
1a	M_t	−2.042	−0.087 (1.93)*	0.792 (4.25)			1.829 (16.85)		0.99	1.05
1b	M_t	−1.590	−0.064 (−0.99)		0.476 (1.74)		1.952 (12.23)		0.99	0.89
1c	M_t	−3.497	−0.195 (2.60)		0.662 (3.75)	0.445 (4.730)			0.99	2.51
1d	M_t	−0.728	0.151 (4.08)		0.234 (1.76)			0.738 (9.48)	0.99	1.51
1e	M_t	−3.578	0.488 (0.720)	0.444 (2.10)		0.233 (2.42)	1.379 (6.68)	0.556 (5.84)	0.99	1.63
1f	M_t	−1.286	0.010 (0.261)	0.339 (2.91)			1.073 (6.92)	0.409 (5.19)	0.99	1.18

Note:
* Figures in parentheses are the calculated t ratios

real income is used the price and income elasticities are −0.09 and 0.79 respectively. The calculated adjustment coefficient for 1e is 0.36 and for 1f it is 0.21.

Table 4.4 presents empirical results of the effects of monetary variables on the consumer expenditure on automobiles. Analysis of the table shows that nearly all the variations in the dependent variable are explained by the independent variables. The calculated t ratios for the regression equations are above the acceptable level in most cases indicating significant coefficients. Positive serial correlations in the residuals are suggested by the D-W statistic in 2b and 2d. Equation 2e shows no positive or negative serial correlations in the residuals. Almost all the regression coefficients have the correct sign as expected *a priori*, except for the coefficient of price variable which has the wrong positive sign although it is highly significant.

A closer look at the coefficients shows that those for both real income and real disposable income have the correct positive signs and in all equations but one they are highly significant. The measure of the yields available on saving and time deposits shows that saving accounts are poor substitutes for automobile purchases. The regression coefficients for this variable was insignificant though it had the correct negative sign. The coefficient of the rate of interest on government securities have the right negative sign and are significant in all the equations presented. This variable was taken as a measure of yields available on financial assets. This result may suggest that the rate of interest on financial assets has a significant effect on consumer expenditures on automobiles. The other monetary variable taken to influence the consumer expenditures on motorcars is demand deposits plus currency in the hands of public, SM. Its coefficients have the expected positive sign in 2a and 2c and is significant at the 1 per cent level in 2c. Inclusion of the variable SM distorted the estimated results, for this reason regressions with this variable were not reported. Coefficients of the lagged dependent variable had the expected positive sign and were highly significant. According to equation 2d the estimated adjustment coefficient is 0.36. The income elasticity of demand for automobiles is 0.72 and 0.60 when real income was used (2a, 2h), and in the region of 0.65 when disposable income is used (equations 2b and 2f). Finally the interest elasticities of the demand for stock ranges from 0.88 to 2.13.

Summary

The stock adjustment model appears to represent the stock demand

Table 4.4 Regression results for consumer expenditure on motorcars in Jordan, 1970–84

Equation number	Dependent variable	Intercept	PM_t	YG_t	YD_t	CA_t	RS_t	RT_t	SM_t	M_{t-1}	R^2	DW
2a	CEM^1	7.537	1.035 (7.60)*	0.719 (3.51)			-0.887 (-2.02)	-0.279 (-0.82)	0.039 (1.43)		0.99	1.61
2b	$CEXM_t$	9.138	1.004 (11.36)		0.656 (2.20)		-2.133 (12.03)				0.99	1.18
2c	$CEXM_t$	-22.404	1.193 (14.43)						2.684 (27.45)		0.99	1.40
2d	$CEXM_t$	7.824						-0.827 (-1.53)		0.569 (2.81)	0.97	1.16
2e	$CEXM_t$	6.053	1.256 (8.08)		0.1428 (0.676)	0.298 (2.82)	-1.168 (-5.00)			0.142 (1.71)	0.99	1.87
2f	$CEXM_t$	62.318			0.670 (3.81)		-2.903 (-2.16)		-4.999 (2.83)		0.96	1.47
2g	$CEXM_t$	2.869	1.207 (13.26)		0.444 (1.98)	0.346 (3.20)	-1.375 (-5.08)				0.99	1.51
2h	$CEXM_t$	5.787	0.903 (8.94)	0.605 (3.21)			-1.426 (-7.48)			0.2291 (3.59)	0.99	1.36

Note:
* Figures in parentheses are the calculated t ratios

for automobiles quite well. A close fit of the statistical model has been obtained. This is evidenced by the high explanatory power, statistical significance and correct signs of most of the regression coefficients.

Our results suggest that the demand for motorcars can be explained as a simple function of income, relative prices and credit availability, where particularly income is found to be an important determinant of the demand for automobiles. The influence of credit availability is also apparent. In many respects these findings are in agreement with evidence presented in the area of demand for consumer durables.

Inclusion of the real rate of interest on government securities and the money supply in the analysis provides some indication of the manner in which monetary operations influence consumer behaviour. Highly significant coefficients for the rate of interest and in some cases for money supply suggest a significant impact of monetary variables on consumer purchases of automobiles.

Appendix 4.1: definition of variables

M_t The stock of motorcars, defined as the number of cars in use at the end of year t

M_{t-1} The stock of motorcars at the end of year $t - 1$

ΔM_t New purchases of motorcars, measured as the new additions of the stocks of cars at the end of year t

PM_t Relative prices of automobiles, average motorcar prices, deflated by the consumer price index

YG_t Gross national product, deflated by the consumer price index

YD_t Disposable income, deflated by the consumer price index

CA_t Credit availability, measured by consumer credit by commercial banks, deflated by the consumer price index

$CEXM_t$ Total consumption expenditures on automobiles, deflated by the consumer price index

$CEXM_{t-1}$ Total consumption expenditures on automobiles at the end of year $t - 1$

RS_t Rate of interest on long-term government securities, in real terms

RT_t Rate of interest on saving and time deposits, in real terms

ΔSM_t Rate of change in SM

POB_t Prices of other goods – the consumer price index is used as a proxy

References

Burstein, M. (1960), 'The demand for household refrigeration in the United States', in A. C. Harberger (ed.), *The Demand for Durable Goods*, University of Chicago Press, Chicago.

Chow, G. C. (1960), 'Statistical demand functions for automobiles and their uses for forecasting', in A. C. Harberger (ed.), *The Demand for Durable Goods*, University of Chicago Press, Chicago.

Hamburger, M. J. (1967), 'Interest rates and the demand for consumer durable goods', *American Economic Review*, Vol. 47, pp. 1,131–53.

Stone, R. and Rowe, D. (1957), 'The market demand for durable goods', *Econometrica*, Vol. 25, pp. 423–43.

Appendix 4.2: background economic data

Table 4A.1 National economic indicators, 1970–84

Year	GNP (million JD)	Disposable income (million JD)	Per capita GNP (JD)	Consumer price index (1976 = 100)
1970	187.0	145.7	123.9	114.2
1971	199.4	146.1	127.7	119.2
1972	221.0	174.0	136.8	126.4
1973	241.5	178.1	144.4	140.6
1974	279.3	206.5	161.4	167.9
1975	376.0	261.4	2,12.8	188.2
1976	560.4	351.6	304.8	209.8
1977	660.1	401.3	346.0	240.3
1978	781.0	437.4	395.2	257.3
1979	921.3	571.7	438.8	293.6
1980	1,185.3	701.2	536.5	362.2
1981	1,501.0	802.1	642.7	351.3
1982	1,695.4	821.2	697.8	377.4
1983	1,848.3	789.6	709.4	396.3
1984	1,854.5	801.3	710.3	411.7

Source: Statistical Yearbook, Department of Statistics, Amman 1985

Table 4A.2 National fiscal indicators, 1970–84

Year	Money supply M_1	M_1	Real r on gov. sec. (RS_t)	Real r on time dept. (RT_t)
1970	92,348.5	2,253.0	4.38	4.30
1971	90,298.5	−2,050.0	4.18	4.18
1972	91,000.0	701.5	4.35	3.99
1973	99,038.4	8,038.4	3.92	3.49
1974	102,420.5	338.1	3.28	2.92
1975	119,343.3	16,922.8	2.92	2.61
1976	131,968.1	12,624.9	2.88	2.34
1977	137,739.1	5,771.0	2.54	2.08
1978	145,888.1	8,148.9	2.37	1.84
1979	160,985.0	15,096.9	2.08	1.53
1980	182,333.2	21,348.2	1.92	1.22
1981	199,731.3	17,398.7	1.78	1.28
1982	208,665.3	8,933.4	1.66	1.19
1983	219,383.5	10,718.2	1.58	1.21
1984	213,564.5	−5,818.9	1.58	1.21

Source: Central Bank of Jordan, Statistical Yearbook, various issues

Chapter five

Jordan's trade and balance of payments problems

Monther Share

Introduction

Jordan's economy has been facing various challenges since independence in 1946. These have to be seen in the context of the limited national resource base of the country. The unstable and occasionally hostile political environment poses even greater difficulties and calls for continuous readjustments.

Despite such unsettling forces, Jordan succeeded in establishing a basic infrastructure and a number of industries. Irrigation and agriculture projects were also undertaken. Progress and expansion in the education and health sectors were among the most noticeable achievements.

Economic growth

During the period 1952–66, gross domestic product (GDP) grew at an average rate of 6.9 per cent and gross national product (GNP) at an average rate of 7.5 per cent per annum. This period witnessed the introduction of development planning into Jordan (Ministry of Planning 1986, p. 2). The Five-Year Plan for Social and Economic Development for 1963–7 was Jordan's first attempt at national development planning. The plan was later revised and changed to the 1964–70 Seven-Year Programme. Reducing the trade deficit was the first of the plan's goals which were listed in order of importance (Jordan Development Board 1964, p. 5). The 1967 war with Israel disrupted development efforts and created new social and economic problems.

Jordan was deprived of an important part of its natural and economic resources as a result of the 1967 war. At the same time it was necessary to allocate scarce resources to military expenditure. Yet economic growth continued. Real GNP grew at an annual average rate of 4.25 per cent between 1967 and 1972 (Ministry of Planning 1986, p. 8).

In 1973 Jordan launched its Three-Year Development Plan aiming at reactivating the economy and alleviating unemployment. The growth rate in real GDP averaged 5.9 per cent per annum as compared with the 8 per cent set by the plan. The GNP real growth rate averaged 7 per cent per annum (Ministry of Planning 1986, p. 11).

This Three-Year Plan was followed by the Five-Year Plan of 1976–80. This plan achieved a real annual rate of growth in GDP of 8.5 per cent, compared to the target rate of 11.9 per cent. GNP real growth rate was 11.9 per cent, compared to the planned rate of 11.5 per cent.

The second Five-Year Plan (1981–5) was formulated in an atmosphere of optimism. Planners assumed a continuation of the positive trends of the 1970s. However, such trends did not prevail. The war in Lebanon, the Gulf War, and the decreases in Arab aid due to the changes in the oil situation and prices, all led to a new set of less favourable conditions. The result was a low real GDP average growth rate of 4.2 per cent per year during the plan period compared with the targeted rate of 11 per cent. The average annual growth rate of real GNP (4.8 per cent) was about half the target rate of 10.9 per cent (Ministry of Planning 1986, p. 28).

Foreign trade: a question of importance

The importance of foreign trade to the less developed economies stems from their inability to produce capital goods and intermediate inputs which are essential for their economic development (Cairncross 1976, p. 713). Such inability is often coupled with very limited resources. Therefore, the needs of the economy and the population, which is usually growing at high rates, will have to be met through importation. Financing imports, more often than not, means a critical challenge to the less developed countries (LDCs). Their export proceeds are insufficient to cover the foreign exchange requirements of the import bill and a trade deficit results.

Trade deficits have been a characteristic feature of Jordan's balance of payments. Table 5.1 indicates that Jordan ran a trade deficit in every single year of the period 1967–85. Jordan's trade deficit dates back to the early days of recording trade statistics in 1936 (Department of Statistics 1984, pp. 2–3).

This persistent imbalance can be attributed to the following factors. First, the limited productive capacity of the country which is constrained by its meager resource endowment. This limitation prevents domestic supply from catching up with the ever-growing domestic demand (Amerah 1982, p. 62). Second, income growth

Table 5.1 Trends in the major items of Jordan's Balance of Payments, 1967–85 (JD millions)

Year	Exports	Imports	Trade balance	Current account	Basic balance	Net official unrequited transfers	Net loans to central government	Workers' remittances inflow	Workers' remittances outflow	Net travel and tourism	Net private investment, short and long run	Net investment income
1967	11.33	54.23	-42.90	26.18	28.16	51.58	1.63	6.55	—	1.50	0.04	3.61
1968	14.26	57.30	-43.04	10.12	15.08	53.07	5.00	4.10	—	-2.40	-0.06	4.92
1969	14.75	67.54	-52.79	-16.28	-10.94	45.79	4.50	6.92	—	-3.45	0.80	6.04
1970	12.17	65.53	-53.36	-5.93	-4.71	39.08	1.42	5.54	—	-4.58	-1.35	6.12
1971	11.44	76.19	-64.75	-21.27	-13.65	35.49	7.84	4.97	—	-3.34	-1.28	4.77
1972	17.01	94.88	-77.87	1.31	8.50	65.96	6.71	7.41	—	-2.97	-0.38	3.34
1973	24.15	107.80	-83.65	3.80	10.25	61.09	7.60	14.80	—	-0.57	-1.14	5.08
1974	49.75	155.68	-105.93	2.94	13.82	84.43	9.47	24.13	—	-0.14	1.06	6.70
1975	48.88	232.94	-184.06	21.47	65.58	138.01	37.42	53.25	—	1.96	6.30	8.23
1976	68.71	338.74	-270.03	17.34	2.68	122.75	-11.35	136.41	6.80	28.72	-3.40	8.25
1977	82.06	453.11	-371.05	-2.46	47.72	166.94	46.40	154.75	15.00	52.80	3.75	7.35
1978	90.92	458.94	-368.02	-85.80	5.10	102.63	73.67	159.38	20.00	40.70	17.23	8.54
1979	120.92	588.32	-467.40	-2.08	57.43	318.05	49.69	180.42	24.00	43.62	7.92	11.04
1980	171.45	714.79	-543.34	111.62	144.87	390.85	21.87	236.68	46.00	47.07	9.28	14.19
1981	242.62	1046.36	-803.74	-13.69	56.56	415.33	23.10	340.89	52.00	59.29	46.78	28.62
1982	264.53	1141.12	-876.59	-118.27	-4.87	363.72	92.57	381.87	62.40	52.20	46.82	32.62
1983	210.59	1101.96	-891.37	-141.32	15.44	289.56	145.88	402.90	72.80	50.62	20.83	16.57
1984	290.66	1069.19	-778.53	-104.13	-39.76	261.70	35.47	475.00	97.50	26.77	10.88	-23.29
1985	310.89	1072.51	-761.62	-99.90	37.74	291.18	127.99	402.92	92.95	37.75	28.90	-35.00

Sources: Central Bank of Jordan 1984, 1987

Table 5.2 Foreign trade and gross national product, 1967–85 (JD millions, current prices)

Year	Exports and imports	GNP (market price)	Foreign trade as % of GNP
1967	65.56	142.5	46.0
1968	71.56	166.4	43.0
1969	82.29	197.4	41.7
1970	77.70	187.0	41.5
1971	87.63	199.4	43.9
1972	111.89	221.0	50.6
1973	131.95	241.5	54.6
1974	205.43	279.3	73.5
1975	281.82	376.0	74.9
1976	407.45	562.4	72.4
1977	535.17	660.1	81.1
1978	549.86	781.0	70.4
1979	709.24	921.3	77.0
1980	886.24	1,190.1	74.5
1981	1,288.98	1,482.7	86.9
1982	1,405.65	1,673.4	84.0
1983	1,312.55	1,769.3	74.2
1984	1,359.85	1,854.5	73.3
1985	1,383.40	1,849.2	74.8

Sources: Central Bank of Jordan 1984, 1987

has developed new needs for the economy and produced a change in the consumption pattern in the country (Ministry of Planning 1986, p. 5). Third, an increasing capacity to import has resulted from increases in workers' remittances, unrequited transfers and capital borrowing. The development of these and other indicators can be seen in Table 5.1. Fourth, Jordan's liberal trade policies encouraged imports and has a prejudicial effect on the trade balance. Fifth, financing development projects, through government expenditure on capital goods and intermediate inputs, added to an already high private demand for imports.

It has been demonstrated that small countries are more dependent on foreign trade than large countries (Kalaf 1971). It is also found with only few exceptions that the size of a country and the openness of its economy are inversely related (Grennes 1984, p. 6). Jordan complies with these rules. Its trade with the rest of the world comprised 46 per cent of its GNP in 1967. This ratio increased gradually to reach a peak of 86.9 per cent in 1981, then stabilized around 74 per cent in the last few years (Table 5.2).

Jordan's foreign trade: trends and developments

Export growth

Between 1967 and 1985, domestic exports rose from JD 9.98 million to JD 255.35 million (Table 5.3). This increase represents a compounded growth rate of 18 per cent per annum. If the period 1967–70 is excluded, a period during which exports fluctuated around a stagnant trend, the growth rate for the remaining years rose to 24 per cent.

Composition of exports

It has been argued that the lack of diversity of economic structure often results in generally undiversified exports (Kalaf 1971, p. 183). Table 5.4 presents a detailed tabulation of the components of Jordan's GDP. It can be seen from the table that the services sector contributed 61.5 per cent to the total GDP in 1967 while commodity producing sectors produced only 38.5 per cent of GDP, of which the value added in agriculture alone was 20.2 per cent. In 1985, the picture remained almost unchanged. Value added by the services sector rose slightly to 62.3 per cent, while that of the productive sectors declined to 37.7 per cent.

However, one important development did emerge. Within the productive sectors, the relative importance of 'mining and manufacturing' rose from 11.9 per cent in 1967 to 18 per cent in 1985. The share of 'construction' almost doubled as well. These achievements came at the expense of the agricultural sector whose share dropped to 8.3 per cent from its previous level of 20.2 per cent. Jordan's economy, therefore, can be safely termed a service economy.

Kalaf's (1971) diversification argument does seem applicable to Jordan. Agricultural products, although dominated by seasonal vagaries, made up 43.7 per cent of Jordan's domestic exports in 1967. This share declined to 9.7 per cent in 1985 with variations along the long-run declining trend. Another major export item is phosphate rock. It comprised about 34.8 per cent of domestic exports in 1967. Phosphate rock exports reached their peak in 1974 and 1975 with a share of 49 per cent of domestic exports in both years. This was a direct result of a substantial increase in world prices of phosphate accompanied by an increase in the quantity exported by Jordan (Mazur 1979, p. 123). Phosphate's share stabilized again at 25.9 per cent of domestic exports in 1985.

The composition of domestic exports underwent a basic change. The relative importance of manufactured exports increased from 18.2 per cent in 1967 to 44.3 per cent in 1985. This may be attributed to the development of the industrial sector. The industrial

Table 5.3 Composition of domestic exports, 1967–85 (JD millions)

Year	Domestic exports	Consumer goods		Intermediate goods		Capital goods		Miscellaneous	
		Value	% of exports	Value	% of exports	Value	% of exports	Value	% of exports
1967	9.98	5.88	58.9	3.81	38.2	0.26	2.6	0.03	0.3
1968	12.17	6.91	56.8	4.59	37.7	0.63	5.2	0.04	0.3
1969	11.92	7.08	59.4	4.06	34.1	0.73	6.1	0.05	0.4
1970	9.32	6.06	65.0	2.59	27.8	0.67	7.2	—	—
1971	8.82	5.45	61.8	2.46	27.9	0.87	9.9	0.04	0.4
1972	12.17	6.20	49.2	3.95	31.3	2.46	19.5	—	—
1973	14.61	6.83	48.7	5.33	38.0	1.82	13.0	0.03	0.3
1974	39.44	13.86	35.1	20.80	52.7	4.77	12.1	0.01	0.1
1975	40.07	16.00	39.9	21.54	53.7	2.53	6.3	—	—
1976	49.55	25.41	51.3	22.05	44.5	2.08	4.2	0.01	0.1
1977	60.25	32.17	53.4	20.56	34.1	7.52	12.5	—	—
1978	64.13	32.63	50.9	23.32	36.4	8.18	12.7	—	—
1979	82.56	42.00	50.9	29.68	35.9	10.87	13.2	0.01	*
1980	120.11	54.23	45.1	51.24	42.7	14.63	12.2	0.01	*
1981	169.03	76.72	45.4	76.70	45.4	15.53	9.2	0.08	*
1982	185.58	88.15	47.6	78.97	42.5	18.43	9.9	0.03	*
1983	160.08	94.24	58.9	59.50	37.2	6.34	3.9	—	—
1984	261.05	167.71	64.2	82.68	31.7	10.66	4.1	—	—
1985	255.35	160.49	62.9	80.77	31.6	14.09	5.5	—	—

Notes:
— No entry
* Less than 0.1%

Sources: Central Bank of Jordan 1984, 1987

Table 5.4 Industrial origin of the gross domestic product 1967–85 (JD millions)

Year	GDP	Value added in agriculture	% of GDP	Value added in mining and manufacturing	% of GDP	Value added in electricity and water supply	% of GDP	Value added in construction	% of GDP	Total productive sectors	% of GDP	Total services sectors	% of GDP
1967	115.6	23.4	20.2	13.8	11.9	1.2	1.0	6.1	5.3	44.5	38.5	71.1	61.5
1968	138.2	16.2	11.7	16.2	11.7	1.5	1.1	9.7	7.0	43.6	31.5	94.6	68.5
1969	162.5	22.5	13.8	18.8	11.6	1.6	1.0	10.7	6.6	53.6	33.0	108.9	67.0
1970	154.7	15.6	10.1	15.9	10.3	1.9	1.2	7.7	5.0	41.1	26.6	113.6	73.4
1971	166.0	23.9	14.4	16.4	9.9	2.2	1.3	7.4	4.5	49.9	30.1	116.1	69.9
1972	182.8	26.6	14.6	18.5	10.1	2.5	1.4	9.2	5.0	56.8	31.1	126.0	68.9
1973	188.9	17.6	9.3	21.2	11.2	2.8	1.5	15.2	8.1	56.8	30.1	132.1	69.9
1974	242.4	30.3	12.5	40.5	16.7	3.0	1.3	16.8	6.9	90.6	37.4	151.8	62.6
1975	303.1	26.0	8.6	56.0	18.5	3.1	1.0	19.2	6.3	104.3	34.4	198.8	65.6
1976	378.4	37.3	9.9	67.8	17.9	3.9	1.0	26.6	7.0	135.6	35.8	242.8	64.2
1977	439.9	41.7	9.5	78.1	17.7	5.5	1.2	36.8	8.4	162.1	36.8	277.8	63.2
1978	551.2	58.6	10.6	94.3	17.1	7.2	1.3	51.0	9.3	211.1	38.3	340.1	61.7
1979	668.6	43.6	6.5	121.6	18.2	10.1	1.5	70.5	10.6	245.8	36.8	422.8	63.2
1980	893.2	69.4	7.8	167.1	18.7	17.1	1.9	97.5	10.9	351.1	39.3	542.1	60.7
1981	1,041.1	75.1	7.2	208.3	20.0	21.0	2.0	110.6	10.6	415.0	39.9	262.1	60.1
1982	1,269.6	81.8	7.0	230.3	19.7	25.3	2.2	121.9	10.4	459.3	39.3	710.3	60.7
1983	1,242.3	110.0	8.8	214.5	17.3	28.3	2.3	126.8	10.2	479.6	38.6	762.7	61.4
1984	1,316.0	99.6	7.6	250.8	19.1	33.5	2.5	127.0	9.6	510.9	38.8	805.1	61.2
1985	1,367.9	113.1	8.3	245.9	18.0	31.5	2.3	124.4	9.1	514.9	37.7	853.0	62.3

Sources: Central Bank of Jordan 1984, 1987

output rose from 100 in the base year, 1979, to 187.8 in 1986 (Central Bank of Jordan 1987, p. 76). Considering domestic exports by economic function (Table 5.3), it can be observed that the share of consumer goods varied from a low of 35.1 per cent to a peak of 65 per cent during the period 1967–85, and they still constituted about 63 per cent of domestic exports in 1985. Intermediate goods' share, including raw materials, varied from 38.2 per cent in 1967 to 31.6 per cent in 1985. They registered their highest share in 1974 and 1975 (52.7 per cent and 53.7 per cent respectively) owing to the aforementioned record phosphate prices in those years. The relative importance of capital goods does seem to have grown significantly over the period; the annual growth rate of their value (22.2 per cent) is higher than that of intermediate goods (17 per cent) or consumer goods (18.4 per cent).

Geographical concentrations of exports

Kuznets (1960, p. 16) contends that small countries tend to have a higher degree of geographical concentration of foreign trade than large countries. This contention seems plausible in the case of Jordan as a small nation. Table 5.5 presents the geographical distribution of Jordan's domestic exports. In 1967 the most popular destination for Jordan's exports was the Arab markets in the region which took 64.9 per cent of the domestic exports. Arab Common Market (ACM) countries, accounted for 22.5 per cent of the total. India came in second place after the Arab countries with 14.3 per cent, followed by the Eastern bloc (8.7 per cent), the European Community (7.6 per cent), Japan (0.3 per cent) and the rest of the world (4.1 per cent). By 1985, geographical distribution of exports changed somewhat. Exports to the ACM increased to 29 per cent of domestic exports while the share of exports to other Arab countries dropped to 22.5 per cent (42.4 per cent in 1967). This however, represents a decline in the overall share of Arab countries which totalled 51.5 per cent compared to 64.9 per cent in 1967. India maintained second place with a moderate increase to 17 per cent followed, as before, by the Eastern bloc with a slight decrease in its share of 0.3 percentage points. The share of Jordan's exports to the European Community was reduced by 4.5 per cent whereas Japan received an increased share of 2.3 per cent. The fourfold increase in the share of the rest of the world (from 4.1 per cent to 15.6 per cent) indicates a reduction in the geographical concentration of Jordan's exports. Nevertheless, they are still highly concentrated in some Arab countries and India.

Export supply elasticity

As Jordan's exports have been growing over time, a tentative estimation is presented of the elasticity of Jordan's export supply to export prices and the exchange rate using a log-linear equation of the following form:

$$\log EX_t = \infty + \beta_1 \log PX_t + \beta \log RC_t + U_t \quad (5.1)$$

where EX is the quantity of exports (quantum index); PX is the exports unit price index; RC is the JD/US dollar yearly average exchange rate; U is the error term; and t is time.

Applying equation (5.1) to Jordan using data for the years 1972–85 yields the following estimated export supply function:

$$\log EX = -11.10 + 1.29* PX + 1.7** RC \quad (5.2)$$
$$(0.248) \quad (1.0155)$$

* significant at all levels   ** significant at the 1 per cent level

$R^2 = 0.766$ $\bar{R}^2 = 0.723$ $F = 18.004$ $DW = 0.64$

Equation (5.2) implies a positive elasticity of exports to price ($\beta_1 = 1.29$). Exports are also elastic and positively responding to changes in the JD/US dollar exchange rate. The exclusion of other relevant explanatory variables may have affected the results, particularly the low DW value. However, a major exercise in this regard is underway but remains outside the scope of the present study.

Imports growth

The value of Jordan's imports rose from JD 54.23 million in 1967 to JD 1,072.51 million in 1985 (Table 5.6), which amounts to 16.6 per cent yearly compounded growth rate. Average propensity to import increased from 38.1 per cent to 58 per cent over the same period.

Marginal propensity to import (MPI) is estimated in equation (5.3):

$$M = -33.72 + 0.65GNP \quad (5.3)$$
$$(0.019)$$
$$R^2 = 0.98 \quad DW = 1.042$$

where M is the marginal propensity to import.

Equation (5.3) implies an MPI equal to 0.65. This means that 65 per cent of any additions to the GNP will be spent on imports. The

Table 5.5   Geographical distribution of domestic exports, 1967–85 (JD millions)

Year	Domestic exports	Arab Common Market		Other Arab countries		EEC		Eastern bloc		India		Japan		Other countries	
		Value	%	Value	%	Value	%	Value	%	Value	%	Value	%	Value	%
1967	9.98	2.25	22.5	4.23	42.4	0.76	7.6	0.87	8.7	1.43	14.3	0.03	0.3	0.41	4.1
1968	12.17	2.68	22.0	5.49	45.1	0.06	0.5	1.19	9.8	1.89	15.5	0.10	0.8	0.76	6.2
1969	11.92	3.11	26.1	5.39	45.2	*	**	1.41	11.8	1.48	12.4	0.03	0.2	0.50	4.2
1970	9.32	3.00	32.2	4.17	44.7	*	**	1.21	13.0	0.25	2.7	0.02	0.2	0.67	7.2
1971	8.82	2.76	31.3	3.92	44.4	0.05	0.4	0.63	7.1	0.96	10.9	0.17	1.9	0.38	4.3
1972	12.61	3.67	29.1	5.48	43.5	*	**	0.41	3.2	1.40	11.1	0.62	4.9	0.98	7.8
1973	14.01	4.42	31.5	5.65	40.3	0.06	0.1	0.35	2.5	1.19	8.5	0.70	5.0	1.70	12.1
1974	39.44	5.93	15.0	12.50	31.7	1.98	4.9	2.04	5.2	6.58	16.7	3.79	9.6	8.54	21.7
1975	40.07	7.03	17.5	9.87	24.6	2.52	5.1	6.39	15.9	1.97	4.9	1.91	4.8	10.92	27.3
1976	49.55	10.08	20.3	13.82	27.9	0.87	1.4	7.29	14.7	1.71	3.4	1.91	3.8	12.22	24.7
1977	60.25	13.62	22.6	22.44	37.2	1.34	2.1	4.17	6.9	3.89	6.4	2.63	4.4	12.63	21.0
1978	64.13	16.44	25.6	26.18	40.8	1.14	1.4	6.45	10.1	3.53	5.5	1.81	2.8	8.38	13.1
1979	82.56	25.93	31.4	29.81	36.1	2.10	1.7	5.33	6.4	6.14	7.4	2.86	3.5	11.35	13.7
1980	120.11	42.45	35.3	30.46	25.4	2.46	1.4	15.15	12.6	8.04	6.7	3.95	3.3	17.96	15.0
1981	169.03	74.75	44.2	39.73	23.5	3.57	1.9	19.47	11.5	10.32	6.1	3.84	2.3	18.46	11.0
1982	185.58	80.56	43.4	42.75	23.0	8.13	5.1	25.41	13.7	16.56	8.9	3.78	2.0	12.95	7.1
1983	160.08	30.58	19.1	56.47	35.3	10.41	4.0	21.22	13.2	13.74	8.6	3.40	2.1	26.54	16.6
1984	261.05	72.05	27.6	60.51	23.2	11.39	4.5	32.78	12.6	34.11	13.1	5.55	2.1	45.64	17.5
1985	255.35	74.17	29.0	57.35	22.5			21.50	8.4	45.31	17.7	5.81	2.3	39.82	15.6

Notes:
* Less than JD 5,000
** Less than 0.1%

Sources: Central Bank of Jordan 1984, 1987

Table 5.6 Composition of imports, 1967–85 (JD millions)

Year	Commodity imports	Consumer goods Value	Consumer goods % of imports	Intermediate goods Value	Intermediate goods % of imports	Capital goods Value	Capital goods % of imports	Miscellaneous Value	Miscellaneous % of imports
1967	54.23	23.87	44.0	13.72	25.3	14.77	27.2	1.87	3.5
1968	57.30	27.61	48.2	12.21	21.3	13.92	24.3	3.56	6.2
1969	67.54	33.89	50.2	14.59	21.6	15.24	22.6	3.82	5.6
1970	65.53	33.02	50.4	15.14	23.1	13.37	20.4	4.00	6.1
1971	76.19	33.44	43.9	13.61	17.9	17.61	23.1	11.53	15.1
1972	94.88	46.29	48.8	18.77	19.8	18.63	19.6	11.19	11.8
1973	107.80	50.60	46.9	22.21	20.6	20.24	18.8	14.75	13.7
1974	155.68	69.63	44.7	30.00	19.3	40.91	26.3	15.04	9.7
1975	232.94	90.51	38.8	57.22	24.6	82.88	35.6	2.33	1.0
1976	338.74	133.33	39.4	90.00	26.6	114.63	33.8	0.78	0.2
1977	453.11	147.18	32.5	121.19	26.7	184.10	40.6	0.64	0.2
1978	458.94	175.67	38.3	117.25	25.5	161.23	35.1	4.79	1.1
1979	588.32	215.21	36.6	179.46	30.5	193.57	32.9	0.08	*
1980	714.79	240.15	33.6	227.09	31.8	246.74	34.5	0.81	0.1
1981	1,046.36	325.21	31.1	305.59	29.2	414.96	39.6	0.60	0.1
1982	1,141.12	368.30	32.3	380.28	33.3	391.40	34.3	1.14	0.1
1983	1,101.96	365.06	33.1	377.79	34.3	310.55	28.2	48.56	4.4
1984	1,069.19	383.21	35.8	419.16	39.2	239.04	22.3	27.78	2.7
1985	1,072.51	369.30	34.4	420.41	39.2	261.07	24.3	21.73	2.1

Note: * Less than 0.1%

Sources: Central Bank of Jordan 1984, 1987

rather high MPI is evidence of a rising domestic demand for imported commodities. Such evidence is supported by the fact that imports were growing at a rate of 16.6 per cent per annum which outpaced the growth rate of the GNP of 14.2 per cent per year over the period of 1967–85. The growth in the value of imports during the period of study may be a result of:

1 the increase in GNP, particularly the contribution of workers' remittances and other transfer payments;
2 the rising demand for capital and intermediate goods to sustain development projects;
3 the increase in world prices;
4 the demonstration effect, which can be detected by the changing consumption patterns in Jordan (Millham 1977, p. 13).

Composition of imports

Table 5.6 gives a detailed account of Jordan's commodity imports. They consist of three major components: consumer, intermediate and capital goods. Imports of consumer goods increased in value from JD 23.87 million in 1967 to JD 369.3 million in 1985. This is equivalent to a growth rate of 15.2 per cent per annum. Their relative importance dropped, however, from 44 per cent in 1967 to 34.4 per cent in 1985. Equation (5.4) shows the estimated MPI for consumer goods:

$$\text{Mcon} = 1.98 + 0.21\text{GNP} \qquad (5.4)$$
$$(0.0043)$$
$$R^2 = 0.98 \qquad DW = 1.099$$

where Mcon is the value of consumer goods imports.

Equation (5.4) implies that one-fifth of any increase in GNP will be directed to expenditure on imported consumer goods.

The share of imported intermediate goods out of total imports increased from 25.3 per cent in 1967 to 39.2 per cent in 1985. These shares reflect the absolute values of JD 13.72 million and JD 420.41 million in 1967 and 1985 respectively. The growth rate of that increase is 19 per cent per year. Equation (5.5) shows the estimated MPI of intermediate goods:

$$\text{Mint} = 35.64 + 0.24\text{GNP} \qquad (5.5)$$
$$(0.0047)$$
$$R^2 = 0.98 \qquad \text{DW} = 1.576$$

where Mint is the value of imported intermediate goods.

Equation (5.5) implies that for every increase in GNP about a quarter will be expended on imported intermediate goods.

The value of capital goods imports grew from JD 14.77 million in 1967 to JD 261.07 million in 1985 or at an average annual rate of 16 per cent. Nevertheless, its relative share in total imports declined from 27.2 per cent to 24.3 per cent between 1967 and 1985. Equation (5.6) also estimates the MPI of capital goods:

$$\text{Mcap} = -2.91 + 0.19\text{GNP} \qquad (5.6)$$
$$(0.02)$$
$$R^2 = 0.84 \qquad \text{DW} = 0.748$$

where Mcap value of capital goods imports.

Again, equation (5.6) implies that just under one-fifth of any increase in GNP will be used to finance the purchase of imported capital goods.

Geographical concentration of imports

The geographical distribution of Jordan's imports is presented in Table 5.7. The data shows that Jordan's largest single supplier is the United States followed by Japan. Jordan's immediate neighbours (the Arab countries) supplied 19.9 per cent of Jordan's imports in 1967. The ACM accounted for 8.8 per cent of total imports. The Arab countries' share increased to 24.5 per cent in 1985 despite a decline of the ACM share to 7.7 per cent. In 1967, Western European countries' share of Jordan's imports was 38.6 per cent of which 35.4 per cent came from the European Community.

In 1985, the share of Western Europe declined to 37.6 per cent and that of the European Community also declined to 29.3 per cent despite a growth of the value of their exports to Jordan by 15.5 per cent per year over the period of study. Imports from the United States maintained their share, around 12 per cent over the period. As regards the Eastern bloc, their share was cut by almost a half between 1967 and 1985 (from 12 per cent to 6.9 per cent). Japan's share, on the other hand, almost doubled (from 3.7 per cent to 6.3 per cent). Thus, like its exports, Jordan's imports are highly concentrated.

Table 5.7 Geographical distribution of imports, 1967–85 (JD millions)

Year	Commodity imports	Arab common market		Other Arab countries		EEC		Other European countries		USA		Eastern bloc		Japan		Other countries	
		Value	%	Value	%	Value	%	Value	%	Value	%	Value	%	Value	%	Value	%
1967	54.23	4.75	8.8	6.01	11.1	19.20	35.4	1.74	3.2	6.77	12.5	6.49	12.0	2.03	3.7	7.24	13.4
1968	57.30	4.51	7.9	6.53	11.4	19.34	33.7	2.38	4.1	6.37	11.1	6.85	11.9	2.89	5.0	8.43	14.7
1969	67.54	7.20	10.7	7.18	10.6	22.33	33.1	2.54	3.8	6.23	9.2	9.43	14.0	5.15	7.6	7.48	11.1
1970	65.53	5.96	9.1	7.14	10.9	22.15	33.8	2.57	3.9	7.38	11.3	9.02	13.8	3.87	5.9	7.44	11.3
1971	76.19	7.05	9.2	9.70	12.7	18.98	24.9	2.95	3.9	18.13	23.8	5.18	6.8	4.19	5.5	10.01	13.1
1972	94.88	7.90	8.3	8.48	8.9	26.98	28.4	3.28	3.5	16.89	17.8	8.24	8.7	4.60	4.8	18.51	19.5
1973	107.80	11.88	11.5	9.84	9.1	30.52	28.3	4.10	3.8	11.26	10.4	7.73	7.2	5.35	5.0	27.12	25.2
1974	155.68	14.41	9.3	12.04	7.7	45.63	39.3	6.90	4.4	17.58	11.3	14.70	9.4	7.38	4.7	37.04	23.8
1975	232.94	14.11	6.1	32.22	13.8	76.97	33.0	16.68	7.2	24.18	10.4	18.74	8.0	17.11	7.3	32.93	14.1
1976	338.74	18.82	5.5	42.07	12.4	125.97	37.2	20.60	6.1	31.05	9.2	25.11	7.4	21.51	6.3	53.61	15.8
1977	453.11	23.07	5.1	49.43	10.9	157.98	34.9	25.94	5.7	67.35	14.9	41.85	9.2	28.72	6.3	58.77	13.0
1978	458.94	23.65	5.1	62.93	13.7	167.93	35.9	31.23	6.8	33.64	7.3	50.16	10.9	30.82	6.7	61.58	13.4
1979	588.32	23.85	4.0	86.78	14.7	211.15	35.9	50.69	8.6	44.26	7.5	51.40	8.7	37.31	6.3	82.88	14.1
1980	714.79	18.91	2.6	130.32	18.2	259.73	36.3	49.53	6.9	61.59	8.6	49.79	6.9	51.34	7.2	93.58	13.1
1981	1,046.36	18.69	1.8	194.38	18.6	339.53	32.4	58.76	5.6	166.67	15.9	81.18	7.7	71.53	6.8	115.62	11.0
1982	1,141.12	16.00	1.4	253.78	22.2	329.59	28.9	69.13	6.0	144.34	12.6	94.83	8.3	87.37	7.6	146.08	12.8
1983	1,101.96	24.51	2.2	226.11	20.5	330.09	29.9	52.73	4.8	131.05	11.9	77.82	7.1	102.89	9.3	156.76	14.2
1984	1,069.19	19.98	1.9	225.72	20.6	319.25	29.8	87.89	8.2	119.26	11.1	64.80	6.1	79.06	7.4	153.23	14.3
1985	1,072.51	83.16	7.7	180.41	16.8	314.55	29.3	88.93	8.3	128.04	11.9	74.38	6.9	67.81	6.3	135.23	12.6

Sources: Central Bank of Jordan 1984, 1987

Import demand elasticity

What are the determinants of the import demand function in Jordan? Here, an attempt to examine these determinants will be conducted using a log-linear regression equation of the following form:

$$\log QM_t = \infty + \beta_1 \log RP_t \; \beta_2 \log RC_t$$
$$+ \beta_3 \log RGNP + U_t \tag{5.7}$$

where QM is the quantity of imports demanded (quantum index); $RP = MPI/CPI$ (where MPI is the imports unit price index and CPI is the consumer price index); RC is the JD/US dollar exchange rate; RGNP is the real gross national product; U is the error term; and t is time.

Equation (5.7) has been estimated using data for the period 1972–85. The results are presented in equation (5.8):

$$\log QM = 1.39 - 0.28^{***} \log RP - 0.62^{**} \log RC$$
$$(0.223) \qquad\qquad (0.318)$$
$$+ 1.38^{*} \log RGNP \tag{5.8}$$
$$(0.098)$$

* significant at all levels
** significant at the 1 per cent level
*** significant at the 2 per cent level

$R^2 = 0.98$ $\bar{R}^2 = 0.973$ $F = 146.658$ $DW = 1.833$

The estimated equation yields the correct negative signs and the correct positive signs for the price elasticity and exchange rate elasticity respectively, and the correct positive sign for the income elasticity of demand for imports. The low price elasticity coefficient (−0.28) is a reflection of the fact that, being a small country, Jordan's quantity of imports would not affect world prices. On the other hand, although still inelastic (−0.62), imports are more responsive to exchange rate changes than to import price changes. Income elasticity (1.38) indicates a strong response to changes in the real income.

Jordan's balance of payments

It has been mentioned above that Jordan's domestic exports grew at a faster rate than its imports over the period 1967–85. However, since exports started from low levels compared with imports, the flimsy differential could not prevent the resultant trade deficit from reaching its present substantial level. In 1985 for example, domestic exports proceeds financed only 29 per cent of the value of imports. The trade deficit in that year was JD 761.62 million, and this amounted to 55.7 per cent of GDP in 1985. As a percentage of GDP, the trade deficit varied from its lowest level of 31 per cent in 1968 to the highest of 77 per cent in 1981. (Detailed statistics of the major items of the balance of payments are shown in Table 5.1.)

In contrast with the trade balance, the services balance always produced a surplus (except in 1968 and 1969). This surplus financed a significant part of the trade deficit. Remittances from Jordanian workers abroad cover a sizeable portion of the deficit. Another source contributing to the financing of the deficit is the unrequited transfers which include Arab and foreign aid and donations (Table 5.1). Thus, as Table 5.1 illustrates, the current account balance depicts a brighter view where the trade deficit for eight of the years under study was turned into a surplus in the current account.

Capital movements in the non-monetary sector indicate foreign investment in Jordan, but in particular they indicate foreign loans to the central government. Net loans to the central government show surpluses except for the year 1976. These loans are earmarked for development projects in contrast with the official aid which is mainly a source of budget support.

The overall balance (basic balance) indicates a surplus in fourteen out of nineteen years covered by the study. Even if earlier periods are considered, the conclusion would still be the same: the problem of balancing Jordan's external payments lies in compensatory financing of the substantial and increasing trade deficit. Raising the funds for the compensatory financing places Jordan under a two-pronged dependency: dependency on foreign aid, and, more recently, dependency on the Gulf labour market (Rivier 1980, p. 21). Official unrequited transfers plus remittances covered 91 per cent of the trade deficit in 1985.

Trade policy

Economic planning in Jordan focuses on achieving a positive growth rate of GNP. Industrialization received great attention, especially import-substituting industries and industries with a high domestic value added. Protective tariffs have been used to encourage industrialization. The general features about trade policy in Jordan include the following:

1 total prohibition of imports of certain strategic commodities such as cement, petroleum products and leather;
2 partial restriction of imports of varous other commodities (the list of restricted imports is subject to periodical revision according to the domestic demand and output conditions); and
3 indirect controls such as import duties (tariffs), which have a protective as well as a fund raising objective.

What consequence did such protective controls have in Jordan? The Three-Year Plan (National Planning Council 1973, p. 112) noted that:

> The prices of some domestic products were higher than those of similar imported ones because some of the existing domestic industries have enjoyed excessive protection advantages and privileges. Hence, these industries have ignored the need to improve the quality of their products or even reduce production costs.

In general, most protected industries took advantage of the protection afforded to them and pursued excessive profits. Moreover, the quality of their products was inferior to their imported substitutes. After the Three-Year Plan (1973–5), the emphasis shifted. Prohibition on the import of many commodities was removed. The focus centered on tariffs only. Some tariffs were reduced to encourage price and quality competition. Tariffs are also a major source of government revenue. In 1985, tariff proceeds made up 28.8 per cent of total domestic revenue. In 1977, they reached 45 per cent of domestic revenue.

Conclusion

The preceding analysis shows that Jordan's balance of payments enjoys a surplus in most of the years under study. However, the trade balance suffers a chronic and increasing deficit. The surplus in the services account, especially remittances, continues to alleviate the trade deficit. Foreign aid and loans eliminate the remaining deficit. This situation results in Jordan's dependency on (a) aid, which is not void of political connotations, and (b) the Gulf labour market. The future of that market for the Jordanian workforce, is just as unpredictable as foreign aid.

Tackling the trade deficit problem should be subject to a well-planned long-term policy. In this regard two major objectives can be identified.

1 *Curtailment of imports*: This objective is easier said than done. It is not possible to reduce imports of capital and intermediate goods which together constitute 63.5 per cent of total imports without hindering development projects and industrialization. As regards imports of consumer goods, measures may be adopted to reduce the inflow of luxury goods. Such measures can be readily effective. But a recommended long-term policy would be the encouragement of import-substituting industries. Import substitution could assume a significant role in Jordan. Two studies by Millham (1977) and Smadi and Amerah (1979) indicate such a possibility. The two studies analysed Jordan's consumer imports and recommended the establishment of a number of import-substituting industries subject, of course, to feasibility studies.

2 *Export promotion*: Efforts must be concentrated on promoting domestic exports, particularly those coming from the manufacturing sector. Marketing and promotional activities lack a sense of professionalism, which adversely affects export promotion efforts and the competitiveness of Jordan's exports in foreign markets. Saket *et al.* (1979) produced a detailed analysis of Jordan's export sector, its structure and problems. The study put forward some recommendations that included setting up an 'Export Council'. They envisaged the council's main task as drawing up 'a national export policy'. The study also suggested that the proposed council become a 'liaison' between the planners and policy makers on one hand, and the exporters and industrialists on the other, in order to integrate the promotion of domestic exports, especially manufactured exports, into the national economic plan.

Finally, one cannot overlook the possibility of exchange rate adjustment to remove balance of payments imbalances. In theory this is possible, and mainly applicable to large countries. Some qualifications are in order, especially as the danger of trade war looms large between the United States and its major trading partners. In the case of Jordan, exchange rate adjustment is a remote possibility, and could be detrimental rather than useful.

Any devaluation of the Jordanian dinar, besides the undesirable effect it may have on the investment environment, is hardly likely to produce any favourable change in the trade balance. The reason is that the domestic demand for imports and the foreign demand for Jordan's exports are inelastic. Moreover, Jordan's productive base cannot be expected to respond positively to such a devaluation particularly as the imported inputs of the manufactured exports will be adversely affected.

Acknowledgements

I would like to thank my colleagues Dr Bani Hani and Dr Hussain Talafha for helpful comments on an earlier draft of this paper. The usual *caveat* applies.

References

Amerah, M. S. (1982), 'Import substitution or export expansion as strategies for growth: a case study of Jordan', unpublished Ph.D. thesis, University of Keele.

Cairncross, A. K. (1976), 'Contribution of trade to development', in G. M. Meier, *Leading Issues in Economic Development*, Oxford University Press, New York, pp. 712-16.

Central Bank of Jordan (1984), *Yearly Statistical Series 1967-83*, Department of Research and Studies, Amman, Jordan.

—— (1987), *Monthly Statistical Bulletin*, Vol. 23, No. 1, Department of Research and Studies, Amman, Jordan.

Department of Statistics (1984), *External Trade Statistics 1984*, Awqaf Islamic Press, Amman, Jordan.

Grennes, T. (1984), *International Economics*, Prentice-Hall, Englewood Cliffs, NJ.

Jordan Development Board (1964), *The Seven Year Program for Economic Development of Jordan 1964-1970*, The Commercial Press, Jerusalem, Jordan.

Kalaf, N. G. (1971), *Economic Implications of the Size of Nations with special reference to Lebanon*, E. J. Brill, Leiden, The Netherlands.

Kuznets, S. (1960), 'Economic growth of small nations', in A. E. Robinson, *Economic Consequences of the Size of Nations*, Macmillan, London.

Mazur, M. P. (1979), *Economic Growth and Development in Jordan*, Croom Helm, London.

Millham, C. B. *et al.* (1977), *Rationalisation of Imports in Jordan*, Economic Research Department, Royal Scientific Society, Amman, Jordan.

Ministry of Planning (1986), *The Five Year Plan for Social and Economic Development 1986-1990*, National Press, Amman, Jordan.

National Planning Council (1973), *The Three Year Development Plan 1973-75*, Amman, Jordan.

Rivier, F. (1980), *Croissance Industrielle dans une Economie Assistée: Le Cas Jordanien*, Presses Universitaires de Lyon, Lyon.

Saket, B. *et al.* (1979), *Developing Manufactured Exports in Jordan*, Economic Research Department, Royal Scientific Society, Amman, Jordan (in Arabic).

Smadi, M. and Amerah, M. (1979), *Composition of Visible Imports: An Industrial Development Potential*, Economic Research Department, Royal Scientific Society, Amman, Jordan.

Part three

Institutions

Chapter six

Inflation, financial intermediation and economic growth in Jordan: 1963–85

Subrata Ghatak and Fawzi Khatib

Introduction

The relationship between economic growth and 'financial re-pression' has become a matter of considerable recent theoretical and empirical investigation (see, for example, McKinnon 1973, 1976; Shaw 1973; Kapur 1976; Wijnbergen 1983, 1984; Ghatak 1981; Galbis 1977; Vogel and Buser 1976; Gupta 1986; and Fry 1978, 1988). Most writers have tried to analyse the implications of a policy of interest rate liberalization on savings, investment and economic growth in less developed countries (LDCs). Most LDCs suffer from capital scarcity, yet interest rates in the money markets of LDCs hardly reflect the opportunity cost of capital, given the interest rate ceilings. Some argue that a higher interest rate in LDCs will have a beneficial effect upon savings, if the economic agents in LDCs respond 'rationally' to price signals. A higher level of savings can then be invested to achieve a higher rate of economic growth.

Empirical evidence available so far from LDCs has lent mixed support to the view that a policy of interest rate liberalization would always raise savings (see, for example, Wijnbergen 1983, 1985; Gupta 1986; Fry 1980, 1988). In theory it is argued that a high interest rate policy could raise the cost of working capital and raise the price mark-up, which would be inflationary as long as a substantial part of investment is financed by working capital. It follows that a high rate of interest would also diminish the level and rate of investment (see Taylor 1983; Wijnbergen 1983, 1984). It has been argued that in countries like South Korea such a phenomenon actually occurred. In Korea, the curb market also played a vital role in reducing investment and economic growth owing to a policy of raising interest rates as the curb market rates increased with a rise in interest rates in the organized sector.

While such debate is of considerable importance for formulating appropriate monetary policies for LDCs, it has tended to neglect an important issue which is related to the analysis of the dynamic process of financial intermediation in open LDCs experiencing inflation. Such an analysis was originally emphasized by Shaw and only a few economists tried to examine the relationship between inflation and financial intermediation (for an exception, see Vogel and Buser 1976). Such a study deserves special attention because monetary policy could be (and has been) quite inflationary in many LDCs (particularly in Latin American countries). Financial repression could take place not only due to a ceiling on interest rates in LDCs but also due to inflation. The real size of the financial sector should then be regarded as a function of inflation.

In this chapter, we will examine the impact of inflation on financial intermediation and economic growth in Jordan between 1963 and 1985. The case of Jordan deserves special attention for the following reasons.

1 Jordan is an LDC which is quite open to the rest of the world.
2 Very little (if anything) is known about the impact of inflation on the financial sector of Jordan.
3 The analysis of the Jordanian case may be of some use for policy formulation for other LDCs.
4 Widespread ceilings on nominal interest rates on deposits make Jordan an interesting case in which to examine the relationships between inflation, financial repression and capital formation.

It is now well acknowledged that, given the ceilings on interest rates, the rate of inflation is a more appropriate measure of the opportunity cost of money holding in most LDCs (see Ghatak 1981 for a summary).

The study of the relationship between inflation and financial intermediation in LDCs can be regarded as very important for the following reasons.

1 Since a high rate of inflation could lead to a highly variable rate of inflation, economic agents could find it very difficult to anticipate and adjust adequately to inflation.
2 Given administered interest rates in many countries, inflation could imply considerable distortions in the allocation of resources.
3 In view of the underdeveloped primary security markets in most LDCs, the role of financial assets is of crucial importance for promoting capital formation. The analysis of the impact of inflation on the growth of financial assets and intermediation then takes on additional significance (McKinnon 1973; Shaw 1973).

In the following sections, we shall first look at the movements of some important financial and real variables in the Jordanian economy. A model will then be set up to test the nature of the relationship between inflation, financial intermediation and capital formation in Jordan. The statistical results of our estimates will then be presented. The final section will draw some conclusions.

Inflation and financial intermediation – a preliminary analysis

Some ideas about financial intermediation and inflation in Jordan can be obtained by looking at Table 6.1. It suggests that the average rate of inflation in Jordan between 1963 and 1985 has been about 7.2 per cent per annum with a standard deviation of about 5 per cent per annum. This was moderate by Third World standards. If we look at the three sub-periods we can actually observe periods of low (1963–72), high (1973–80) and modest (1981–5) rates of inflation. In the first period, low rates of inflation are associated with increasing rates of real investment. Such a period is also related to a steady rise in demand and time deposits. In contrast, in the second period, we observe high rates of inflation (though not as high as has been seen in many other LDCs) and high rates of investment. Such phenomena may perhaps be explained by the inflow of foreign aid to Jordan. Thus, although the rate of inflation in Jordan during the 1970s reflected the impact of the rise in oil price, such a rise in oil price also conferred on Jordan some important benefits as shown in the rise of the proportion of foreign aid, income and investment.

From 1980 to 1985, the fall in real investment and the share of investment in income is particularly noticeable along with the decline in the proportion of aid to income. The trends in currency holdings and demand deposits have been positive throughout the whole period under investigation. Such trends do not validate 'conventional wisdom' as the rate of inflation and currency and demand deposits are supposed to be negatively correlated.

The real rate of interest has been positive up to 1968, then it remained negative throughout the 1970s and early 1980s. With the fall in the rate of inflation in the 1980s, the real rate of interest became positive again since 1983.

With these preliminary remarks, we will present the statistical form of the model in the next section to test more rigorously the nature and significance of the association between inflation and financial intermediation in Jordan.

Table 6.1 Trends in financial indicators, 1963–85

Year	INF	C/D	TS/D	C/P	D	TS/P	I/P	I/Y	i – P*	AID/Y
1963	2.07	124.39	86.59	41.63	33	28.89	40.82	14.53	1.04	13
1964	2.03	137.84	153.89	46.04	33	51.40	37.60	11.71	1.04	17
1965	2.09	126.68	94.23	51.67	40	38.43	46.86	13.24	1.79	16
1966	2.05	118.02	84.82	58.33	49	41.92	53.27	14.92	1.79	18
1967	2.05	217.38	92.41	99.08	45	42.12	46.15	16.84	3.31	37
1968	0.20	260.45	95.90	117.69	45	43.33	50.00	16.23	0.28	32
1969	6.91	286.31	100.40	127.30	44	44.64	63.93	18.14	-0.12	23
1970	6.93	358.39	116.96	138.31	38	45.13	42.28	13.48	-1.79	21
1971	4.73	332.04	116.40	131.76	39	46.19	48.73	15.40	-0.42	18
1972	5.69	243.19	99.70	121.60	50	49.95	54.18	16.43	-2.41	30
Mean	3.63	220.47	104.13	93.34	42	43.20	43.38	15.09	0.45	23
S.D.	2.47	90.23	20.57	39.37	5	6.27	7.60	1.92	1.72	3
1973	11.23	233.21	91.87	129.97	55	51.20	62.93	19.54	-5.95	26
1974	19.42	204.34	88.85	129.72	63	56.40	71.01	22.63	-13.61	31
1975	12.09	162.32	81.66	138.95	85	69.90	87.90	23.38	-5.98	37
1976	11.48	139.70	95.15	145.36	104	99.01	135.32	26.71	-5.07	22

	INF	C	D	TS	P	I	Y	i	P*	AID
1977	14.54	131.46	104.20	148.02	112	117.32	155.12	29.84	-7.99	25
1978	7.07	140.76	176.97	160.18	113	201.39	162.77	28.55	-1.91	13
1979	14.11	139.58	192.60	176.53	126	243.59	188.78	31.97	-7.48	34
1980	11.10	144.64	214.07	203.25	140	300.81	229.94	33.43	-4.72	33
Mean	12.63	162.00	130.67	154.00	100	142.45	136.72	27.01	-6.59	28
S.D.	3.56	36.93	54.19	25.29	29	94.33	59.24	4.85	3.39	7
1981	7.69	142.47	288.44	213.63	149	342.54	292.64	38.09	-5.34	29
1982	7.43	148.03	254.17	227.04	153	389.86	288.41	35.68	-1.33	22
1983	5.01	146.02	285.82	240.02	164	469.81	233.86	28.42	2.15	16
1984	3.79	152.49	343.04	240.05	157	540.02	217.19	25.88	3.44	15
1985	1.24	176.70	401.86	204.89	115	465.99	160.45	23.08	4.00	17
Mean	5.03	153.14	302.67	225.13	148	441.64	238.51	30.23	0.58	20
S.D.	2.68	13.66	70.03	15.73	18	76.76	54.75	6.42	3.91	5
Overall mean	7.22	185.50	156.52	143.09	85	164.34	120.44	22.53	-1.97	24
Overall S.D.	5.07	69.25	91.35	59.84	46	168.05	85.50	7.90	4.42	7

Notes:
INF: rate of inflation; C: currency; D: demand deposits; TS: time and saving deposits; P: prices; I: gross investment; Y: GNP; i: nominal interest rates; P*: expected rate of inflation; AID: foreign aid

The statistical form of the model

The following statistical model has been proposed to analyse the relationship between the size of the financial sector, inflation and investment. As investment is one of the prime movers of the economy, it is argued that a rise in financial intermediation should have a favourable impact on investment and economic growth.

Definition of variables

C   public holdings of currency
D   public holdings of demand deposits
TS   public holdings of time and saving deposits
Y   gross national product
I   gross investment
R   commercial bank reserves
P   prices (the consumer price index)
D   dummy variable (1) for the years 1967–73 and otherwise
t   actual time
t − 1: time lagged one year

The behavioural equations

$$\log C/Y = a_0 + a_1 \log (\Delta P/P_{t-1})_t + a_2 \log (Y/P)_t + a_3 D \qquad (6.1)$$

$$\log C/Y = a_0 + a_1 [\log (\Delta P/P_{t-1})_t + \log (\Delta P/P_{t-1})_{t-1}]/2 \qquad (6.2)$$
$$+ a_2 [\log(Y/P)_t + \log (Y/P)_{t-1}]/2 + a_3 D$$

$$\log D/Y = b_0 + b_1 \log (\Delta P/P_{t-1})_t + b_2 \log (Y/P)_t \qquad (6.3)$$

$$\log D/Y = b_0 + b_1 [\log (\Delta P/P_{t-1})_t + \log (\Delta P/P_{t-1})_{t-1})]/2 \qquad (6.4)$$
$$+ b_2 [\log (Y/P)_{t-1}]/2$$

$$\log TS/Y = c_0 + c_1 \log (\Delta P/P_{t-1})_t + c_2 \log (Y/P)_t \qquad (6.5)$$

$$\log TS/Y = c_0 + c_1 [\log (\Delta P/P_{t-1})_t + \log (\Delta P/P_{t-1})_{t-1}]/2 \qquad (6.6)$$
$$+ c_2 [\log (Y/P)_{t-1} + \log (Y/P)_{t-1}]/2$$

where $a_1 < 0$ $a_2 > 0$ $a_3 > 0$
              $b_1 < 0$ $b_2 > 0$
              $c_1 < 0$ $c_2 > 0$

To investigate the public demand for financial assets equations 6.1–6.6 are formulated. In equation (6.1), the demand for currency is a function of real income, Y/P, the 'scale variable' and the rate of inflation, $\Delta P/P_{t-1}$ as the opportunity cost variable. A positive association is expected between C/Y and the real income whereas the price coefficient is expected to be negative. Given the volatile period which the country witnessed during 1967–73 (the Arab–Israeli war in 1967 and the civil war in 1970), a dummy variable with *a priori* positive sign is suggested. However, the dummy variable will be tested in each equation.

In equation (6.2) the same specification is repeated but with a moving average of two years for each variable. This might reduce fluctuations among variables and improve the fit. The demand deposits functions (equations (6.3) and (6.4)) are also proposed on the basis of same arguments.

Equations (6.5) and (6.6) are of much importance as far as the intermediation process is concerned. Variations in inflation rates are expected to have a negative effect on the volume of time and saving deposits held with commercial banks. Again, the *a priori* sign is expected to be negative with inflation and positive with income.

To investigate the relationship between capital formation and financial intermediation, we assume the ratio of investment to the gross national product is a function of the growth of monetary assets which comprise currency (C), demand deposits (D), and time and saving deposits (TS) as a proportion of income, as well as of the ratio of income to demand and time savings. The last ratio approximates the ratio of nonmonetary to monetary assets and hence represents an index of financial repression. *A priori*, the variable is greater if financial liberalization and intermediation exerts a positive impact on economic growth. It is, of course, assumed that there is a stable and monotonic relationship between non-monetary assets and output. Hence, we can write:

$$\log (I/Y) = f_0 + f_1 \log (\Delta C/Y)_t + f_2 \log (\Delta D/Y)_t + f_3 \log (\Delta TS/Y)_t + f_4 \log [R/(C + D + TS)] + f_5 \log (Y/D + DS) \quad (6.7)$$

The variable $R/(C + D + TS)$ is really a proxy of the index of financial diversification. It is known that differing effects of C, D and TS (different forms of money) on capital formation are due in part to differing reserve requirements (see, for example, Vogel and Buser 1976). Hence, the ratio, $R/(C + D + TS)$ is used to capture the impact of intertemporal variations in aggregate reserve requirements. *A priori*, we expect:

$$f_1 < 0 \qquad f_2 > 0 \qquad f_3 > 0 \qquad f_4 < 0 \qquad f_5 < 0$$

In fact, it is the sign and significance of f_5 which is of particular interest to us. The model is estimated by Ordinary Least Square regression technique and in logarithm form. The statistical results (in two alternative specifications) are presented in equations 6.5 and 6.6.

Tables 6.2 and 6.3 indicate that the inflation rates affect negatively the behaviour of C, D and TS. Apparently, the statistical fit in all equations is good and between 77 and 99 per cent of total variance of the dependent variables are explained.

All variables have their *a priori* signs and their coefficients are significant at the 5 per cent level and less except for the inflation rate in the demand deposits equation which despite its correct sign, is insignificant in equation (6.3). When a moving average of two years was tested, the coefficient is significant in the currency equation. It is worth noting that between 1967 and 1972, Jordan witnessed a period of considerable political instability. Given the DW statistics, the possibilities of autocorrelation is rejected in all equations.

With respect to the investment function, the positive correlation between capital formation and financial intermediation is confirmed. More than 80 per cent of the variation in the ratio of investment to income is explained by the growth of monetary assets (among other variables). The ratio of the non-monetary to monetary assets has its *a priori* sign and its coefficient is highly significant. As a proxy for the degree of financial liberalizations it could lead to more intermediation and increase the availability of investable funds. This argument was supported by the positive and high correlation between the $\Delta TS/Y$ variable and I/Y.

However, since the variables $\Delta C/Y$ and $\Delta D/Y$ in the investment equation are very insignificant, we have dropped them from the model.

Conclusions

The following conclusions can be drawn on the basis of our study on Jordan.

1 The relationship between inflation and currency holdings is positive and highly significant.
2 The relationship between inflation and demand deposits is negative. However, the coefficient is significant only at the 10 per cent level. A highly significant and positive relationship has been found between real income and demand deposits.

Table 6.2 Model estimates (in log function)

Eqn no.	Constant	$(\Delta P/P)_t$	$(\Delta Y/P)_t$	$[(\Delta P/P)_t + (AP/P)_{t-1}]/2$	$[(Y/P)_t + (Y/P)_{t-1}]/2$	R^2	DW	F	SEE
6.1	-.79	.091	.650			.77	1.47	21.06	.169
6.2	-1.08			-.17 (-3.30)	.67 (7.71)	.82	1.55	27.59	.151
6.3	-.02	-0.83 (-1.13)	.39 (2.81)			.99	1.43	608.78	.102
6.4	-.05			.09 (-1.39)	.41 (2.90)	.99	1.44	617.42	.101
6.5	-8.38	.058 (-1.68)	.61 (12.38)			.90	1.36	80.30	.173
6.6	-9.16			.04 (-2.78)	.59 (14.55)	.93	1.39	113.44	.147

Table 6.3 The investment equation (in log function)

Eqn no.	Constant	$\Delta TS/Y$	$R/C + D + YS$	$Y/D + TS$	R^2	DW	F	SEE
6.1	.134	.087 (2.22)	-.360 (-2.17)	-.361 (-4.12)	.81	1.75	24.74	.139

3 The assumed negative association between inflation and savings and time deposits has been confirmed and found to be highly significant. The relationship between the time savings and real income has been found to be positive and very significant. The real income elasticity of time and saving deposits is less than unity. If other variables are constant a 5 per cent rise in real income should raise time and saving deposits by 3 per cent.

4 The expected positive correlation between time and saving deposits and investment and the negative association between the ratio of non-monetary to monetary assets has been confirmed. Given the high level of significance in t-values, it is very likely that an increase in the degree of financial intermediation along with a rise in time and saving deposits should have a beneficial effect on the ratio of investment to income.

References

Fry, M. (1978), 'Money and capital: financial deepening in economic development', *Journal of Money, Credit and Banking*, Vol. 10, No. 4, pp. 464–75.
—— (1980), 'Saving, investment growth and the cost of financial repression', *World Development*, Vol. 8.
—— (1988), *Finance and Economic Development*, Oxford University Press, Oxford.
Galbis, V. (1977), 'Financial intermediation and economic growth in less developed countries', in P. C. I. Ayre (ed.), *Finance in Developing Countries*, Frank Cass, London.
Ghatak, S, (1981). 'Monetary economics in developing countries', Macmillan, London and New York.
Gupta, K. (1986), *Financial Repression and Economic Growth*, Croom Helm, London.
Kapur, B. (1976), 'Alternative stabilization policies for less developed economies', *Journal of Political Economy*, Vol. 84, p. 4, August.
McKinnon, R. (1973), *Money and Credit in Economic Development*, Brooking Institute, USA.
—— (ed.) (1976), *Money and Finance in Economic Growth and Development*, Oxford University Press, Oxford.
Shaw, Edward S. (1973), *Financial Deepening in Economic Development*, Oxford University Press, New York.
Taylor, L. (1983), *Structuralist Macroeconomies*, Basic Books, New York.

Vogel, R. and Buser, S. (1976), 'Inflation, financial repression and capital formation in Latin America', in R. McKinnon (ed.), *Money and Finance in Economic Growth and Development*, Marcel Dekkar, New York.

Wijnbergen, S. Van (1983), 'Interest rate management in less developed countries', *Journal of Monetary Economics*, Vol. 12, p. 3, September.

—— (1984), 'Exchange rate management and stabilization policies in developing countries', University of Warwick Discussion Paper.

Chapter seven

Islamic banking – the Jordanian experience*
Rodney Wilson

The subject of Islamic finance has received increasing attention in recent years, both from Muslim scholars and from those in the West with an interest in Islamic affairs. Much of the writing is of a theoretical nature, however, and it is only recently that the results of empirical investigations have started to appear. This paper is intended as a modest contribution to this empirical literature.

There are several reasons why the Jordanian experience is of special interest, and why it is worth examining in some detail.

1 Jordan, despite its small size, is one of the most developed Islamic countries, where the majority of the population use banks. The Kingdom's gross national product per capita of $2,000 understates its level of development, as Jordan has perhaps the best educated and most highly qualified population in the entire Islamic world.

2 The economy is very open, with international transactions of considerable importance, reflecting Jordan's geographical position, market size and economic structure. Much banking business therefore involves trade finance, and the handling of remittances, which are still of considerable importance for the Jordanian economy, despite the oil recession in the Gulf.

3 The banking laws are liberal, with the major banks being privately owned. Foreign banks are permitted to operate, although most business is handled by domestically owned banks. There is much competition in the financial sector, involving both the banks themselves, money changers, who handle a large portion of remittance transactions, and business involving the West Bank where Jordanian banks no longer operate.[1]

*An earlier version of this chapter appeared in the *Arab Law Quarterly*, Vol. 2, Part 3, August 1987, pp. 207–29.

4 Islamic banking is well established in Jordan, with the Jordan Islamic Bank for Finance and Investment founded in 1978, and operating since September 1979. It has a more extensive branch network than any other national Islamic bank. There is also the Islamic Investment House in Amman, which has built up a significant investment portfolio, but which has run into difficulties. There are lessons from its experience for other Islamic financial institutions.

5 There has been little written about Islamic banking in Jordan, despite the seven years of experience with modern Islamic finance. Ahmed El Ashker has written extensively on the Egyptian experience of Islamic banking, and a shortened version of his thesis has been published. Mohammed Bashir has written on the Sudanese experience (see Bashir 1984 for a summary of the main findings of his thesis). I have written myself on Jordanian banking, but not hitherto on Islamic banking in the Kingdom. (For a description and analysis of banking trends in Jordan see Wilson 1986.)

Jordan's current financial position

The Jordanian economy has been remarkably resilient for over three decades, despite the traumatic experiences of the Israeli occupation of the West Bank in 1967, the civil war in 1970, the difficult relations with Syria, and the spillover effects from the Gulf War involving Iraq, Jordan's major trading partner. Growth rates have been high, often averaging over 10 per cent per annum, well above those of neighbouring states such as Syria and Iraq. The government's policy of encouraging private initiative and enterprise seems to have paid off, with a flourishing small business sector, and a diversified range of light consumer orientated industries which serve both Jordan and Iraq. The economy's main weakness has always been the trade imbalance, with export receipts covering only 20 to 30 per cent of import payments. Until recently this was not a problem as the foreign exchange gap was covered by remittances and aid flows from abroad, initially from Britain and the United States, but in recent years mainly from Saudi Arabia and the Gulf. With the oil recession in the Gulf, aid inflows have fallen sharply. Those from Kuwait in 1985 fell to a quarter of the previous year's level, and in the case of Saudi Arabia, the major donor, the decline exceeded 50 per cent. Early indications suggested aid disbursements will be even lower in 1986, as aid to Iraq is being given priority over assistance to Jordan, owing to the former's critical situation because of the Gulf War.

At the same time remittances are falling sharply, the value

declining by over a quarter in 1985. Although remittances in 1986 were better than expected, prospects are poor. The demand for foreign labour has declined sharply in the Gulf, partly reflecting the completion of labour intensive infrastructural projects, but also as a result of the fall in investment caused by the fall in oil revenues. Even if the oil situation improves, it seems unlikely that there will be any substantial recruitment of new workers from Jordan, as the pressures are now great to indigenize employment in the Gulf, especially as some of the states now face a problem of youth unemployment. Even those Jordanian passport holders working in administration and teaching are finding their services are no longer required when contracts come up for renewal.

The Jordanian banking scene

It is important to be aware of these disturbing economic trends when assessing the prospects for banking in Jordan, including those for the Islamic banks. The future growth of the economy and banking business will inevitably be affected by developments in the international civil market, even though Jordan itself is not an exporter of oil. Much will also depend on the outcome of the Gulf War, given Iraq's significance as a market for Jordan. In view of Jordan's ability to overcome the gravest of crises in the past however, it would be unwise to take too gloomy a view of the future.

Jordan's educated citizens have a remarkable aptitude to seize whatever opportunities arise, and to ensure that profitable business results. The demise of Beirut as a banking centre, for example, helped Amman to develop as a centre for Middle Eastern and Arab operations, given the stable political environment, and the liberal economic climate. Similarly the state control of virtually all economic activity in Syria and Iraq, including the nationalized banking sector, has helped Jordan attract capital and enterprise from these states which could not flourish under tightly regulated conditions.

Jordan is the home of one major international bank, the Arab Bank, and eight primarily local banks which serve the domestic market. Although in terms of paid up capital the Arab Bank is four times larger than any other Jordanian bank, this merely reflects the size of the international operations of this essentially Palestinian institution. Domestically, the Jordan National Bank is more significant in terms of deposits and lending, and other institutions such as the Cairo Amman Bank, the Jordan Kuwait Bank and the Petra Bank do almost as much business.[2]

Riba transactions in Jordan[3]

In the mid-1970s almost half the bank deposits with the commercial banks were in demand or current accounts on which zero or minimal interest was paid. By 1985, however, this proportion had fallen to below one-quarter, reflecting the increased competition in the banking sector for deposits (Wilson 1986). Most deposits are now in the form of term deposits for a fixed period or savings deposits which also earn interst. Non-residents, mainly Jordanian expatriates working in the Gulf, seem particularly keen to maintain interest-earning deposits, as only 15 per cent held demand deposits in 1985. This may reflect their lesser need for transactions balances, as they return to Jordan relatively infrequently.

As far as an asset deployment is concerned, the commercial banks advance almost half their funds in the form of loans on which interest is payable, some through overdraft facilities, but an increasing amount through structured term lending. Around 10 per cent of bank assets are held in interest-earning government bills and bonds, and around 15 per cent are held in foreign assets, again mainly interest-yielding securities. Less than 2 per cent of all commercial bank advances are in the form of direct investment.

Around a quarter of commercial bank advances are in the form of trade finance, mostly credits to cover imports, although some are for purely domestic commerce. A similar proportion of commercial bank advances are for construction finance, although this proportion has been falling, reflecting the recession in the construction industry, which has affected even domestic house building and home extensions. Personal lending has increased in significance however, and now accounts for over a tenth of all commercial bank credit.

Although interest transactions are the prevalent form of bank business in Jordan, rates remain relatively low, reflecting the Kingdom's modest rate of inflation, and the stability of the Jordanian dinar. Interest rates on savings and time deposits are in the 4–8.5 per cent range, depending on the deposit terms, and borrowers are seldom charged more than 10 per cent. The authorities have been concerned to keep interest rates down in order to curtail business overheads, although this has been largely through exhortations rather than by direct regulation via monetary policy.[4] Nevertheless this policy seems to have worked, and relations between the commercial banks and the Central Bank are mainly close, the latter's role being to exercise effective control, while at the same time ensuring that sound banking standards are adhered to.

Origins of Islamic banking in Jordan

The Central Bank has been accommodating to the introduction of Islamic banking into the Kingdom, and responded positively to the initial suggestions which were made concerning this type of banking. While not wishing to see the banking system Islamized, the authorities were sensitive to the wishes of those who wanted Islamic financial services, and it was recognized that many believers were unhappy with the kind of banking facilities offered by the *riba* commercial banks. It was, therefore, thought that provision should be made for a plural system, which would accommodate both *riba* and *halal* (permitted) financial transactions, the latter being the only type permissible under the *sharia* (religious law). Accordingly, law no. 13 of 1978 was drafted, published in the official gazette no. 2733 of 1 April. It was this law that provided for the establishment of the Jordan Islamic Bank for Finance and Investment.

In framing this legislation the Finance Ministry sought the advice of *sharia* legal experts, as well as the Central Bank staff concerned with bank regulation. The initiative for the law, however, came as a result of an approach made to the Jordanian authorities by Sheikh Saleh Kamel of the Al Baraka Group, with backing from within Saudi Arabia. The law defines the type of deposits which the bank can receive, and the forms of advances which it is permitted to make under the *sharia*. The functions, objectives, management structures and capital provisions are all set out under the establishment law.

Several types of deposits are permitted. Trust deposits are like current account deposits which earn no return, but which are repayable in full by the bank on demand. Joint investment accounts can be opened by individuals or business who wish to share in the bank's profits (or losses). The return on these deposits is not guaranteed, as such a guarantee would contravene Islamic law.[5] Indeed there may be a zero return, as section 22(a) of the establishment law indicates, but in practice this has never happened. There are three kinds of joint investment accounts: savings account, notice accounts and fixed accounts. Money can be withdrawn from savings accounts subject to ten days advance notice. The depositor gets a 50 per cent profit share, however, on his or her balance. Notice accounts, as their name implies, are subject to a longer minimum notice of withdrawal – three months – but depositors get a 70 per cent profit share on their balances. With fixed accounts depositors get a 90 per cent profit share, but funds are illiquid in the short term, the minimum deposit period being a year.

The Jordan Islamic Bank also provides specific investment accounts for clients seeking to invest in particular projects, with the bank acting as the client's agent or investment manager. The bank shares in any profits from the investment, but is not liable to participate in any losses. This type of service provides a model for Islamic fund management, and represents a successful innovation in Islamic financial field by the Jordanian bank. The bank may also provide *muqaradah* (bonds), which maintain their face value, but entitle the holder to a share of the profits on the funds in which the money raised through the bond issues have been utilized. Such bonds have not yet been issued, but the provision of such a facility under the establishment law gives the bank increased flexibility.

The law provides for advances to be made by the bank on the *mudarabah* profit-sharing principle, as well as through decreasing participation. The bank's share of the project gradually diminishes over time. Short term finance for trade purposes can be advanced through repurchasing schemes, as is the case with other Islamic banks.

The Jordan Islamic Bank

Capital structure

The authorized share capital of the Jordan Islamic Bank was JD 4 million,[6] with shareholdings restricted to a maximum of 5 per cent of the total capital under law no. 13 of 1978. The initial paid up capital was JD 1 million, most of which was raised by public subscription apart from the funds invested by the founder owners. Each year until 1983 a further JD 1 million was paid up until the whole authorized capital was subscribed. The founder subscribers were entitled to increase their participation in line with their initial subscriptions each year until 1983, but not all did so. By December 1980 only JD 273 was unsettled, but by 1981 this had risen to JD 168,492 representing almost 17 per cent of that year's settlements. The position improved the following year, however, as only JD 56,983 was left unsubscribed out of the fourth capital issue. All of these shares were readily taken up by new purchasers who were keen to become owner participants in the bank because of its increasingly favourable reputation.

In 1985 some amendments to the bank's establishment law were made when the bank's permanent law no. 65 was passed. The major change provided for an increase in the bank's authorized capital to JD 6 million, a decision which was ratified by the General Assembly of the Bank at a meeting on 21 December 1985. All the bank's shareholders are entitled to attend the General Assembly. This decision was taken partly as a result of the development of the bank's business, and the need to have an adequate capital base. In addition, however, the Central Bank of Jordan issued new regulations requiring the minimum capital of all Jordanian banks to be JD 5 million. During the first half of 1986 the new authorized capital was duly paid up, most being subscribed by the existing shareholders. Under Jordanian law existing shareholders are given the first option of purchase when the company's capital is increased, and they have fifteen days to exercise their right. Most chose to do so, as the bank's shares had steadily increased in value, and proved a sound investment. The shareholders were confident in the management, and there was a ready market for existing shares. The number of shareholders of course varies, but the majority are private rather than institutional investors. The management estimated that there were over 5,000 shareholders in 1986, with the average nominal holding therefore being JD 1,200, although the shares themselves were worth twice this amount.

Sheikh Saleh Kamel of Saudi Arabia is Chairman of the Board of Directors, but his holding in the bank is below JD 250,000. The Al Baraka Investment and Development Company has a similar shareholding, it being a Jordanian company which is wholly owned by the Al Baraka International Group. Over 95 per cent of the capital is Jordanian owned. The bank is not a member of the International Association of Islamic Banks, which tends to be dominated by Prince Mohammed bin Faisal's Islamic banks. Like other Al Baraka associates, the bank prefers to remain independent of this grouping, although in its overseas business it will deal with other Islamic banks, including the Faisal Islamic Banks, in preference to secular commercial banks. All the bank's operations are fully in accordance with the *sharia*, and Sheikh Abdul Hamid Essayeh, a respected Jordanian religious authority, acts as the *sharia* consultant.

Share values

Shares in the Jordan Islamic Bank have been actively traded since the creation of the company in 1979. Dealings in bank shares account for around 70 per cent of transactions in the Amman Financial Market, an exchange which has become the second most important in the Arab Middle East after Cairo in terms of the value of transactions. Kuwait used to be the leading market in the region, but dealings remain depressed following the Souk Al-Manakh débâcle in 1982. The volume of dealings in shares in the Jordan

Table 7.1 Equity position of the Jordan Islamic Bank

	Value of shares traded (JD thousands)	Number of shares traded (thousands)	Average share price[1] (JD)	Yield[2] (%)
1979	542	503	1.078	0.0
1980	4,059	2,757	1.472	0.0
1981	3,886	2,732	1.423	3.51
1982	6,402	2,517	2.544	3.14
1983	7,261	2,310	3.143	2.54
1984	6,693	2,015	3.322	2.71
1985	826	308	2.678	3.36
1986[3]	186	82	2.268	ND[4]

Notes:
1 Nominal value is JD 1,000
2 Calculated on the basis of shareholders dividend in relation to the actual average share price
3 January to June
4 ND – not declared

Sources: Jordan Islamic Bank 1979-85; Central Bank of Jordan 1986

Islamic Bank peaked in 1980 and 1981 as Table 7.1 shows, but since then the amount of trading has fallen. In 1980 it was the second most traded company on the Amman Financial Market after the Jordan and Gulf Bank, but more recently dealings have declined. The initial high volume of transactions partly reflected the enormous amount of interest in this new type of financial institution by market participants. Shareholders today tend to regard their holdings as long term, however, rather than tradable instruments which can be sold to realize capital gains.

There is a willingness to hold on to the shares even when their value declines as shareholders feel themselves committed to the bank. As a capital asset the shares have done relatively well in any case. As Figure 7.1 shows, share prices in the Jordan Islamic Bank have consistently outperformed the index for all shares. Prices rose more than twice the general share index over the 1979-86 period, and although bank shares did better than those for manufacturing and distributive trades, the value of shares in the Jordan Islamic Bank increased by almost 50 per cent more than banks on average. It was only during the 1980-1 period that the shares in the Jordan Islamic Bank performed less adequately, but this reflected the uncertainties of the early settling down period. Nevertheless, during this period the overwhelming majority of founder shareholders willingly subscribed to the increases in paid up capital as already indicated.

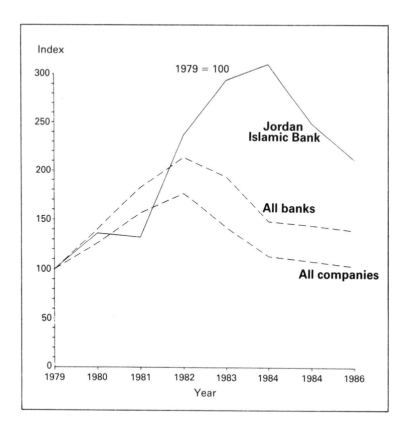

Figure 7.1   Jordan Islamic Bank share prices

Sources: Central Bank of Jordan, Monthly Statistical Bulletin and Amman Financial Market

Deposit growth

The Jordan Islamic Bank started from a modest deposit base as might be expected for a new and novel kind of financial institution. Jordanians tend to be conservative, especially in financial matters, and preferred to adopt a 'wait and see' approach before depositing their own funds. The initial publicity that surrounded the opening of the new bank brought only a limited public response, and most of the initial depositors were the bank's own investors. The management was content to have a slow buildup of business initially, as it would not have been easy to employ a sudden surge in deposits profitably in any case. Advertising was rejected as a means of attracting clients, instead the management's policy was that the bank's reputation could best be spread by word of mouth from existing satisfied customers to their relatives and friends.

It would, of course, have been easy to expand deposits rapidly by targeting a few affluent customers and larger businesses which could have deposited substantial sums. In Jordan there are several thousand such people, some of whom are extremely devout in their religious observance. Management's aim, however, was to establish a wide deposit base by attracting as many customers of modest means as possible. This inevitably meant more administrative effort, and raised bank overheads. The advantage of such a policy was that the deposit base would be more stable, avoiding the possibility of some affluent customer deciding to withdraw all his funds at once. One year after opening, by the end of 1980, there were around 5,000 depositors, and by 1986 the number had grown to 65,000.[7] The average size of deposit is under JD 2,000 and some clients have deposits of JD 200 or less. The size of deposits has tended to fall over the time despite the aggregate growth, a trend which the management is pleased to see. The aim is to make the institution a people's bank for the *Umma* – the community of believers.

The major means of expanding the deposit base was by establishing a branch network throughout Jordan. There are now thirteen branches of the bank, from Irbid in the north to Aqaba in the south. Five of the branches are in Amman, where over a third of Jordan's population is concentrated, including most of its more affluent citizens. The spread of branches in the region may have contributed to the decline in the average value of deposits, but it means that the bank is regarded as a truly national institution. Further branches are planned, including one at Mafraq in the north, one at Salt, high above the Jordan Valley, and possibly one at Azraq in the east. Jordan is, of course, a limited market, and the geographical possibilities are soon exhausted, but the management plan is to open a new branch each year, at least for the next five years. The bank has no ambitions outside Jordan, being an essentially national institution.[8]

Types of deposit

Figure 7.2 illustrates the growth of deposits since the Jordan Islamic Bank's inception. Initially, trust accounts were the most popular, these being current accounts on which cheques can be drawn as already described. The management was keen to encourage such transaction accounts, which earned no return, until the bank could build up an investment portfolio. Since 1980, however, joint investment accounts have become more significant, and it is this type of account which has come to dominate in terms of deposits. The percentage of total deposits accounted for by joint investment accounts rose from 54 per cent in 1980 to almost 62 per cent in 1983, and over 70 per cent by 1986. Of various types of joint investment account offered, the fixed-term account has proved the most popular, as it earns the highest return: 90 per cent of the declared profit proportion. Over 90 per cent of the joint investment deposits are of this type.

From the bank's point of view this dominance of fixed-term accounts means a secure deposit base. At least a year's notice must be given for funds to be withdrawn, and in practice the amount under notice is extremely low. The bank can, therefore, back projects on a long-term basis, secure in the knowledge that most of its funding is also long term. There is little need to worry about unanticipated calls for funds, as in the case of *riba* commercial banks. Depositors know, however, that if an unexpected need arises, and there are unforeseen expenses such as hospital bills to be paid, then the bank will provide help. The bank maintains a *Qird Hasan*, an interest free loan from a social purpose fund to help the needy. A total of 595 loans were granted from this fund on an interest free basis in 1985, these being worth JD 238,321. The bank has started to accept *Qird Hasan* deposits which must be specifically used to alleviate social hardship. In 1985 a total of JD 14,628 was deposited by sixty-eight customers on this charitable basis.

The management are keen to attract specified investment accounts, which as Figure 7.2 shows have grown steadily since 1983. By 1986 these accounted for over 10 per cent of deposits, and the management's objective is to increase these accounts to over one-fifth of deposits by 1990. With this type of deposit, funds are invested in specified investment projects which the depositor requests, and the rate of return directly depends on the particular project being funded, rather than the bank's overall profit. The depositor has, therefore, a greater degree of choice, but he or she bears the risk, and makes the gain (or loss).[9] The bank's role is to provide financial management for the project. It ensures that the funds are properly used, and that the interests of the investor are protected. The bank is, therefore, an investment services manager, bringing the parties in need of funds in touch with those with surplus funds.

Many customers maintain more than one type of deposit, running a trust account for their transactions' needs, while at the same time placing longer-term funds in joint or specified investment

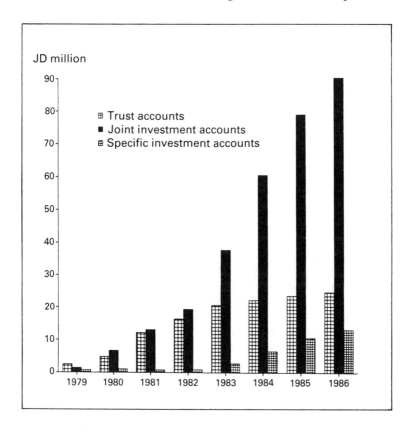

Figure 7.2   Jordan Islamic Bank deposit growth
Sources: Jordan Islamic Bank Annual Reports

accounts. Some of these long-term accounts are precautionary balances, to cover items such as medical expenses, although in Jordan, given the emphasis on education, many of the balances are to cover future school and university fees. This is a major expenditure item for most middle-class households, but through savings, the cost can be met over a longer period of time. Needs can be reasonably well anticipated in advance with educational fees, and for this purpose a joint investment account with a fixed one-year notice provides the ideal investment vehicle.

Role of the Jordan Islamic Bank compared to other banks

The extent to which Islamic banks contribute to the institutional-ization of savings has long been debated. It is through this process that a positive contribution to development can be made by matching savings with investment needs. Funds are employed in a systematic fashion using some form of rate of return criterion, thereby ensuring a more optimal use of resources. A major contribution to this process is made if Islamic banks encourage those who were not previously in the banking habit to use their services. Many Muslims were hesitant to use *riba*-based financial instititions, but Islamic banks provide them with a *halal* system of finance, to which there is no religious objection. Indeed, for believers, dealing with such institutions is preferable to personal hoarding, which, like *riba* transactions, is condemned in the Koran.

The Jordan Islamic Bank seems to have attracted several thousand customers who were not previously in the banking habit, although the exact number cannot be assessed precisely, as clients are not asked such questions when they open accounts. It seems likely that many trust (current) account holders are in this position, a quarter of the total. Some may have used *riba* banks in the past, and then closed their accounts when the Jordan Islamic Bank opened, but this probably only applies in a small minority of cases. Bank customer loyalty is as significant in Jordan as elsewhere. Few with trust accounts with the Jordan Islamic Bank maintain current accounts with other banks however, as the holding of multiple accounts which earn no return is extremely wasteful.

Many clients of the Jordan Islamic Bank who maintain only joint investment accounts also have current accounts with other banks. This applies especially in the case of business customers. The accounts with the Jordan Islamic Bank are viewed as long-term investments, whereas the other accounts are transactions balances. For individuals this is less likely to be the case, and they may not need current accounts. Jordan remains, like other Arab countries, an essentially cash-based society as far as personal transactions are concerned, with cheques and credit cards used much less than in the West.[10] In these circumstances banks are regarded primarily as savings institutions. Even foreign exchange transactions, apart from those for large amounts, and letters of credit seldom go through the banking system. Moneychangers handle most foreign exchange deals, including remittances, which were very important, and continue to have some significance for the Jordanian economy.

The Jordan Islamic Bank has probably not contributed as much to the spread of banking as some of the Islamic banks in the

Gulf, simply because most Jordanians with significant means already banked prior to its establishment. The bank has made a more significant contribution to the spread of banking in the provincial centres where it established branches, rather than in Amman, which was financially more sophisticated. Overall it would seem most appropriate to suggest that the Jordan Islamic Bank has tended to complement the activities of the *riba* banks rather than being a substitute for them, but this reflects the Jordanian financial environment, rather than any shortcomings in the bank itself.

The Jordan Islamic Bank is continuing to expand its deposits rapidly in spite of the recession which Jordan is experiencing. Table 7.2 shows recent deposit growth, which has been extremely rapid, especially for joint investment accounts. These are growing much more rapidly than trust accounts, perhaps reflecting the fact that the new customers being attracted are lower income earners who do not require chequing and other similar facilities. The bank seems to be doing better than *riba*-based banks in terms of deposit growth, particularly with regard to time deposits. No comparison was possible for specified investment accounts, as other Jordanian banks to not offer such deposit facilities.

Asset deployment

Most of the Jordan Islamic Bank's funds are placed in Islamic investments on a profit-sharing basis. Figure 7.3 shows the growth of the bank's assets, with almost JD 80 million invested on an Islamic basis by 1986, and over JD 45 million in cash holdings. Initially cash holdings predominated, as Islamic investments take time to arrange, but by 1980 Islamic investments were already more significant. The proportion of bank assets accounted for by Islamic investments amounted to over 54 per cent by 1983, and by 1986 this figure had risen to almost 56 per cent out of a total asset portfolio exceeding JD 142 million. These Islamic investments mostly consist of *mudarabah* advances to business clients on the profit-sharing principle. About 20 per cent are trade credits provided through the purchase of goods on behalf of clients, who repurchase the goods when they in turn have arranged sales. This figure also includes leasing arrangements on the *ijara* (leasing contract) Islamic principle. The leasing is for a specified period, at the end of which the client will make a final payment and take over the ownership of the goods in question.

The relatively high holdings of cash by the bank should be noted. In 1983 this proportion was 26 per cent, and in 1986 the figure had risen to almost 32 per cent. This refers partly to cash in hand, but it

Table 7.2 Recent trends in deposit growth in the Jordanian Islamic Bank for finance and investment accounts

Accounts	Trust accounts	Joint investment accounts	Specified investment accounts
Deposit value (JD)			
Dec. 1984	22,297,948	60,570,798	6,610,710
June 1985	24,696,330	68,977,848	9,895,949
Dec. 1985	23,745,917	79,118,479	10,703,701
June 1986	24,876,300	90,400,921	13,228,938
Deposit growth (%)			
Dec. 1984–Dec. 1985	6.5[1] (−10.2)[2]	30.6[1] (15.0)[2]	61.9
June 1985–June 1986	0.7[1] (0.5)[2]	31.0[1] (9.8)[2]	33.7
Deposit shares (%)			
Dec. 1984	24.9	67.7	7.4
June 1986	19.4	70.3	10.3

Notes:
1 Demand deposits in all commercial banks
2 Time deposits in all commercial banks

Sources: Jordan Islamic Bank 1985, 1986; Central Bank of Jordan 1986

also includes deposits with other commercial banks and the Central Bank of Jordan. These inter-bank deposits are placed on a non-interest-earning basis. The high level of cash reserves partly reflects the conservative policy of the bank's management, and the desire to maintain adequate liquidity. Cash holdings are higher than the management would like, however, partly reflecting the recession in the Jordanian economy, and the lack of investment opportunities in the present climate. A proportion of around one-quarter is considered optimum, but the management does not wish to make high risk advances, and views the additional cash as a welcome hedge during this period of business uncertainty.

Islamic community finance

The specified investments identified separately in Figure 7.3 are also, of course, undertaken on an Islamic basis, and the essential principle involved is *mudarabah* or profit sharing. These investments, nevertheless, have to be distinguished from the more general

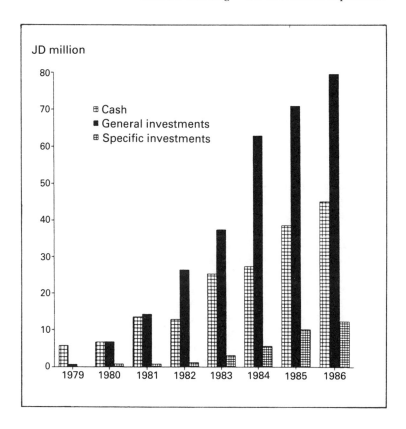

Figure 7.3 Jordan Islamic Bank asset holdings

Sources: Jordan Islamic Bank Annual Reports

type of Islamic investments already discussed, which take the form of portfolio investment in the sense that the Jordan Islamic Bank has only a minority stake in the enterprises it is supporting. With specified investments the bank itself is the instigator of the investment, and wholly owns and controls the projects involved. This can, therefore, be regarded as direct investment. The major instance of this type of investment is the Al-Rawdah housing project in north Amman. The bank acquired a plot of 40 dunums opposite the Al Rai daily newspaper offices in the north of Amman for housing development for middle-income citizens in 1981, and a larger plot the same year in the south of the capital near Jabal Al-Hashimi.

This was for a comprehensive housing scheme for low-income citizens.

Work was started on the smaller plot in north Amman first, with the preliminary study completed within a few months of the plot being acquired. Construction started in October 1983. A commercial centre containing a supermarket and other shops is being built together with thirty villas and seven residential buildings containing apartments. A mosque, community hall, and school are being constructed. Disbursements have accounted for almost 87.4 per cent of the funds invested in the specified investment accounts by 1986, the remaining sum being accounted for by the land purchase at Jabal Al-Hashimi for the low-income housing scheme. Some of the investors are hoping to live in this new Islamic community themselves, which will be a very attractive residential suburb of Amman. This ambitious project has taken up much of the bank's efforts in the last few years, but once the villas and apartments are occupied, returns will start to come in, and the bank plans to go ahead with the development of the Jabal Al-Hashimi site as well as other specific projects. As Table 7.3 shows, the assets accounted for by specific investments continue to grow rapidly, reflecting these housing developments.

If specific investment funds from depositors continue to grow as rapidly as recently then a corresponding buildup of the bank's specific investment will occur. The Jordan Islamic Bank will be well placed to undertake further large direct investments in housing and other fields, and the experience learnt from the Al-Rawdah scheme should be invaluable.

General investment policy

Figure 7.4 shows the distribution of funds by the Jordan Islamic Bank. This refers to the allocation of the Islamic investment funds already discussed, rather than the specified investments which have been in housing to date as indicated in the previous section. Most of the bank's lending has been to industry, mainly small manufacturing establishments producing plastics, soaps, medicines and other products which are sold mostly in the local market and in neighbouring Arab countries such as Iraq. The bank has been much more involved in industrial lending then other Jordanian banks, as many of its depositors are those involved in manufacturing. It is hoped to increase investment exposure in manufacturing, as this sector has been more buoyant.

Advances for trade are second in importace, as Figure 7.4 shows, most of this being on a resale basis as already discussed. This type

Table 7.3 Assets of the Jordan Islamic Bank for finance and investment

	Cash	General investments	Specific investments	Fixed assets
Asset value (JD)				
Dec. 1984	27,555,017	63,013,403	5,636,284	3,842,930
Dec. 1985	33,442,402	66,404,051	4,111,218	4,472,492
Dec. 1985	38,855,419	71,013,906	10,107,048	4,865,563
June 1986	45,362,485	79,650,758	12,279,117	4,969,438
Asset growth (%)				
Dec. 1984–Dec. 1985	41.0	12.7	79.3	26.6
June 1985–June 1986	35.6	19.9	34.8	11.1
Asset shares (%)*				
Dec. 1984	27.0	61.7	5.5	3.8
June 1986	31.2	54.8	8.5	34.0

Note:
* Does not add to 100 per cent as other assets such as securities, non-interest yielding bills, etc., excluded

Sources: Jordan Islamic Bank 1979–85; Central Bank of Jordan 1986

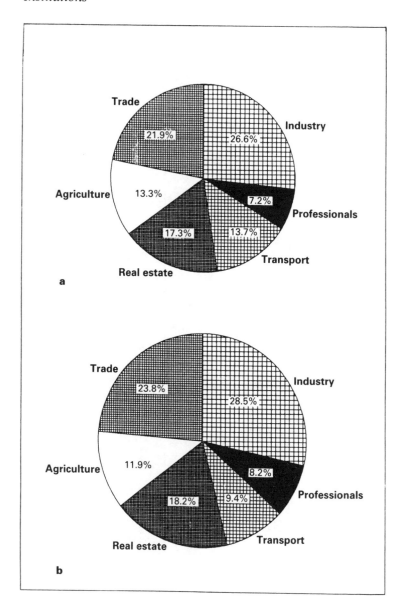

Figure 7.4 Distribution of funds by Jordan Islamic Bank: (a) 1984 total lending = JD 63 million; (b) 1985 total lending = JD 71 million

Sources: Jordan Islamic Bank Data Base

of advance is more liquid than industrial investments which tend to be long term, the period for trade advances typically being one year or less, and often as short as three months. Jordan's imports are being curtailed because of balance of payments difficulties, and the bank's management accept that trade finance, which usually covers imports, will at best maintain its share in the years ahead. Lending for real estate acquisition has continued to increase. With real estate values depressed, the bank's view is that this is a good time to invest, as property will appreciate once the economy moves out of recession. This seems a reasonable judgement, as prices are no longer falling, and the expectation is for a market improvement. The financial institutions that invested in real estate speculation at the height of the boom in the 1970s were the only ones that got into difficulties over asset valuations when the boom ended. The Jordan Islamic Bank avoids speculative investments however, as this would be against the institution's principles. Rather the emphasis is on aiding believers to acquire property at reasonable prices for their own long term use, and that of other believers.

Investment in transport undertakings declined over the 1984–5 period in relative terms as Figure 7.4 shows, largely reflecting the difficulties in Iraq's trade in which most of the transportation companies are involved. The future demand for this type of advance is difficult to predict, as much depends on Iraq's position in the Gulf War. The bank would like to invest more in agricultural projects, but the Kingdom's agriculture is experiencing marketing difficulties after the rapid expansion of production in the Jordan Valley in the 1970s. Saudi Arabia has a surplus of its own heavily subsidized wheat production, and some of the other Gulf states are producing tomatoes and other produce at great expense in greenhouse units. The advances to individuals are mainly to professionals such as doctors and dentists, for the purchase of equipment. The bank hopes to advance more to this type of client, as they are extremely reliable, and know exactly how to use their advances productively.

Returns on investment

The revenue which the Jordan Islamic Bank earns on its investment compares favourably with the earnings of other financial institutions. Figure 7.5 shows the returns since 1980, which are expressed in money values. The decline over the 1982–4 period merely reflects the drop in the rate of inflation, and in real terms the return is higher. Inflation has declined from over 7 per cent in the early 1980s to under 4 per cent per annum.[11] This means a real rate

155

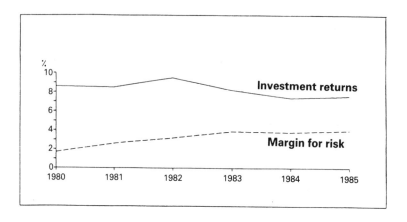

Figure 7.5   Returns on Islamic investments and risk provision
Sources: Jordan Islamic Bank Annual Reports 1979–85 and Interim Statement for 1986

of return of 3.5 per cent over the 1984–5 period, which is quite adequate by Jordanian standards. Higher returns can of course be earned by more risky investments, but the bank's management tends to be prudent in its asset deployment policy, as already indicated. Furthermore the bank is keen to back socially constructive projects, rather than ventures of dubious national value to Jordan.

Figure 7.5 also shows the margin for risk which the bank sets aside in case of default by those funded. In practice the calls on these reserves are very limited, as the banks clients, being committed Muslims, are honest in their dealings, and are fully aware of their responsibilities towards the bank and its depositors. The bank has perhaps the best clientele in Jordan in terms of the customers to whom it makes advances. Nevertheless, in business, problems often arise which are unforseeable, as this is the nature of any investment undertaking. Therefore the bank likes to adopt a safety first approach, and allow an adequate margin of funds to cover contingencies. With the favourable repayments record, and good return on investment, it has been possible to establish a large contingency fund for investment risk, which stood at over JD 3 million in 1986. A specific portion of the bank's cash assets are earmarked for this fund.

Distribution of profits

Figure 7.6 shows the profits which have been distributed to investors. These are, of course, determined by the bank's own investment returns. They compare favourably with the interest paid by *riba*-based commercial banks, the returns being consistently above the rate of inflation. The return has been calculated on the basis of 90 per cent of the declared dividend, the rate earned by those holding fixed-term joint investment accounts, which, as already indicated, account for the overwhelming proportion of investment deposits. This return is above the interest which most of those holding time deposits with the *riba*-based banks earn. Only those who deposit very large amounts with the Jordanian commercial banks can earn higher returns. The Central Bank of Jordan until 1982 set a minimum rate which *riba*-based banks paid to those with time and savings deposits. Following concern that this was raising interest rates for borrowers, the Central Bank decided to set a maximum rather than a minimum rate. Both rates are shown in Figure 7.6 for the respective time period for which they applied by the long broken lines above and below the profit return on Islamic investments. The broken lines indicate the actual maximum and minimum which the commercial banks paid during periods when these were not enforceable by statutory limits. Overall, it seems that investors with the Jordan Islamic Bank have fared well, and the bank has been able to reward them adequately while still maintaining a cautious investment strategy.

Staffing issues

The Jordan Islamic Bank recruited most of its initial senior staff from other Jordanian banks and the financial services sector, as the emphasis was on the hiring of competent experienced personnel. There was little need to recruit abroad given the wealth of banking talent within Jordan, some of whom were enthusiastic about the new type of financial institution as it meant they could pursue a banking career which was in harmony with their religious beliefs. Most had university degrees as well as professional banking qualifications.

Further down the seniority ladder, school leavers were recruited for clerical and other tasks, and the bank developed its own training programme. Within the bank's new headquarters building in the Sheisani district of Amman there are a lecture room and teaching facilities. Specialist courses are provided for the bank's staff on

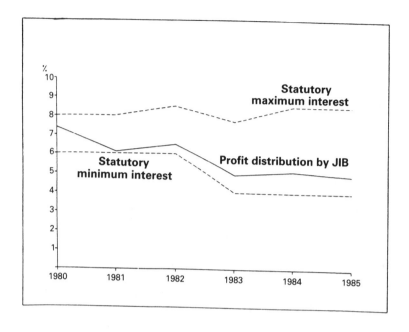

Figure 7.6 Profits for distribution to joint investment account holders compared to interest payments by *riba* banks

Sources: Jordan Islamic Bank Annual Reports 1979–85 and Interim Statement for 1986

Islamic banking procedures and techniques. Employees have also been sent to the Banking Institute of the Central Bank of Jordan for training. The bank has also cooperated with local educational institutions including the University of Jordan, and has offered traineeships in Islamic banking to a number of economics and business studies students, some of whom have subsequently been taken on by the bank. Scholarships in Islamic finance are also offered to outstanding students which are tenable at the University of Jordan on a sandwich course principle combining academic study with practical training. Recruitment is generally presenting no problems, with many more applicants than jobs at all levels. Jordan with its well-educated workforce now faces the problem of graduate unemployment. The bank is therefore giving priority to graduate recruitment, although, of course, given its small size, it can only hire a limited number of graduates each year from Jordanian universities.

The Islamic Investment House

The encouraging success of the Jordan Islamic Bank contrasts with that of the Kingdom's other major Islamic financial institution, the Islamic Investment House. This institution was founded on 10 September 1981 with an authorized capital of JD 4 million, the same amount as the Jordan Islamic Bank. It received its permit to operate from the Central Bank of Jordan on 28 December 1981. Very comprehensive regulations were drawn up for the working of the institution, even more detailed in fact than those for the Jordan Islamic Bank. The institution was partly founded as a result of a Kuwaiti initiative, with Mr Tukhaim Fahd Al-Tukhaim as chairman. Most of the directors were Jordanian however, including Mr Khairy Ayyoub Al Hammoury, the Vice Chairman and General Manager. Sheik Motlaq Al-Mohtaseb, a prominent Jordanian religious authority, was appointed as the *sharia* advisor.

The aims of the institution were similar to those of the Jordan Islamic Bank, as it was intended to provide financial services for both investors and those in need of funds on a *riba*-free basis. From the start, however, the institution was regarded as a vehicle for those with substantial funds to invest, rather than an ordinary deposit bank. As its name suggested, it was primarily an investment house, although the use of the word house in the title was partly because some Muslims object to any reference to banks.[12]

The Islamic Investment House did not establish a branch network however, although it offered similar types of accounts to the Jordan Islamic Bank, including demand deposits, and three kinds of joint investment deposit. Initially in 1982 only demand deposits were accepted, and JD 729,971 was deposited. By 1983 when joint investment deposits started to be accepted, demand deposits fell to JD 633,251, as some investors switched to profit-earning deposits. Notice deposits proved the most popular as with the Jordan Islamic Bank, these accounting for around 90 per cent of the JD 1.5 million in joint investment accounts in 1983. By 1984 this figure had grown to over JD 5.5 million, including JD 628,000 deposited in foreign currency. This represented about 9 per cent of the amount invested in the Jordan Islamic Bank.

Investment policy

The Islamic Investment House pursued an active investment policy with the limited funds it had at its disposal. The investments undertaken were imaginative, and at first sight seemed sound projects to back. A 30 per cent stake was acquired in the ship 'Farah' which carries passengers, cars and trucks from Aqaba to other Red Sea ports including Jeddah in Saudi Arabia, and more recently Neuiba in Egypt. Advances were also given to house purchasers, who repaid by instalments over a ten-year period. Over 150 advances were given for such purchases. The Islamic Investment House also financed the building of villas in the Zayy and Al-Ghour areas of Amman for rental.

In 1983 an agreement was signed between the Islamic Investment House and the Tukhaim International Exchange Company of Kuwait for the House to manage the latter company in return for a share of its profits. This company was also controlled by the Islamic Finance House's Chairman, Mr Tukhaim Fahd Al-Tukhaim. The purpose of this agreement was to facilitate money transfers between Kuwait and Jordan. The House also invested in Jordanian industrial companies, including the Jordan Steel Industries Company and the Vegetable Processing and Preservative Company. In addition a plot of 1,500 dunums was acquired for market gardening through greenhouse cultivation of vegetables, and it was planned to use part of the plot for a dairy farm, and another part for lamb fattening.

All these ambitious projects were supervised by the Islamic Investment House's small staff of fifteen in 1982, and thirty-five by 1983–4. A high proportion of the House's deposits were invested, only 22.7 per cent of assets being liquid cash or bank deposits in 1982. The following year this proportion declined to 11 per cent, although in 1984 there was a slight increase to 13.7 per cent. This left only a small margin to meet unexpected withdrawals by depositors. These were less than half the proportion of cash reserves held by the much more prudent management of the Jordan Islamic Bank. Clearly with hindsight it appears the Islamic Investment House was not adequately covered to meet contingencies.[13]

The financial crisis

The worsening recession in the Jordanian economy and the neighbouring Arab states had diastrous consequences for the Islamic Investment House. Problems started to appear in 1983, but the House was committed to the projects it was backing, and did not want to let its clients down. The real estate ventures were particularly unfortunate, as there were problems letting the villas in Zayy and Al-Ghour, as the market became depressed, and there were few newcomers seeking this type of rather expensive rented accommodation. Many of those who had been given advances for house purchase were unable to repay the instalments to the House, as

Table 7.4 Returns to deposits with the Islamic Investment House and Jordan Islamic Bank

	Islamic Investment House		Jordan Islamic Bank	
	1983	1984	1983	1984
Investment deposits	5.4	5.5	2.7	2.8
Notice deposits	6.3	6.5	3.8	4.0
Fixed deposits	8.1	8.3	4.9	5.1

Sources: Islamic Investment House 1983, 1984; Jordan Islamic Bank 1983, 1984

their incomes had fallen with the recession, and a large proportion were dependent on income from the Gulf.

The fall in remittances with the oil recession and the dismissal of Jordanian workers in Saudi Arabia and the Gulf, affected the business of the Tukhaim International Exchange Company, whose profits were sharply reduced. Furthermore the recession even affected the profitability of the ship 'Farah' which had fewer passengers and vehicles to carry. In spite of these setbacks, the Islamic Investment House tried to maintain a high return to depositors, as the management realized that funds might be withdrawn if the rates did not stay competitive with those offered by the Jordan Islamic Bank. Profits paid out were as shown in Table 7.4 for 1983 and 1984. These were in fact higher than those for the Jordan Islamic Bank, being over 60 per cent greater for the one-year fixed-term deposits in which most account holders invested. Those investing with the Islamic Investment House may have expected a higher return however, as placing money with a small institution always implies a greater risk.

With low profits on its investments, and the need to pay out high returns to its account holdings, the Islamic Investment House got into serious difficulties in 1984. A rumour spread that it could no longer meet withdrawals by depositors, although this was unfounded. Nevertheless, the value of its shares started to decline rapidly, and the Central Bank of Jordan feared that the situation might become critical if it did not step in.[14] Share dealings in the Islamic Investment House were suspended, and the House was prohibited from taking further deposits. The value of existing deposits was guaranteed by the Central Bank, but no dividend was paid out in 1985. The institution has, in practice, become a closed fund, although depositors will be able to get their funds back in instalments if they wish. Most are holding on however, as the Islamic Investment House hopes to pay dividends again in the future when the economic situation improves.

Investors cannot complain too much, as the Islamic Investment House has tried to honour its commitments, and they have not lost their deposits. Rather, all they have forgone are the dividend receipts. Their deposits were placed on a profit-sharing basis, however, and with no profits there can be no gain. This must be a lesson for the investors, but the principle of sharing in hardship as well as in good fortune is, after all, an important tenet of Islam.

Despite the setbacks which the Islamic Investment House has experienced, the Jordanian experience of Islamic banking has been on the whole one of success, with the Jordan Islamic Bank emerging as a major domestic financial institution. It now ranks sixth in terms of the value of assets as far as Jordanian banks are concerned, and it is the second fastest growing Jordanian bank after the Bank of Jordan and the Gulf. It accounts for over 5 per cent of the total assets of the Jordanian banking system.[15]

The Jordan Islamic Bank has also been successful in encouraging many believers to use its services as a *riba*-free bank rather than hoarding. It ranks fifth in Jordan in terms of deposits, and its deposits are growing at a more rapid rate than any other major Jordanian bank. Its financial caution has proved justified given the experience of the Islamic Investment House. The Jordan Islamic Bank ranks seventh in its holding of liquid assets as a proportion of deposits out of eighteen major Jordanian financial institutions, a position which the management intends to maintain. Yet it was the eleventh most profitable institution in gross (pre-tax) terms, and ninth in terms of net profit in relation to paid-up dividend.

This ratio was a reasonable 16.6 per cent. All this augurs well for the future of Islamic banking in Jordan, which after seven years is already well-established and prospering. Jordan is likely to maintain a plural banking system, with *riba* and *halal* institutions existing side by side, but the experience of the Jordan Islamic bank shows that this type of bank can function effectively, serve its clients well, and compete in the market with the other institutions while strictly adhering to Islamic principles.

Glossary

hala	permitted
haram	forbidden
ijara	leasing contract
mudarabah	equity sharing between bank and client
muqardah	Islamic bonds on which no interest is earned but the value of which varies with the anticipated (variable) profit share

Qird Hasan	interest-free loan to those in need
riba	interest or usury (see note 3)
Sharia	religious law
Umma	community of believers

Notes

1 The Israeli military authorities prohibited Jordanian banks from operating in the West Bank after 1976, but recently the Cairo Amman Bank was granted permission to re-open its Ramallah branch.
2 Information from the bank's annual reports up to 1985.
3 There is no consensus on the definition of *riba*, which means an addition to a principle sum of capital. Most Islamic scholars equate *riba* with interest, rather than just usury. For a discussion see Wilson 1983.
4 Up to 1982 there was a statutory minimum for returns on savings and time deposits, but this was subsequently changed to a statutory maximum.
5 The value of deposits is, however, guaranteed, so there can be no loss of principal.
6 JD 1 = $0.34 = £0.50 = DM 0.17 (October 1986).
7 Information supplied by the bank's management.
8 The question of opening branches in the West Bank or Gaza has not been considered, but the position will be reviewed if several Jordanian banks establish branches. There are plans for an independent Islamic bank in Gaza, controlled by local residents.
9 There is, of course, no spread of risk.
10 Credit cards, mainly the Visa type, are issued by a number of Jordanian commercial banks, but they are mainly used during overseas travel. The Jordan Islamic Bank cannot issue such cards, as interest is charged on debt outstanding. A charge card, which is paid in full monthly on the American Express principle, remains a possibility, but the question of penalty clauses for non-repayment has not yet been resolved. These could be regarded as a form of *riba*.
11 Official figures cited by the Central Bank of Jordan. This refers to the general index. Prices of clothing and imported consumer durables rose faster than the general index.
12 The word being Italian in origin, and referring to a table (banco) on which the merchants of Lombardy carried out financial transactions, usually on an interest basis.
13 Details in the Institution's annual reports up to 1984, there being none for 1985.
14 The House could not increase its share capital to JD 5 million as the Central Bank then stipulated for all banks, although as the House did not regard itself as a bank, this was less of a problem. Nevertheless, the regulation had implications for the House as a deposit taker.
15 According to the Jordanian Banker's Magazine's rankings for 1985.

163

References

Bashir, M. (1984), 'Successful development of Islamic banks', *Journal of Research in Islamic Economics*, Vol. I, No. 2, pp. 63–72.

Central Bank of Jordan (1986), *Monthly Statistical Bulletin*, June, Amman.

Islamic Investment House (1983), *Second Annual Report*, Amman.

—— (1984), *Third Annual Report*, Amman.

Jordan Islamic Bank (1979–85), *Annual Reports*, Amman.

—— (1983), *Fifth Annual Report*, Amman.

—— (1984), *Sixth Annual Report*, Amman.

—— (1985), *Seventh Annual Report*, Amman.

—— (1986), *Balance Sheet*, June, Amman.

Wilson, R. (1986), 'The role of commercial banking in the Jordanian economy', in A. Bardan and B. Khader (eds), *The Economic Development of Jordan*, Croom Helm, London.

Part four

Politics in Jordan

Chapter eight

Jordan in the 1980s: legitimacy, entity and identity

Yezid Sayigh

To a student of Middle Eastern politics, Jordan presents an intriguing case: how has a country of such recent formation, and with such scarce natural and demographic resources, survived the buffeting of several wars and the presence of strong, often hostile neighbours? There are many elements to the answer, but the central one concerns the triad of legitimacy, entity and identity, to which this chapter addresses itself.

The chapter's first contention is that legitimacy, both of the Hashemite monarchy and of the Jordanian nation-state, is no longer in question or under challenge. Secondly, after a long period of flux, the concept of a specifically Jordanian entity, combining the Transjordanian and Palestinian communities under Hashemite rule, has been progressively consolidated over the last two decades. The Arab–Israeli war of June 1967 and the Jordanian civil war of 1970–1 were major turning points in Jordan's recent history, deciding the internal balance of power and accelerating the development of the Jordanian state. Further aiding the development of the state and economy in Jordan in the 1970s and early 1980s was its internal stability, the changes in inter-Arab politics, the truce with Israel, and the availability of Arab oil wealth. All these factors have contributed to the consolidation of the Jordanian entity, by winning it broad acceptance and allegiance within the various sectors of the population. By the same token, a concept of Jordanian identity is gradually evolving, but its future success remains in doubt. This is due to the dynamics of the Jordanian–Palestinian relationship, whereby absorbing the Palestinians has been both a requisite of Jordan's modern development and a source of great internal tension.

The chapter's third contention, therefore, is that the Palestinian dimension retains the ability to impede the development of a separate Jordanian identity based on a Palestinian–Transjordanian mixture, although the continued survival and viability of the Jordanian nation-state is itself no longer in doubt.

167

The quest for legitimacy

After establishing the Emirate of Transjordan in 1921, the Hashemite throne had to defend the legitimacy of its rule to its population and to other Arab rulers. Indeed, the Hashemites had to struggle to confirm the legitimacy of the existence of Jordan as such. Parallel to these efforts, the Hashemites sought to define the new Jordanian entity they had constructed, and to determine its foundations, *raison d'être* and boundaries. In turn, asserting legitimacy and entity depended to a large degree on the development of a specifically Jordanian identity, an identity based in most countries on shared ideology, history and social culture.

The progress of these three elements – legitimacy, entity and identity – has not occurred at an equal pace. Indeed, their interrelationship notwithstanding, each has tended to develop within a different phase in Jordanian modern history. Thus, legitimacy was the key concern under the Emirate (1921–45) and during the first post-independence phase in 1946–67. A second, transitional phase in 1967–70 witnessed intense flux, as the question of power was resolved and the foundations for Jordanian entity and identity were laid. Defining the parameters of the modern nation-state of Jordan has been the central concern since the early 1970s therefore, in contrast to the issue of legitimacy, which has no longer been at stake since 1967.

Perceptions of the reasons for Jordan's existence may vary, from the reminder that there is an unbroken history of human settlement in that area to less charitable views, but the question phrased by one Western scholar is still pertinent: 'How can a political system created only recently [1922], and almost fortuitously by British diplomats as a by-product of more important strategic decisions find legitimacy as an indigenous, traditional polity?' (Hudson 1977, p. 210). Jordan's founder, Emir Abdullah, spent the formative years of the Emirate consolidating his internal legitimacy. This included warding off Wahhabi attacks and suppressing revolts by indigenous clans, such as the Huweitat and 'Udwan, during the 1920s. Other minor incidents occurred as late as 1937, when local inhabitants joined Palestinian irregulars seeking refuge from the British Mandate in the 'Ajlun mountains (Mahafthah 1973, pp. 147–8). That legitimacy was an issue at stake is also indicated by Abdullah's choice of the small trading town of Amman as capital, rather than the established centres of Salt and Irbid, and by his early reliance on non-Jordanians[1] to occupy senior political, military and administrative posts. British officers commanded the Arab Legion and Palestinians acted as prime ministers and advisors (the family names Mufti, Hashin, Touqan and Rifa'i are among the most prominent). Moreover, most of the twenty non-Jordanian Arab officers who ever held senior rank in the Public Security forces (out of fifty in 1927–77) did so in this phase.

By 1946, when formal independence was declared by the Hashemite Kingdom of Jordan, the monarchy had successfully coopted the Transjordanian community within the new state structure. The challenge to legitimacy now came instead from the Palestinians and other Arab governments, especially after Abdullah's Act of Union between the East and West Banks of Jordan in 1950. Significantly, whereas the British presence in the interwar period had largely isolated Transjordan from the immediate effects of external conflicts, allowing Abdullah to concentrate on achieving internal stability, the dissolution of such constraints in the Arab independence period put Hashemite legitimacy to a renewed test. Thus, in addition to the universal problems confronting Arab governments over their stability and legitimacy were the added difficulties Jordan faced in legitimizing its creation as a country, its bonds with the West, its lack of a unifying past and its special relationship with the Palestine question (Hudson 1977, pp. 209–19). A major problem was to justify the emergence of yet another Arab country in a fragmented Arab world, particularly as Abdullah had raised the banner of Arab unity and continued to believe in a Greater Syria until his death. Ironically, it was this apparent threat to the entity and legitimacy of Jordan's Arab neighbours that went furthest in alienating them, while its close ties with Great Britain and then the United States exposed the Kingdom to the charge that it was no more than an artifice, a tool of the West (Cremeans 1963, p. 104).

However, the monarchy's success in overcoming the twin challenges of internal opposition and external subversion during the 1950s, and then the twin pressures of autonomous Palestinian nationalism (in the form of the nascent clandestine guerrilla groups and the PLO) and the inter-Arab 'cold war' in the first half of the 1960s, went far in imposing general acceptance of the legitimacy of both the Hashemite throne and the Jordanian state. Final re-inforcement came in June 1967. The Six-Day War weakened the ability of Arab governments to intervene in the affairs of sister states, especially to the extent of undermining their physical survival (Vatikiotis 1971, p. 169). This resulted partly from their loss of political credibility and partly from their own internal moral and physical debilitation. Consensus politics grew stronger in inter-

Arab relations, based on mutual tolerance. For Jordan this revolved around newfound warm ties with Nasser's Egypt; other former critics were also less inclined to denounce Hashemite rule as they were striving to assert their own authority and legitimacy at home, especially if they were themselves minority governments.

The decline of Arab interventionism was also influenced by the public statements of Israeli leaders declaring that they would consider as *casus belli* any attempt by an Arab state more powerful than Jordan or Lebanon to take control of either of these and change the balance of power on Israel's eastern or northern border. The lessons of 1967 were forcefully demonstrated in 1970, when both American and Israeli military action was threatened to halt Syrian intervention in the Jordanian civil war, and when the Iraqi and Syrian governments consequently refused to authorize involvement by forces under their control on behalf of the Palestinian movement. Significantly, though both Iraq and Syria were vociferous in their denunciation of the Jordanian action, they directed their accusations at 'certain factions' within the government and army, but not at the King himself or at the institution of the monarchy. As this shift in Arab attitudes coincided with the final resolution of the internal struggle over power and the allegiance of Jordan's Palestinians, the question of legitimacy ceased to be an active threat to the throne's stability and security. The rest of this chapter therefore turns to the concepts of entity and identity, which have been the focus of much leadership effort since 1970, and which retain appreciable potential to disrupt the development of modern Jordan.

Entity and identity

Given the complexity of Jordan's demographic composition and the extent of its vulnerability to external events, social and political ideology has always been an important driving force in its history. This explains why the issues of Arab nationalism, Palestine and the Arab–Israeli conflict have been so emotive, and why the throne's official history, public stands and ideology have also been so crucial to maintaining internal stability (Vatikiotis 1984, p. 159). Thus, the core concepts of 'entity' and 'legitimacy' form basic criteria in understanding Jordanian politics.

The Jordanian political entity was originally set up from the top downwards, with an army and a mini-bureaucracy in being even before a coherent body politic or unified society as such existed. Given the miniscule and heterogeneous population, and the general absence of intrinsic features that could distinguish and give form to the new emirate, it was largely the movement of neighbouring political systems to define themselves and delineate their borders that defined the Jordanian entity. Specifically, what designated the heterogeneous inhabitants of Transjordan as one sociopolitical unit was the dismemberment of the Ottoman Empire and the demarcation of separate polities in Syria, Iraq, Palestine and Saudi Arabia. This is not to belittle the existence of established communities – with their own historic, social, economic and political ties – in the territory that became Jordan, but to remember that the Hashemites' original political 'project' was to found a united Arab kingdom based in Damascus, and that Abdullah only settled in Ma'an after being turned back from Syria by the French army.

Possibly the most important instance of the demarcation process was the effect on Jordan of the creation of Israel. One scholar has gone as far as concluding that the presence of Jordan as a state is contingent on the existence of Israel (Vatikiotis 1966, p. 139), though at least it can be said that 'Israel helped define the Jordanian entity'. (The implication here is solely that the existence of Israel as an exclusive Jewish state helped distinguish Jordan from Palestine, a distinction that remains a matter of contention, as Ariel Sharon's plan for 'Palestinianizing' Jordan shows.)

In summary, the historical elements of the formation of Jordan have been negative, not positive, a fact which goes far in explaining the sensitivity of Jordanians to any questioning of their identity, and their leadership's continuing attempt to inculcate a sense of their own history into the Jordanian popular mind. The latter effort is expressed in repeated statements by Jordanian leaders, officials and academics recounting specific instances of Jordanian history stretching back centuries in time (Tal 1978). For instance, in his address to the Rabat Arab Summit Conference in 1974 (which recognized the PLO as sole legitimate Palestinian representative), King Hussein devoted a large part of his address to an account of Jordan's modern history. A more recent example is a talk by Crown Prince Hassan at the University of Jordan in March 1984, in which he emphasized the importance of Jordanian history, referring to battles in Islamic and pre-Islamic periods. Furthermore, although less marked of late, members of the royal family have often stressed their tribal, Islamic and Arab nationalist credentials to their constituency in times of trouble. These, and other themes, have all played a part not only in reinforcing the throne's legitimacy, but also in inculcating a sense of 'belonging' to the Jordanian entity among the citizenry. This is a citizenry which in the not too distant past saw itself as southern Syrian or northern Hejazi rather than Jordanian (Cremeans 1963, p. 1,032), and in some views still

171

threatened the Kingdom with dismemberment (dividing between Saudi Arabia and Syria) as late as 1976 (Vatikiotis 1984, p. 94).

The last 'negative' element in defining the modern Jordanian entity was its loss of the West Bank to Israel during the war of June 1967. This removed an area that had long troubled the throne because it contained a politically active, all-Palestinian population that stretched central control. Furthermore, Jordan's return to the borders it had occupied up to 1948 (that is the East Bank) not only mollified the Arab states that had originally opposed the union of the two Banks, but even involved them in support of Jordan's claim to the West Bank under the guise of 'restoring the Arab territories occupied by Israel in 1967'. Most importantly, the Jordanian government was accepted as the legal authority in the East Bank and as a viable partner in Arab circles, winning it financial, military and diplomatic/political support. This was reflected, for example, in the allocation of a substantial annual grant to Jordan by the Khartoum Arab Summit, the stationing of Iraqi and Saudi Arabian troops in the Kingdom, and mediation/conciliation activity between the government and Palestinian guerrillas by Egyptian, Iraqi, Syrian and Algerian emissaries.

The transition was not an easy one, however, and Jordan entered a turbulent phase after the 1967 war, as it absorbed the effects of the West Bank's loss, the influx of 300,000 Palestinian refugees and the rise of the Palestine Resistance Movement (PRM). The loyalty and allegiance of various sectors of the population was put to the test, especially as the PRM won widespread support within public and official circles both inside and outside Jordan. Indeed, the guerrillas initially had the support of army personnel, including Transjordanians and bedouins, and managed to recruit some clans into its armed militias. Certain cabinet ministers were considered guerilla sympathizers, and appointments were often made deliberately to include such persons in the government. In the September 1970 confrontation, the PRM was even able to establish 'liberated provinces' administered by Transjordanians, while attracting appreciable numbers of deserters from the army. In his letter of appointment of Wasfi Tal as Prime Minister, a month after the showdown, King Hussein noted the vacillation and mixed allegiance of 'many people' in central organs and the general public, 'as if the thread that tied them to this country were finer than a strand in a cobweb'.

In contrast to the negative input of the 1967 war, the 1970-1 civil war provided a positive input to entity formation in Jordan, in so far as it was the result of an assertive initiative by the Jordanian leadership rather than an external event. On one hand, the events leading to, and including, the civil war witnessed consolidation of

Transjordanian support for the throne, particularly within the army, as well as alienation of sections of the Palestinian community from the guerillas. Moreover, the confrontation served to 'sift' allegiances, removing or isolating anyone whose political loyalty was not to the throne and government. In overview, in the contest of wills and strength, Jordan proved the stronger (at least within the East Bank) politically and institutionally as much as militarily. On the other hand, resolving the question of power in Jordan allowed the state and economy to develop more fully and more rapidly. This was largely because the identity of those holding authority had been clearly defined, and so coherent policies could be formulated. State organs gained new-found unity of purpose as well as the opportunity to implement policy, thanks to the disengagement from political conflict and the imposition of internal security. Internal stability also encouraged a substantial revival of Western financial and economic assistance.

Entity construction in the 1970s and 1980s

Since the end of the civil war, the Jordanian entity has gained greatly in form and definition. In contrast to the impetus imparted by that war, however, which stemmed from resolving the identity of power in Jordan, the progress of entity formation in the past fifteen years has consisted of other, more constructive elements. Three main strands are apparent: gains in Jordan's external political situation; socioeconomic development; and changes in citizen–state relations.

In the first case, Jordanian–Western ties have remained strong since 1970, in contrast to the nadir of the 1967–70 period. Jordanian–Arab ties have also generally been good since 1973, following a two-year 'freeze'. Thus, Jordan has enjoyed good political relations with the Arabs and West simultaneously, an unthinkable achievement before 1967. It has been active in Arab regional bodies, and has played an active mediatory role in several conflicts, as well as offering security and military assistance to several Gulf states, North Yemen and Libya. This situation is partly a result of changes in the regional environment and balance of forces and in the mode of inter-Arab politics, but it is also a result of Jordan's own success in asserting and protecting itself. Most importantly, the nature of Jordanian interaction with its external environment both reflects and reinforces the degree to which its actual and conceptual boundaries have been consolidated.

Second, the successive social and economic development plans since 1972 have had a major impact on the progress of the

Jordanian entity. The extension of services and infrastructure and the expansion of agricultural, industrial and mineral production have all increased the incentives for political stability while bringing the economy nearer to maturity. Indeed, the direct connection between socioeconomic development and internal security is deliberate, and openly confirmed by official sources. Significantly, Jordan's rapid economic growth took place following the 1974 oil boom, which not only provided sources of finance and a conducive regional political climate but also encouraged a surge in labour migration. The pattern is by no means new for Jordan, but since the early 1970s tens of thousands more Jordanian citizens have migrated to the Arab oil states. This has strengthened Arab ties with the donor state, Jordan, and created vested interests in its survival and viability, while reducing economic strains and political tensions within the Kingdom itself. As the springboard for such demographic and economic movements and as the recipient of material rewards (and as a final destination of earnings and remittances), Jordan has been confirmed as a cogent entity. The central role of the state in obtaining and distributing financial resources has further reinforced the identification in the popular and official mind of the Jordanian entity with state and citizen.

Third, the effects of the state's expanded role and of socioeconomic development have been to alter citizen–citizen and citizen–state relations. Jordan has witnessed a decline of tribes, clans and families as the vehicle for social and political action, as the twin processes of modernization and urbanization[2] have progressed, under various stimuli (McLaurin and Jureidini 1984). This is particularly so for the Transjordanian community, which has a higher rate of employment in the public sector (both civilian and military). However, the Palestinian community has been influenced as well, especially as much of its income-generating ability – through labour migration, professional services and commerce – comes by virtue of Jordan's good standing with other Arab countries. Moreover, the government regulates much of the activity of the private sector through price and importation controls, increasing the interdependence between citizen and state. Finally, if anything, Jordan is important to many of its citizens because it provides them with a passport; as is the case with hundreds of thousands of Jordanian passport-holders in the West Bank and Arab Gulf who are not and for many years have not been East Bank residents. Thus, the functional relationship that has grown over the last decade and a half between the state and population has also reinforced the fact of a specifically Jordanian entity.

The Palestinian dimension

Parallel to the impact of social, economic and political developments, another theme has influenced the formation of the Jordanian entity. This has been the interaction between the Jordanian leadership and the Palestine phenomenon. Historically, a major problem for the Hashemite throne since its very inception has been to assert Jordan's distinctiveness from Palestine and delineate its separate boundaries. Among the obstacles to such an effort were historical social and economic ties across the Jordan River and administrative bonds. More serious was Britain's initial inclusion of Transjordan in the Palestine Mandate, and the insistence of Jordanian and Palestinian leaders, at various times since, that both peoples form an indivisible whole. The absorption of a large number of Palestinians from the West Bank within the Kingdom after 1948 further obscured the issue. The principle of unity had to be emphasized, although regionalist (*qutriyyah*) politics were in fact in operation. This is not to revive the hostile debate over the intentions and motivations of Jordanian policy towards the Palestinians, but to stress the fact that the dynamics of Jordanian–Palestinian unity have always been complicated, involving as much conflict as convergence – a sort of 'unity of opposites'.

The central observation to make of the Jordanian–Palestinian relationship is that the Jordanian leadership, whatever its identity and politics, has had to maintain a major involvement in the Palestine conflict. This is due to the imperatives of history and geography, but as much also to the absorption of a large number of Palestinians within the East Bank population (at least 50 per cent by Transjordanian admission). The 1950 Act of Union (between the East and West Banks) effectively internalized an external conflict – creating a symbiotic relationship between internal and external in Jordan. The Jordanian government could only hope to control its Palestinian citizens in the long term if it could manage those issues that concerned and mobilized them: Palestinian rights, the West Bank and relations with the PLO. Failure in this regard would lead to a growing divergence of interests and aims between the Palestinian base and the Jordanian establishment a divergence that the existence of an autonomous Palestinian body (such as the PRM or PLO) would exacerbate. However, as both the Palestinians and the Palestine problem extend beyond Jordan and involve many other actors, the Hashemite throne has in effect been seeking to control a phenomenon that resides only partially under its direct sovereignty.

Adding to its difficulties, the Jordanian leadership has had to contend with two more problems. One is the possible emergence of an autonomous society and political system in the West Bank, while the other is the action and rival appeal of independent Palestinian nationalism, embodied since 1964 in the PRM and PLO. Whatever the motivations and circumstances, Jordanian policy has been consistently opposed to the emergence of a separate Palestinian entity, especially (though not exclusively) one based on the West Bank. This was at the heart of Jordanian opposition to Ahmad Hilmi Pasha's All Palestine Government and Hajj Amin Husseini's Higher Arab Committee, to Iraqi proposals during 1959–63 for an independent Palestinian republic, and to the formation of the PLO. This hostility arises from political and security considerations, but also from the difficulty of defining and distinguishing each entity and of setting the balance of power between them. In this context specifically, the loss of the West Bank in 1967 was more bearable because it removed a potential base for a Palestinian entity while strengthening the physical, political and moral foundations of the Jordanian entity in the East Bank.

In contrast to this negative input, the Palestinian dimension has also had a positive impact on the development of the Jordanian entity. Palestinians have swelled the population and expanded the economy, reinforcing the attributes that any country needs for its viability and credibility. At least in terms of the broader vision of the Hashemite family, if not necessarily in the opinion of part of the Transjordanian community, the inclusion of Palestinian manpower has been instrumental in the success of the Jordanian 'project' and of the internal balance contrived within it. The constant problem has been, however, to gain the advantages of absorbing a large number of Palestinians without becoming destabilized by the Palestine conflict. Jordanian policy since 1948 may thus be described as a mixture of two postures: an offensive one designed to absorb assets, whether demographic or territorial, and a defensive one designed to ward off the pressures of autonomous Palestinian nationalism and entity formation. Seen this way, much of Jordan's diplomatic and political activity relating to the West Bank (primarily) and the PLO (secondarily) since 1967 has been a form of 'forward defence', in which the Jordanian leadership sought, until 1988, not only to maintain its stake and legitimize its claim to the West Bank and Palestinian representation, but also to retain the strategic initiative and thus control the direction of the conflict, diverting and preempting potential threats. Moreover, despite the Rabat decision of 1974 in effect making the PLO responsible for the West Bank's fate (and absolving Jordan of responsibility in Arab eyes), Jordan has kept its options open at the international level, so as to remain a viable interlocutor in any settlement of the Arab–Israeli conflict.

Internally, the question has been how to deal with the Palestinian inhabitants of Jordan. These divide roughly into three main waves of migrants, with differing material interests and political perceptions and varying degrees of attachment to Jordan. However, assuming equal political loyalty, what is significant in this context is that granting Palestinian citizens a full stake in the Jordanian system alters its nature and affects the position of the Transjordanian community within it too. By the same token, any lesser status for the Palestinians imbues Jordan with a more overtly Transjordanian character and leads to internal conflict. To this extent, the success of the venture to form a lasting, specifically Jordanian entity, and identity depends on creating a synthesis, although failure to do so does not mean the end of the modern nation-state of Jordan. One might posit that the success of the synthesis would embody the Hashemite vision, while its failure would still leave intact the Transjordanian entity which has provided the backbone of modern Jordan (although the Transjordanians are not its sole constituent or beneficiary).

Naturally, the process of synthesis, or of setting the internal balance, is not easy, nor is it a simple mechanical task. For example, the 1970–1 civil war assisted the process of synthesis by forcing a realization (not universally a reluctant one) on the Palestinians that ultimate power was not theirs as a community. Conversely, the war also demonstrated to the throne Jordan's continued vulnerability and the extent to which the Palestine issue could threaten the Jordanian state from within. This led to a dual policy. First, there was the insistence that the question of identity, as well as that of allegiance to the entity, be resolved, reflected in a policy of 'Jordanization'. A second approach underlay the first and provided a fallback to it in case it failed. This was a policy of containment, reflected in a reduction in the relative numbers and authority of Palestinians in certain sectors and in an attempt to nullify or divert political activists. A question therefore arises: has the development of the modern state and entity of Jordan been underlain by a long-term policy of limiting Palestinian influence, albeit without halting the absorption of the Palestinians within society?

Here perceptions play a major part. Many Palestinians see deliberate patterns in official behaviour or at least confirm the existence of effective (though unintentional or unmalicious) divisions that end in Palestinian preponderance in the private economic sector and Transjordanian domination of the Army, security and state sectors. Officials deny the existence of any discrimination or purposeful, systematic policies that might strengthen or weaken specific communities, though they confirm the need to control potentially explosive political issues. Many Transjordanians assert, conversely, that Palestinians control the economy and threaten security and that there is a need to defend against encroachment, although some distinguish between the intentions of Jordanian and non-Jordanian Palestinians. Interestingly, Transjordanians who are favourably disposed and unfavourably disposed toward the Kingdom's Palestinians are both opposed to formal arrangements that tend to distinguish between East Bank residents, such as the 1986 electoral law, although the reasons for opposition may differ.

Assessments and perceptions of the intentions of each community and of its position in the system may differ, but for all practical purposes Jordan's Palestinian community has largely adhered to the concepts of Jordanian entity and identity. However, this applies to a particular form of Jordanian entity and identity. When Jordanian public opinion was mobilized to face the Syrian military buildup on the common border in Autumn 1980, Palestinian citizens rallied in defence of Jordan. To this extent, there is a clear concept of shared entity, but it is the Palestine issue specifically that has the potential to provoke disagreement about how to define common identity. Cases in point are the various changes instituted in West Bank parliamentary representation since 1974, and the recent request that Jordanian citizens indicate their place of origin on official forms. Coming as they have in the wake of broader events, such as the breakdown of the Jordan–PLO Amman Accord and the inauguration of the Jordanian development plan for the Occupied Territories, such measures hold significant political implications, whatever their administrative justifications. Thus, the Jordanian entity and identity into which the Palestinians are assimilating are viable in so far as they permit modification and accommodation, a neccessity that might not meet with the approval of all Transjordanians, although it is essential to Hashemite policy since 1948.

In historic overview, the Hashemites' insistence on absorbing and welding both communities into one society has been responsible for the present degree of stability in Jordan. Ultimately, if the key to the Hashemite throne's early success in establishing its authority was its command of the state and army, then its long-term success lay in the balance it contrived, determining the place of each socioeconomic group or ethnic community within the country's social, economic and political life. This balance functioned well in much of the 1950–67 period and in the 1970s, but under certain external pressures, which involved Jordan's Palestinian community, the system reverted to its basically Transjordanian character. Seen differently, although the balance struck allowed the Jordanian leadership both to absorb the Palestinians and to consolidate the security and legitimacy of throne and national entity, it also institutionalized and perpetuated the elements of conflict and defined the Jordanian balance as constituted and finally influenced by them.

Jordanian unity and identity: conclusions and prospects

In overview, the specifically Jordanian entity has been consolidated since 1967, thanks to four main developments. First, although most (but not all) sections of the Jordanian leadership insist on restoring the West Bank, its loss has actively helped develop the distinct character of the East Bank. The uneasy marriage of both banks in 1948–87 embodied a basic dichotomy, which resulted in constant divergence between the Hashemite throne and the Palestinian constituency over external and internal policies. Whatever damage the loss of the area to Israel may have caused to Jordan (from which the economy has experienced a remarkable recovery), therefore, this dichotomy at least was partly resolved. Second, the resolution of the effective competition for power in 1970 not only strengthened the government's physical control over the Palestinian community but changed the latter's attitude towards its Jordanian identity. Since the 1970s, many Palestinians have come to view themselves as Jordanian, a process aided by the material rewards of participation in the system and by constant repression of political activists (especially in affiliation to the PLO). Third has been the qualitative and quantitative growth in the role of the state in all spheres. The harmonization of policy and the growing convergence of interests between citizens and state have in particular reinforced Jordan's image. Finally, 'lubricating' and accelerating the process of acceptance and consolidation has been economic prosperity, which offered citizens a stake in Jordan's welfare and allowed the state to increase its relevance to the population.

None the less, the Jordanian entity is still in transition, and so remains under threat. The sources of danger are already implied in the preceding paragraph. At the immediate level, the disproportionate role of the state and of what may prove to have been only temporary economic growth, suggests the possibility of a regression should any setbacks befall the political and economic structures of Jordan. Jordanian dependence on external financial support remains high, despite several development plans, whether to fund government budgets and economic projects or to reduce unemployment and raise liquidity and per capita income through labour migration. The downward trend of Arab aid and workers' remittances since 1981, and the return of growing numbers of migrants themselves since 1983, both indicate potential problems of major import. Compounding the situation is the fact that government policies have neutralized or even dissolved the foundations for mass political activity, while the state has acquired a disproportionately large role in social and political life – Jordan is 'top-heavy'. This imbalance is problematic partly because it runs counter to the popular demands for a share in the Jordanian political process generated by socioeconomic development, and partly because broad political participation by the population is necessary to consolidate the Jordanian entity. In Jordan's case especially, the historical circumstances of its formation require it to reinforce legitimacy, entity and identity by inviting participation, though this then risks altering the form and direction of the country – a catch-22 situation.

It may be suggested that internal economic and political problems are insufficient to place a national entity in jeopardy. However, in the Jordanian case such pressures are particularly potent because they tend to coincide with the Jordanian–Palestinian divide. For instance, a large part, probably the greater by far, of the expatriate Jordanian community in the Gulf comes from the West Bank or the Palestinian community of the East Bank. Migration in the past therefore helped ease Jordinian–Palestinian tensions, and, by the same token, reverse migration will increase the number of unemployed in both Banks, create competition over resources with the Transjordanians, and feed political discontent. There is a certain amount of oversimplification here, and the Jordanian government is bound to seek solutions regardless of ethnic origin, but the core implication is that political activism and Palestinian nationalism are likely to grow, with negative effects on Jordanian entity formation.

Of equal importance is the fact that whatever Jordan's internal situation, the competition over the West Bank and the conflict over Palestine continue. As mentioned earlier, regardless of the actual motivations and circumstances of Jordan's absorption of the West Bank in 1948–50, it is evident that the Kingdom benefited strategically in terms of the inter-Arab balance of forces, as well as demographically and even economically in the long run. More importantly, no third state came into being between Jordan and Israel. The emergence of a Palestinian entity remains a remote possibility, given Israel's grip on the territory, but it is also the focus of the PLO's efforts, as well as being a central demand of large parts of the Arab and world communities. Thus the issue cannot be ignored by the Jordanian leadership. Furthermore, the basis for Jordanian political control over the West Bank has been seriously eroded, due to the birth and politicization of entire generations of Palestinians under Israeli rule, raising the prospect of spillover into the East Bank. The vitality of the West Bank issue, especially in light of the PLO's dogged survival and popularity, will thus continue to influence Jordan's internal and external policy formulation.

In final conclusion, what has kept entity and identity in Jordan from settling permanently has been the Palestinian dimension. The Jordanian leadership has long since obtained Arab recognition of its legitimacy, but continues to search for a formula that will retain the Palestinians within the Kingdom without threatening the security and stability of the entire Jordanian structure. By that token the foundations of the present nature and future form of the Jordanian entity and identity were laid during the transitional period of 1967–70. As a result of its momentous events, a shift occurred in Palestinian attitudes towards the Jordanian state, though not necessarily in Palestinian perceptions of the Jordanian system. Rather than a crude balance of power imposing its priorities, as might be said of the 1950–67 period, the Jordanian entity has come to offer a stake to the Palestinians since 1970, assisted by strong economic incentives. None the less, underlying the new *modus vivendi* has also been the conclusion, by the Jordanian leadership, that its own security and the stability of the Jordanian entity should not be as vulnerable to Palestinian activism as was the case in the mid-1950s or in 1967–70. This assessment has been reflected in various policies which, though not positively discriminatory, have sought to ensure the dependability of state organs and personnel and to broaden the skilled manpower base (to avoid excessive dependence on one community). That the Palestinian dimension is entangled with other considerations, imbuing them with added potency, is indicated by developments in 1986 such as the Yarmouk University incident (see Chapter 9, p. 192), the conflict with the PLO, and renewed distinction between East and West Bankers. A further indication is the disagreement within Transjordanian circles over Jordan's position in the Arab–Israeli conflict and *vis-à-vis* the Palestine issue, one result of which has been to strengthen the feeling that there may be a divergence of long-term vision between the Hashemite throne and indigenous community of Jordan.

Having highlighted the background to Jordanian vulnerability on the issues of entity and identity, it is this chapter's conclusion that the modern nation-state of Jordan has passed the point at which its form and future are in serious doubt. Not that entity and identity have been finally defined and universally accepted by all sectors of the Jordanian population, nor that there are no potential threats to the current stability, but that the last two decades have witnessed a basic shift from a totally defensive posture to a more confident, assertive stance by the Jordanian leadership. The core element is perception: how members of the Jordanian family view themselves and their sub-national groupings, and how they are viewed by non-Jordanians. In turn, perceptions are influenced by the position each community occupies relative to the political system and to the structure of power in Jordan and by the nature and mechanics of the relationship of each community to the throne. Thus, there are elements of conflict inherent to the system, especially in the broader context of Arab political rivalry and economic decline and of competition/conflict with Israel and the PLO over the West Bank and Palestinian representation. Combined with the continued ambivalence of Jordanian identity, it is likely that Jordan will experience more conflict, internal and external, before the basis for belonging to the Jordanian entity is fully defined for all its citizens.

Notes

1 In this chapter, the term 'Jordanian' refers loosely to anything or anyone pertaining to the country of Jordan as it stands in its boundaries since 1967. The terms 'Transjordanian' or 'East Banker' will refer specifically to the original inhabitants of the area that first became the Emirate of Transjordan.
2 These two terms are used in a neutral sense to depict changes in residence and living and employment patterns, without assigning positive or negative connotations.

References

Cremeans, C. D. (1963), *The Arabs and the World*, Praeger, New York.
Hudson, M. C. (1977), *Arab Politics: The Search for Legitimacy*, Yale University Press, New Haven.
Mahafthah, A. (1973), *Al-'Alaqat al-Urduniyyah-al-Britaniyyah, min Ta'sis al'Imarah hatta Ilgha'al-Mu'ahadah (Jordanian-British Relations, from the Establishment of the Emirate to the Abrogation of the Treaty, 1921-1957)*, Dar An-Nahar, Beirut.
McLaurin, R. D. and Jureidini, P. (1984), *Jordan: The Impact of Social Change on the Role of the Tribes*, Praeger, New York.

Tal, B. (1978), *Al-Urdun, Muhawalah lil-Fihm (Jordan: An Attempt to Understand)*, Dazr al-Liwa', Amman.

Vatikiotis, P. J. (1966), *Politics and the Military in Jordan*, Praeger, New York.

—— (1971), Conflict in the Middle East, Allen & Unwin, London.

—— (1984), *Arab and Regional Politics in the Middle East*, Croom Helm, London.

Chapter nine

Politics and the 1986 electoral law in Jordan
Philip J. Robins

Introduction

In the Arab world substantive political activity tends to be confined to the informal sphere of interaction. The formal domain, such as popular assemblies, party conferences and the media are often sterile affairs drained of political argument. They rarely give insights into the political system nor cast light on the balance of power relations. Owing to this prevailing political culture, it is difficult for researchers to determine exactly where power lies in Arab polities and the areas from which ruling regimes perceive threats to their position to exist. This is compounded by the fact that documentation relating to the informal decision-making process often does not exist.

The publication of a 1986 electoral law in Jordan is important in this context. It is a rare example of a formal document which throws light on the general power relations in the polity. It is also one of the few formal documents to be published in the Kingdom which gives a sure indication as to the direction of thinking of the ruling élite. Its importance is all the more real because of the comprehensiveness of the document which, by virtue of its function, deals with a number of political issues. The existence of an old electoral law facilitates ready comparison of the changes which have taken place in the polity over the intervening period.

Due to the nature of representation in Jordan in the past, any 1986 electoral law has primarily to address itself to the delicate position of the Palestinian community in the country. The law also has something to tell us about the position of religious and ethnic minorities and the tribes within the political system, as well as the rural–urban dichotomy. In order to extract full significance from the law it must also be considered in its context, both historical and contemporary. In the latter respect, the law has much to say about the attitude of the authorities towards ideological currents within the Kingdom.

A second reason for undertaking an analysis of the law at this stage is the impending question of a general election on the East Bank. Parliament was formally reconvened after a lengthy hiatus in January 1984. According to the constitution (Article 68 ii) a general election shall take place during the four months preceding the end of the term of the house. This makes a general election due between September 1987 and January 1988. There is a provision by which the King may extend the life of the Chamber of Deputies by not more than two years (Article 68 i). Of course the King also has the power to postpone indefinitely the introduction of the law or even to prorogue parliament once again. But that he must do something cannot be disputed.

In looking at the new electoral law in the Kingdom I propose to begin by briefly examining the attitude in Transjordan and Jordan of successive authorities to the electoral process and the notion of popular representation. I will then proceed to sketch the political context in which the new electoral law was drawn up and the steps which resulted in its adoption. I will attempt to draw conclusions about the motives behind its formulation. Finally, I will analyse the new law thematically in comparison with its predecessor, mindful of the changes which have been introduced.

Electoral process in Jordan

The legislative councils

The Transjordanian state's first experience of national elections occurred in April 1929. This beginning was not auspicious. The British mandate authorities had decided on the necessity of some assembly to give the regime a constitutional character. They also wanted some form of popular endorsement of the Anglo-Transjordanian agreement in order to bestow legitimacy upon the relationship of Britain and the mandated territory. Neither the British authorities nor Emir Abdallah were enthusiastic about such a development. The British Resident was loathe to see political power dissipated more than was absolutely necessary. He fought hard for the council to be known as the 'Legislative Assembly' rather than the 'Representative Assembly' as was the popular desire. The Emir, who had been trying painstakingly to build up his power base in the area since November 1920, resented any concessions which reduced his power. As one writer has said of Abdallah, the Emir's 'inherent nature and upbringing made him eminently suitable for the role of an autocrat' (Abidi 1965, p. 13).

The assembly that emerged was heavily subordinate to the executive council, the head of state and the British Resident in ascending order. The Organic Law (Seton 1931, p. 397), which was published in April 1928, provided that the Executive Council should be given *ex officio* status *en masse* on the Legislative Assembly, meaning that it occupied six out of the total twenty-two places. Moreover, the chief minister was also to chair the assembly giving him control over the agenda and the course of debates. The subsequent electoral law (Seton 1931, p. 248) prescribed that the other assembly members, the fourteen representing geographical constituencies, were to be elected indirectly; the primary election, open to all non-bedouin male citizens aged 18 and over, resulted in an electoral college which then selected the final members. A communal feature was built into this process with three of the fourteen having to be Christians and two places being allocated to the Caucasian community. This element was in marked disproportion to the sizes of the respective minority communities. The final two places were reserved for the nomadic tribes of the desert, via a process which concentrated even more leverage in the hands of the Emir. The two bedouin members were chosen by two ten-strong tribal commissions appointed by the Emir.

The relationship between the Emir and the assembly was strictly regulated in the Organic Law. First, the Emir had the right to appoint and dismiss the chief minister and his team at will. The Executive Council was in no way accountable to the assembly. In direct relation to the assembly, the Emir had the power to convene, adjourn, prorogue and dissolve it, though with certain safeguards as to the period before another assembly had to be elected. Furthermore, the Emir had to give his assent to bills passed by the assembly; this permitted him to return any bills with which he did not agree to the assembly within one year. In turn, the Emir was subject to the vigilance of the British Resident. As one political scientist analysing the period put it 'Whereas the 1928 agreement enabled the British government to control the Emir, the Organic Law enabled the Emir to control the governed' (Aruri 1972, p. 77).

Early years of the Kingdom

In March 1946, the mandate was formally brought to an end and a new treaty signed with Britain. Two months later the state was declared independent and the Hashemite Kingdom of Jordan was created. In 1946 a constitution (Davis 1953, p. 235) was adopted to replace the Organic Law. The reduction of British influence was something to which the Emir had been looking forward; he was not eager, especially with the country in such a docile state, to begin sharing power. Consequently, the legislature did not gain any substantial power *vis-à-vis* the executive.

The 1947 electoral law (Davis 1953, p. 253) provided for the establishment of a bicameral legislature. The Chamber of Deputies was to have twenty members, to be drawn from nine constituent districts, and selected by one direct election. The King, however, was to choose the speaker of the house. As before, the cabinet was only responsible to the monarch. The character of the Chamber of Notables more overtly betrayed the atmosphere of paternalism that then pervaded the political system. It consisted of ten members who were appointed by the King for an eight-year term 'from among persons who held the confidence of the people' (Khatib 1975, p. 108).

Other obstacles were placed before the elected assembly to marginalize its role. Under the new constitution, the cabinet, with the authorization of the King, was allowed to consider the budget to be valid, even if the lower house had refused to pass the budget law. It also gave the cabinet the right to issue provisional laws in the absence of the Chamber of Deputies.

In December 1949, the appropriate article in the electoral law was amended in order to enfranchise the Palestinians who were, in April the following year, to be added *de jure* to the Kingdom. Equal parity was to be given to the 'western region' in the Chamber of Deputies which had twenty seats allocated for it. No such formal provision was made in the Chamber of Notables for the automatic representation of Palestinians.

As in the late 1920s, opposition was voiced by those who disagreed with the emasculation of the elected chamber. In 1947 two of the deputies were persistent critics of the constitution and the electoral law. They demanded both that the cabinet be responsible to parliament and not the monarch, and the full authority to carry out a proper legislative function. In December, 1947 the two critics were joined by four other deputies voicing similar demands. Though the proceedings of the Chamber of Deputies show that these demands were regular issues on the agenda, the executive found it easy to ignore them.

The fusion of the two banks of the Jordan disrupted the prevailing pattern of political relations. The Chamber of Deputies was enlarged and, with the addition of representatives from the more politically sophisticated Palestinian community, became more ambitious when it was formed anew in the spring of 1950. It was partly the frustration that it felt against the restrictions placed on it executing the conventional functions of a legislature that led it to refuse to pass the central government budget in May 1951. This was an affront to Abdallah's conception of a parliament and he dissolved the chamber. His assassination two months later prematurely brought to a close this clash of perceptions over the notion of the legislature.

1952 Constitution

The short reign of King Talal began with instructions issued by the monarch to his prime minister to seek a vote of confidence from the newly elected lower house. This new approach of enhancing rather than trying to stifle the legislature persisted long enough to be enshrined in the 1952 constitution, and to have some important amendments added to it two years later. Generally speaking, the substance of this constitution is still on the statue books in the Kingdom today. Under that document, the prime minister and his ministers were made collectively and individually responsible to the Chamber of Deputies. Each new administration had to seek a confidence vote after outlining its forthcoming programme, and a two-thirds majority of deputies could bring down a government. The deputies in turn were empowered to impeach ministers. There was also a reduced period of six months for the monarch to object to legislation while the deputies were endowed with a potential override to the royal veto. The chamber was also given greater authority over financial and foreign affairs. Generally speaking, there were fewer devices through which the throne could stymie the role of parliament.

The liberal process reversed

However, the climate of liberalism in which the constitution was drawn up proved short-lived. With the growth of radical, trans-statal ideologies in the early 1950s, Jordanian governments soon sought to subvert some of the important provisions of the constitution. Shorn of the obstructive, procedural means to do this, in relation to the Chamber of Deputies the cabinet had to resort to underhand tactics. In 1954, for instance, there was widespread interference in the general election for the lower house. Intimidation of the opposition candidates and supporters was common, while the army was used as a vote bank with which to try to defeat candidates deemed undesirable. As the domestic political situation deteriorated in the mid-1950s and civil strife periodically erupted, the King tried to conciliate the moderate opposition by relinquishing an element of his political power. Free elections were therefore held in 1956 and a cabinet was formed by Sulaiman Nabulsi, the leader of the pan-Arabist National Socialist Party.

This power-sharing arrangement between King Hussein and his ambitious premier was always uneasy and eventually short-lived. After the dismissal of the Nabulsi government the opposition attempted to force the King to climb down. A national congress of the radical opposition forces was convened at Nablus, which included twenty-three members of the lower house, and a long list of demands drawn up. With his personal power, and possibly his throne and state at stake, the young King replied with draconian measures. Assured of the support of the organs of coercion, Hussein's new government was able to institute what one author has called a 'Reign of Terror' (Aruri 1972, p. 146). It enforced a curfew which in turn allowed it to introduce martial law, dissolve all political parties, impose censorship, purge the bureaucracy and carry out wholesale arrests. Parliament was permitted to serve its full term, but only after some seventeen deputies were forced to resign or had their seats in the house terminated as a result of executive pressure (Jreisat 1968, p. 62).

This successful iron-fisted action was a potent illustration of the weak institutional position of the legislature in Jordanian politics and the unstoppable power of the executive. In time, most of the draconian measures were rescinded, although a formal ban on political parties still exists at the time of writing. Nevertheless, the threat of their reimposition still casts a shadow over the assembly. Evidence of a renewed willingness of the executive to interfere in the composition of the lower house was displayed in the 1963 and 1967 elections. This usually took the form of indirect interferences, such as prohibiting a candidate from travelling freely within a constituency and showing official displeasure to deter voters from returning him (Azm 1985). Sometimes the interference was direct, such as occurred in one notorious case involving the poll for the central bedouin deputy in 1967 (Amman-based diplomat 1986). Another of the provisions given to parliament under the constitution, namely the right to bring down a government, was simultaneously exercised and effectively undermined in April 1963. The King was so angry at the effrontery of the parliament in witholding a confidence vote in the government of the day, led by Samir Al Rifa, that he dissolved it and called a new poll.

The last elections for the Chamber of Deputies took place in April 1967. When the mandate of the assembly ran out in 1971 no new elections were possible owing to the occupation by Israel of the

West Bank. The house was summoned to an emergency meeting in November 1974 in the wake of an Arab summit in Rabat. The latter summit had recognized the PLO as the sole legitimate representative of the Palestinian people in the face of opposition by King Hussein. The King reasoned that if the PLO was so designated to represent the Palestinians, there was no place in a Jordanian elected assembly for representatives of Palestinians. The house met long enough to pass a constitutional amendment empowering the monarch to postpone elections under compelling circumstances. It also met briefly in 1976 to pass another amendment. With demands growing on the East Bank for a greater input into politics a National Consultative Council, whose members were chosen by the King, was formed in 1978. Towards the end of its third term, this was dissolved to permit the return of the elected house of parliament.

Historical conclusion

A legislature was reluctantly introduced as part of the formal political process. Except for a brief period, the regime has been reluctant to devolve power to the legislature, and has been uncomfortable with its presence. Initially, the executive had many formal safeguards over the actions of the legislature. These included control over the choice of representatives, the business of the assembly and the right to veto its legislative output. Most of these provisions disappeared with the introduction of the 1952 constitution. From that time up to the 1967 war, the executive pursued one of three courses with regard to the electoral process. There was the brief interlude of complete impartiality, which characterized the general election of 1956. There was the draconian intervention which marked the period immediately following April 1957 and which effectively ended with the abolition of martial law in November of the next year. Finally, there was the period of interference, often indirect although not always so, which was the trademark of the remaining years to 1967.

Introduction of electoral law

Recall of parliament

King Hussein recalled parliament on 5 January 1984. Arthur Day writing recently has stated that the recall of parliament was 'a political, not a constitutional, act' (Day 1986, p. 41). He cites two main reasons for this move. First, bringing back parliament would assuage some of those criticizing the King for the lack of democracy in the country. As one senior Jordanian official was quoted in the local press: 'we in Jordan feel that it is not realistic to expect our own political development to be forever frozen because of lack of progress on resolving the Palestinian issue' (*Jordan Times*, 7 January 1984). Second, Day points to manoeuvring by Hussein to press the PLO to join with Jordan in diplomacy towards a peace settlement with Israel. He was both drawing attention to the fact that the concession the PLO had extracted from the Kingdom at Rabat had not brought them any nearer to their political objectives, and putting pressure on the organization by challenging their exclusive position.

The political context

In his speech from the throne of 2 November 1985, King Hussein said that his government would soon submit to parliament a new electoral law. In a short reference to the subject the King said that the 'genuine democracy' that this would bring should be founded on the principle of decision making at the grass-roots level (*Jordan Times*, 3 November 1985). In order to understand the real objectives in introducing a new electoral law with its individual provisions, a brief look at the context in which it was brought in is necessary.

The notion of introducing a new electoral law was not a new one. It had been brewing under the premiership of Mudar Badran (Farraj 1986). However what this deputy called the 'catalytic' (ibid.) effect in speeding its introduction was the by-election held in the Kingdom in March 1984. The first act of the newly recalled lower house had been to pass a constitutional amendment allowing elections to take place on the East Bank but not, due to the Israeli occupation, on the West Bank. The eight members who had died since the 1967 poll would be replaced by direct election. The newly elected deputies and their forty-six fellows would themselves in turn elect new members to fill the six vacant seats for representatives from the West Bank.

Of the eight places to be filled in the East Bank, two were those specifically reserved for Christians, making six seats open to contest by Muslims. The election campaign was free of government interference and resulted in the election of three candidates who ran on an overtly Islamic platform. The election to fill the one vacant seat in the constituency of Amman attracted the most interest because of its large population and its status as the capital. Laith Al Shbailat, a former president of the Jordan Engineers' Association, was returned here ahead of thirty-five rivals.

He polled 18,458 votes, nearly double the total received by his nearest rival, Barjas Al Hadid, who was a close relative of the previous incumbent.

The town of Irbid in the north, Jordan's second city, had been identified with growing Islamicist views. A slate of candidates identified with the Islamic current had been returned in the municipal elections of the previous December. There had also been agitation on the campus of the nearby Yarmouk University for a more pious regime, particularly regarding the segregation of the sexes. At the forefront of this campaign was a former lecturer by the name of Dr Ahmad Al Kufahi. Despite this backdrop, few predicted his runaway victory. He was returned with a majority of 10,687 over Dr Qasim Ubaidat, a candidate identified with the nationalist left (Tal 1984). In a field of nineteen, Kufahi received over 30 per cent of the vote. The third Islamicist winner was in the southern seat of Tafilah where Dr Abdallah Al Akailah, a lecturer at the University of Jordan and member of the Muslim Brotherhood, defeated two other candidates. The government had permitted free elections in order to gain an indicator as to public opinion. There was considerable shock among the political establishment at the outcome of the poll.

There was also considerable dismay on the part of those whose traditional fiefdoms had been lost as a result of the by-elections. Nowhere was this more apparent than in the constituency of Amman. Although the electoral districts in Jordan tended to be large, multi-member constituencies, there had only been one seat at stake in the capital. The previous incumbent had been Muhammad Minwar Al Hadid, from the Hadid section of the Balqa tribes. With their considerable influence based on land owned in and to the south of Amman, a Hadid had occupied a place in the Chamber of Deputies since 1947. The section was also identified as being close to the Hashemite ruling family – ever since 1923 when the section supported Emir Abdallah against a rebellion of most of the Balqa tribes led by Sultan Al Adwazn. The Hadid had viewed the seat as a family right (Hadid 1984); its eventual loss amounted to an affront to their honour. The effect of the loss of the seat on the Hadid was profound; some of its leading members were driven to enter the realm of ideological politics and some joined the United Democratic Association of Dr Jamal Al Shair. If few of the old families who strongly supported the monarchy had lost seats in the by-election, the lesson was not wasted on most of them. A groundswell built up amongst them for electoral change to protect their influence.

There was soon evidence that the electoral victories would make life uncomfortable for the government. Day notes that the three elected Islamicist members combined with three or four other deputies to form a bloc in the lower house. This loose bloc chose certain populist issues on which to attack the government of the day and its predecessors. These included human rights issues (such as the imprisonment of political prisoners), the activities of the General Intelligence Department, the continuance of martial law and public sector corruption. An example of this was the last meeting of the Chamber of Deputies before the summer recess on 15 May 1986. During the session, some seventeen deputies spoke, many of them criticizing the practice of the confiscation of students' passports as a way of applying political pressure. Dr Akailah and Mr Shbailat concentrated their attack on the GID. This was meant to cause maximum embarassment to Prime Minister Ahmad Ubaidat who was a former interior minister and head of the department. The Prime Minister was only able to stem the tide by specifically outlining the security threats that the Kingdom was suffering. Thus he had been forced to reveal the instability and strain to which the country was prone.

The birth of the new law

Following the speech from the throne on 2 November 1986, a ten-man committee of the prime ministry was established to formulate the individual clauses. This committee included the Prime Minister and his deputy, the Minister of Justice and the Minister of the Interior, and two non-cabinet members (Tal 1986). The brief timescale involved suggests that much of the work on the bill had already been completed. The substantive content of the law seems certain to have emanated from the Palace (Farraj 1986) while work on drafting the bill had already been undertaken by the previous administration (Ubaidat 1986). The bill was then forwarded to the Chamber of Deputies Legal Committee which met regularly between 7 January and 25 March 1986. Members of the cabinet and particularly the Prime Minister were regular attendants at the meetings to consider the clauses of the new bill.

The Legal Committee went on to amend over twenty-two articles of the seventy-five article bill, with the Islamicists being acknowledged as having led the lobby in support of amendments (Amman-based diplomat 1986) However, the vast majority of these were procedural alterations. The bill went before the Chamber of Deputies on 27 March and was passed after only around one and a half hours debate. There was one amendment accepted by the Prime Minister, Zaid Al Rifai, at this stage. The original article had stipulated that members of illegal political organizations would not be allowed to run in parliamentary elections. This had worried liberals as well as radicals since a handful of loose political associations had been permitted to evolve over the last ten years in the Kingdom, though political parties remained proscribed. The clause was amended to say that 'illegal parties' referred to 'those organizations whose goals contradict the Jordanian Constitution' (*Jordan Times*, 29 March 1986).

Only two deputies voted against the bill, Mr Shbailat and the Ba'athist Muslim deputy for Karak, Riyadh Al Nawaisah. The majority of those who might have been expected to demur refrained from doing so, according to a local journalist who closely follows parliamentary affairs, as part of the compromise over the membership of political organizations amendment. The Senate duly passed the bill on 26 April after consideration by its legal committee. During the formalities of the debate Ahmad Ubaidat voiced his considerable reservations on the form of the bill. This speech incurred the anger of his incumbent successor who instructed the media not to carry details of the address. Indeed, public discussion of the bill was kept to a minimum owing to the increased control of the press which prevailed at the time.

Changes in the electoral law

The Palestinian question

Equal representation

In a state where a majority of the citizens are Palestinian it is self-evident that any attempt at formal political change will have a Palestinian dimension to it. The new electoral law addressed the issue of Palestinian representation directly. Its provisions also had implications for the long-running competition between the PLO and King Hussein to speak on behalf of the Palestinian people. Inevitably, it was this subject which became and still continues to be the most controversial in the new law.

According to the law adopted in 1960, thirty deputies, half of the total number, were elected from seven constituencies on the West Bank. Electors could only vote once, but they had the right to register wherever they lived, regardless of residence. Therefore it was possible for Palestinians working on the East Bank to register and vote in elections held in their family homes. The occupation of the West Bank made it impossible for elections to the Jordanian parliament to be held there. The March 1984 by-elections established the principle that while all residents on the East Bank were free to vote, only those identified as East Bankers could nominate themselves as candidates.

The principle of equal representation of the two Banks was introduced in 1950 to emphasize the joint commitment of the Hashemite regime to the Jordanian and Palestinian people alike. But, under this cloak of equality, the clear Palestinian majority in the Kingdom had been obscured. In drawing up the new law, the regime was clearly in a quandary. The depopulation of the West Bank since 1967 and the boom in the population of the East Bank made the continuation of such a balance untenable. A more proportionate division of seats would have been along the lines of those advocated by a promiment leftist Palestinian lawyer Ibrahim Bakr. In a memorandum on the bill addressed to the dean of the Jordanian Bar Association (Bakr 1986), Mr Bakr advocated between 61 and 70 per cent of the seats being allocated to the East Bank. Yet to have changed the formal balance in favour of the East Bank would have diminished the King's chances of reestablishing himself as a credible spokesman for the Palestinian people. Moreover, it would have helped entrench the political alienation felt in the Kingdom by Palestinians since the Rabat summit decision of 1974. Indeed, it would have been construed as another device to ensure that political posts were occupied increasingly by East Bankers.

Refugee camp constituencies

The formula adopted in the law to try to surmount both of these problems was to give the Palestinian refugee camps on the East Bank formal representatives, but to include this element in the block allocation of seats to the West Bank. Each of the eleven refugee camps on the East Bank were apportioned one deputy and these seats were classified as part of the seventy-one seats allocated for West Bank representatives. Together with the seventy-one seats allotted for the East Bank (excluding the refugee camps), the new total number of members of the Chamber of Deputies was increased from sixty to 142. That this move was purely an electoral device is illustrated by the fact that the refugee camps on the West Bank were not similarly elevated to the level of constituencies.

The neatness of this arithmetical trick did not bring immunity from criticism. Mr Bakr, for instance, noted that the bill for all practical purposes acknowledged the inequality between the two Banks. He then stressed the strangeness of a situation whereby constituencies which are located on one Bank are deemed to be part of the other.

But the most widespread criticism was reserved for the decision to create refugee camp constituencies. This move was deemed unwise because it implied the permanence of the camps. Even though the camps in question had been in existence since the 1948 and 1967 Arab–Israeli wars, their transient nature is synonymous with a declaration that the Palestinian question has not been solved. To give any impression that the camps are permanent constructs is to imply that there is no longer any hope for the refugees to return to their homes in Palestine.

This was by no means an obscure and theoretical political point, but one which was taken up by almost all shades of political opinion in Jordan. Indeed, it was a pillar of the East Bank establishment, Ahmad Ubaidat, who made one of the strongest criticisms of this clause in a controversial speech to the Senate during discussion of the bill. He made this very point by warning that such a proposal would 'change the camps into towns' (Ubaidat 1986). In saying this he articulated a familiar East Bank fear about the state of Jordan losing its demographic and political identity to the Palestinians. However, he went further to synthesize East Bank and Palestinian fears of a peace settlement with Israel which would leave both communities dissatisfied. In Ubaidat's view, the 'creation of constituencies in both these camps represents the will of settlement that both communities refuse' (Ubaidat 1986). The consequence of such a settlement would inevitably be discontent on the part of the Palestinians and instability in Jordan. He also warned that this kind of measure would help bring about the resolution of the Palestinian issue on unfavourable grounds.

Refugees and East Bank elections

Moderate Palestinian critics of the move concentrated on a different aspect of the same question. The Christian member for Jerusalem, Dr Fuad Farraj, was concerned about the tension that it might perpetuate and fuel between Palestinians resident on the East Bank and the indigenous population (Farraj 1986). He expressed the view that effort should be expended to water down the differences between the communities rather than formalizing the divisions. He regarded this part of the law as promoting the formal 'segregation' of the two communities; of fractionalizing rather than cementing relations. He also believed that it removed an important area of cooperation. In the March 1984 by-election, East Bank candidates in whose constituency there existed a refugee camp had to go out to woo the voters therein. It also provided a valuable point of contract and enable the candidates to stay in touch with the issues that were of importance to the camp leaders. Dr. Farraj believed that this would remove a valuable chance for dialogue between the camps and their East Bank neighbours.

Though this indeed may have been a reasonable point in theory, there is no doubt that the creation of refugee camp constituencies was double-edged. It also held the advantage of removing a source of dissatisfaction from among the aspiring East Bank political élite, especially those relying primarily on kinship rather than on an ideological base of support. Those standing in constituencies housing large refugee camps resented having to seek the refugee vote in order to try to get elected. Furthermore, they felt that they were less likely to receive the votes of refugees than the ideological candidates of both leftist and religious persuasion. Though the turn-out in the 1984 by-election was not great among the camps, this perception seems to have been accurate. An analysis of the by-elections published in the *Al Ra'i* newspaper noted 'that part of the refugees voted in support for [sic] leftist candidates, and others, supported candidates with strong religious orientation' (reprinted *Jordan Times*, 25 July 1984).

Undoubtedly, part of this resentment also focused on the influence of the PLO. Although it is difficult to isolate the influence which the organization did have on, for example, the by-elections, its existence as a factor certainly made the traditional candidates wary. The notion that the outcome of an East Bank election may depend on the line of the PLO was anathema to many candidates. In the March 1984 by-election the PLO was racked by divisions in the wake of the Fatah revolt of May 1983 and the visit to Cairo of Yassir Arafat the previous December. Consequently it did not play a prominent role. The columnist quoted before confirms this point: 'The Palestinian refugees in the camps were divided, due to the division in the Fatah movement of the Palestine Liberation Organization'. However, this would not always necessarily be the case. In closing down the offices of Fatah in the Kingdom and expelling the deputy commander of the PLO forces, Khalil Al Wazir (Abu Jihad), in July 1986, King Hussein said there had been interference in the Kingdom's internal affairs. Specifically he said there was a 'conclusive evidence of PLO attempts to influence the outcome of a recent by-election in the north of the country' (*Financial Times*, 16 July 1986) in a reference to the controversial poll in Irbid the previous month.

Inequality of camp representation

As already pointed out, some refugee camps, namely those on the West Bank, were not singled out at all to have special representatives. From this one must conclude that the policy of creating special camp constituencies for the East Bank had nothing to do *per se* with ensuring that the voice of the refugees could be heard in the legislature.

Even within the pattern of camp representation on the East Bank, anomalies abound. The chief one is clearly the wide discrepancy in the number of people each member is supposed to be representing. The refugee camps on the East Bank are not homogeneous in terms of population or area. According to the official United Nations Relief and Works Agency (UNRWA) statistics published at the end of June 1985, the largest camp was Baqaa with 54,307 refugees and the smallest Al Talbiyyah with 1,508 inhabitants. Despite this great difference in population, each camp was allocated one member to represent it in the chamber.

The result of this approach is that it is the more populous camps like Baqaa, Amman New Camp (Wahdat), Jabal Hussein and Marka which are underrepresented, while the less numerous ones are overrepresented. It is no coincidence that it is the more numerous camps, especially Baqaa, Wahdat and Jabal Hussein, which are the most highly politicized and disaffected (Amman-based diplomat 1986).

The system of allocation appears to be an attempt by the regime to have the best of both worlds. The allocation of seats to the camps enables it to maintain the illusion of dual representation, while satisfying a grievance of its traditional base of support on the East Bank. At the same time, the pattern of representation granted to the camps is aimed at minimizing the likelihood of the emergence of a refugee bloc or the election of candidates who are markedly critical of it. It will prove easier for the regime to influence the elections in the smaller camps. Failing that it will be easier to coopt the elected representative through the use of resource allocation. If the member cooperates, he will have patronage appointments to bestow on his constituents and better services for the camp. If he does not, these can be withdrawn, thus reducing the likelihood of his election in the next poll. Even if such devices fail in the larger camps, the handful of members will be swamped in a chamber of 142 where procedural devices can be used more successfully to limit the use of parliament as a political platform.

Elected deputies to choose West Bank members*

Having directly elected the seventy-one deputies for the East Bank and the eleven representing the refugee camps, the electoral process turns to the selection of the sixty West Bank members proper. Since the recall of parliament, vacant West Bank seats have been filled by the existing deputies from both Banks electing candidates. The selection of the West Bank members in the future is a refinement of this process. Half of these are to be chosen by the eighty-two deputies already elected and the remaining half to be chosen by the 112 members, that is the eighty-two and the thirty elected by them.

There is acute sensitivity amongst PLO supporters at any moves by the Jordanian regime to increase the independent Palestinian presence in the representative apparatus. Any such moves reawaken fears that King Hussein might by trying to create an alternative leadership and grooming it to play a role, at the PLO's expense, in the peace process. Consequently, it was the view of many Palestinians that the West Bank should be omitted from the Jordanian representative machinery (Bakr 1986). This split process for choosing the West Bank members effectively acknowledges the weakness of any pretensions by the regime in this direction. The fact that the West Bank deputies are being elected primarily by East Bank members is unlikely to increase their legitimacy with the Palestinians living under occupation, whom they are supposed to be representing. It seems that the idea of a split process is little more than a gesture designed to obscure the fact that the West Bank deputies will not have been elected by Palestinians. The fallibility of this process will no doubt go a long way towards negating the argument that parliament is more representative of the Palestinians because of the large increase in the number of deputies.

Criticism of the procedure by which the elected deputies choose their sixty West Bank colleagues also emanated from those who fear the ideological emasculation of the chamber. If as expected the East Bank contingent is dominated by those who are socially and politically conservative, they will almost certainly choose West Bank deputies of similar background and outlook. This in turn, argue many liberals as well as radicals, will help stifle the few representatives who have a more active contribution to make to a Western conception of parliamentary life (Muashar 1986).

*Editor's comment: This section was written in 1987 and it has been retained even though it has been overtaken by events. The opinion was relevant at the time of writing and as such provides an important insight into circumstances in 1987.

Size and distribution of seats

Smaller constituencies favour kinship groups

The new law sought to undermine the dominance of the old multi-member constituencies which had characterized the pattern of representation on the East Bank since the inception of the Kingdom. But the West Bank was omitted from this substantive change, reinforcing the conclusion that it was executed with some specific political objective in mind for the East Bank. The old electoral boundary system was not replaced by a clearly-defined new formula. The new prescription consisted of a hotchpotch combination of small electoral districts and proportionately smaller multi-member constituencies based on large urban areas or residual rural areas. This accounted for sixty-five of the East Bank seats with the balance being made up of bedouin representatives from the *badia* region.

Eleven of the smaller electoral districts, like Wadi Musa and Dhiban, formed single member constituencies. While it would be an exaggeration to label them rotten boroughs, the districts had clearly been chosen in order to ensure that an important kinship group dominating the area should have an almost automatic place in the chamber. One member of the original drafting committee was frank about the motives. The creation of such constituencies would ensure that tribes like the Bani Hamida, who are to be found around the town of Dhiban, would return a deputy from amongst their number. Similarly the numerous Bani Hasan tribe, who stretch from Zarqa to Mafraq, to the edge of Jarash, would have greater representation because of such a demarcation rather than having their numbers dissipated as in past polls (Tal 1986). The creation of two or three member constituencies, such as in Ajlun and Jarash, was also expected to cement such a tendency.

The general view in Jordan appeared to be that the creation of smaller constituencies had favoured kinship groups like tribes and families. The formulation of constituencies on this basis appeared to be tantamount to a reward to the traditional supporters of the regime. Mr Ubaidat implied as much when he referred to the favouritism which had been shown to certain groups in certain constituencies (Ubaidat 1986). Undoubtedly, in the wake of the March 1984, by-elections, this bias was a response to the demands being made by such groups stung as they were by the electoral success of the ideological candidates. The fact that the regime did not introduce a comprehensive system of single member constituencies robbed it of the justification that the new system would promote better identification between a deputy and his constituents. Moreover, the formation on 1 January 1987 of a Greater

Amman Council to provide services in the past supplied by smaller administrative units indicates that decentralization is not a uniform policy goal in the Kingdom.

Similarly, few doubted that the creation of these smaller constituencies was a device to increase the ability of the regime to interfere in local politics. For example, one Christian Palestinian politician, disinterested in the machinations of rural East Bank politics, was forthright in reading such a motive into the change (Farraj 1986). As with the small Palestinian refugee camps, the ability of the regime to manipulate the electoral process and to coopt elected members was increased.

The overriding political consequence of such a change in the size of constituencies appears to be the effect it will have on ideological candidates. The same deputy was clear in identifying the Islamicist candidates and the 'dormant' political groups, like the Communist Party of Jordan, as the likely losers. The creation of these 'kinship seats' will, it is hoped, lead to the reinvigoration of the family or tribal collectivity as a political unit. The wish of the regime must also be that the increased number of deputies will bring certain smaller kinship groups nearer to the political process and as such boost their status and local standing. This in turn will, so the reasoning goes, reduce the potential for alienation which has made the Islamic candidates popular as the focus of protest votes. This is all conjecture. What is beyond doubt is that in smaller constituencies where a particular family or tribe is powerful or numerically strong it will be markedly more difficult for ideological candidates to garner the necessary votes to capture these seats.

Rural bias is maintained

The creation of smaller constituencies is part of a more general objective aimed at increasing the proportionate representation of rural areas at the expense of the cities and even some of the large towns. This is no accident of geography nor is it a negligible imbalance. Rather, the legislature in Jordan has throughout its past been weighted in favour of rural representation, the rationale for which has been that the rural peoples are more traditional in their support for the regime and those living in urban areas less uncritical. In the new electoral law this tendency has been strengthened. The main target of the new law has been the large cities of Amman and Zarqa, where there are weighty majorities of poorer Palestinian workers and artisans, and where unemployment is increasing as a political problem. Both have been the victims of blatant gerrymandering for which no justification exists nor is given.

That the law does create an imbalance there is no doubt, even allowing for the difficulties in exactly measuring representative proportions. For instance, although the urban-dominated Amman governorate possesses 41.1 per cent of the total East Bank population including the refugee camps, the law has only allocated it 25.6 per cent of the eighty-two seats, that is the East Bank element combined with the eleven seats for the camps. If one extracts the population of the camps from the governorate and simply uses the formal seventy-one seat East Bank allocation, then one is left with 38.7 per cent of the population represented by 23.9 per cent of the East Bank deputies. In fact the underrepresentation of the city of Amman is even greater than this. In 1983, the city of Amman accounted for 29.8 per cent of the population yet under the new law it has been allotted just 9.9 per cent of the total number of East Bank seats. The attempt to minimize the likelihood of the election from the capital of members adhering to radical ideologies is further increased by the fact that of the seven places allocated to the city, one is reserved exclusively for a Christian and one for a member of the Caucasian community. A similar imbalance applies in the governorate of Zarqa which has 15.9 per cent of the East Bank's total population, but has only been allocated 7.3 per cent of the eighty-two seats allotted to those resident on the East Bank. Extracting those living in the camps and their seats, one is left with 14.5 per cent of the population represented by just 5.6 per cent of the seats.

The predominantly rural areas of the south, which historically have been the strongest supporters of the regime, by contrast have been allocated a disproportionately greater number of seats. The Karak governorate, for instance, is overrepresented by more than three times. It possesses 4.2 per cent of the population yet 12.7 per cent of the total East Bank seats. The Tafilah governorate is also three times overrepresented while the electoral areas of the Maan and Aqaba governorates combined receive twice as many seats in proportion to their population.

The minorities

The Christians

The Christians are the only confessional minority group of any significance in a state composed mainly of Sunni Muslims. They are well integrated into the society and share the political culture of their Muslim compatriots. However, for all the good relations which have existed historically between the two communities there is a self-consciousness of being different. The *millet* system, which protected the Christian community when the country was part of the Ottoman Empire, has effectively been retained. The Christians have their own religious courts to pronounce over matters of personal status and have always enjoyed seats set aside for them in the successive legislatures in the state.

The Christians have also always enjoyed representation disproportionate to their numbers. In the early 1960s, when they formed some 6.5 per cent of the population, they were given nine seats or 15 per cent representation in the sixty-member chamber (Aruri 1972, p. 41). While the Christians have by no means been politically passive, there has been a perception that, as a minority, they are less of a threat than other constituencies in the state. Constitutionally, Islam is the religion of the state. Neither the head of state nor the prime minister could be of any faith other than Islam, and the Christians do not have the numbers to upset the status quo. Christians tend thus to be seen as potential allies rather than threats. Furthermore, Christians have tended to prosper as merchants and businessmen, making them natural allies of order and stability. In particular, there is a general perception within the Christian community that King Hussein is well disposed towards them and he has assumed the role of a protector.

The new law maintains this privileged position for the Christians. Altogether, the community, which now forms about 6 per cent of the total population, has been allocated seventeen seats out of 142, or just under 12 per cent of the total strength. This represents a slight reduction compared to before, but this has not stopped the special status from being attacked. One renowned lawyer and columnist, Walid Saadi, in an unpublished article criticized this practice as being against the constitution, which prescribes no discrimination on the grounds of race, language or religion. 'The fact that previous electoral laws made provisions for elections on the basis of religion does not bestow constitutionality on the new law', he wrote. Illustrating the nervousness which has been felt in Jordan since the civil war began in Lebanon, he concludes by asking the question: 'do we wish to sow the seeds for a future Lebanon in our midst?'

The Islamicist deputy, Laith Al Shbailat, also took up the question of minority representation but, due to its highly sensitive nature, only did so in a memorandum published at the time of the debate on the bill rather than raising it orally. He criticized the notion of sectarian representation as being likewise against the constitution. However, he went on to make the point that if there does have to be special representation for the Christian community then it should be in proportion to the size of that community as established during the 1979 census, which was the most recent authoritative population survey conducted in the Kingdom. His explanation for the regime's continued patronage of minority confessional and ethnic groups was that the minorities always tend to side with the government (Shbailat 1986).

The wariness and reluctance of the Christian community to relinquish its formal position of privilege is beyond dispute. Even one of the articulate, younger members of the community who is passionately committed to the notion of democracy was only willing to contemplate an end to this special status if there was a trade-off with the legalization of political parties (Muashar 1986).

The Caucasians

The Caucasians, who came to Transjordan at the behest of the Ottomans in the days of the Empire, form the only significant ethnic minority living in the state. They consist of two groups: the larger Circassian community of some 25,000 who are Sunni Muslims and the smaller Shishan community numbering around 2,000 who adhere to the Shiah sect of the same faith. Although they have their own language and culture, after some hundred years of residing in the area they are fast becoming assimilated. The Caucasians were introduced into the area for overtly political reasons. The Turks wanted to establish a political constituency in a turbulent area to act as a constant source of support. With the demise of the Ottoman Empire, the Caucasians transferred their allegiance to the Hashemites. Like the Christians, they have been granted a position of a favoured minority. In return for unswerving support, they have been rewarded with patronage in the senior ranks of, in particular, the air force, the General Intelligence Department and the bureaucracy.

This favouritism has been carried over into the ranks of the legislature. The 1928 electoral law granted them one seat in the Legislative Council for every 5,000 inhabitants compared with one seat for every 27,000 inhabitants for the Muslim Arab community (Aruri 1972, p. 40). The Caucasian community continued to enjoy seats specially allocated under the electoral laws that followed. The 1986 law was no exception. Three such seats were reserved in the Amman city, Wadi Al Sir and Zarqa constituencies compared to the two which exist under the present arrangements. Although this marked a proportionate reduction in seats from 6.6 per cent of the East Bank allocation to 4.2 per cent, it is still more than the 1 per cent of the population that they form.

Criticism of the specific allocation of seats for the Caucasian community came from the same quarters and from similar perspectives as that aimed at the Christian allocation. If the attacks are less strident it is because of the fewer numbers involved and because there is greater consciousness of the Christians as a minority.

The bedouins

It has not been fashionable in writing about Jordan to include the bedouin in the chapters on 'the minorities'. Yet the bedouin, which for these purposes means those tribesmen living in the *badia* districts of the country, lend themselves to analysis as a favoured minority. In classifying them as a minority, I refer to them as such in a geoeconomic sense rather than as a confessional or ethnic minority. They are favoured in so far as they have their own *millet* in the *badia* or desert regions. Tribal law still takes precedence over the civil legal system in this area, a fact which has been strengthened by King Hussein's letter of 27 January 1985 which criticized newspaper attacks on the norms and traditions of the bedouin. They are also allocated separate seats in the chamber in a way much akin to the Christian and Caucasian communities.

Under the new law, the bedouin will be represented by six deputies, twice the number as under the previous law, but proportionately slightly less. Two each will be drawn from the northern, central and southern tribes.

Of course, those living in the *badia* regions cannot be described as being favoured in quite the same way as the other minorities described above. Though they are privileged with respect to the legal, political and cultural spheres, the ordinary tribesmen at least have fared less well with regards to their economic well-being. While most of the rest of the Kingdom enjoyed to some degree the benefits which accrued from the regional economic boom of the 1970s, the *badia* districts on the whole did not. The state was slow to act as a distributive mechanism in relation to these parts, and it is only recently that the *badia* has started to enjoy even such meagre benefits of development as electrification. It is against such a background and remembering the role played in the past by the bedouin as the bedrock of the regime that one can consider the continuing favours bestowed upon the leaders of these communities.

Conclusion

The 1986 electoral law falls firmly within the context of electoral legislation and practice as experienced almost uninterruptedly throughout the history of the state. Despite the scantily avowed official aims of the new electoral law, a hidden agenda of goals has been set for it. These real objectives fall into three categories: first, the restriction of representation in those geographical areas and amongst those ideological groups deemed likely to be critical of the regime; second, the strengthening of rural kinship groups both as a reward for past political allegiance and to help blunten the impact of the former; and third, to give greater weight to the regime as a mouthpiece for residents of refugee camps and those Palestinians living under occupation. The synthesis of these ends is likely to produce a docile and manipulated Chamber of Deputies functioning within a brittle shell of representative democracy.

Acknowledgements

I should like to thank Tim Niblock and Helen Robins for reading a first draft of this paper and for their valuable comments.

References

Abidi, A. H. H. (1965), *Jordan: A Political Study*, Asia Publishing House, London.

Amman-based diplomat (1986), interview with author, 5 October.

Aruri, N. H. (1972), *Jordan: Study in Political Development*, Martinus Nijhoff, The Hague.

Azm, Y. (1985), interview with author, 1 October.

Bakr, I. (1986), memorandum to Jordan Bar Association, 2 February.

Davis, H. M. (1953), *Constitutions, Electoral Laws, Treaties of States in the Near and Middle East*, Duke University Press, Durham, NC.

Day, A. R. (1986), *East Bank/West Bank*, Council on Foreign Relations, New York.

Farraj, F. (1986), interview with author, 12 November.

Hadid, B. (1984), interview with author, 29 February.

Jreisat, J. E. (1968), 'Provincial administration in Jordan: a study of institution-building', unpublished doctoral thesis.

Khatib, A. (1975), 'The Jordanian legislature in political development perspective', unpublished doctoral thesis.

Muashar, M. (1986a), interview with author, 6 October.

——, M. (1986b), 'Looking forward to 1988', *Jordan Times*, 20 September.

Saadi, W. (undated), 'Let's talk again about the new electoral law', unpublished article.

Sabbagh, R. (1986), interview with author, 17 September.
Seton, C. R. W. (ed.) (1931), *Legislation of Transjordan 1918–1930*, Crown Agents for the Colonies, London.
Shbailat, L. (1986), interview with author, 9 September.
— —, L. (undated), memorandum on the new electoral bill.
Talal, King (1952), *The Constitution of the Hashemite Kingdom of Jordan*, Amman.
Tal, M. (1984), interview with author, 22 February.
—— (1986), interview with author, 5 October.
Ubaidat, A. (1986), Text of speech to Senate, 27 April.

Part five

International Relations

Chapter ten

The Arab–Israeli and Iran–Iraq conflicts: a view from Jordan

Kamel Abu Jaber

Introduction

Many Arab intellectuals and decision makers are slowly being convinced that the Iran–Iraq conflict reflects a test of wills between different concepts of life and different civilizations. Historical, military, political, economic and even personality factors are intertwined in the conflict to give the impression that these are not mere border disputes or limited conflicts. Arab culture in the Middle East seems to be surrounded by hostile forces that wish to reduce it, if not altogether change it drastically.

The assumptions and the constants of both the Gulf War and the Arab–Israeli conflict have not changed over the years, although the variables have. Neither on the regional nor on the international levels do the Arabs seem to have genuine allies; their current sense of fear and insecurity emanates from this assessment of the situation.

Each month seems to unfold its own quota of dramatic and tragic events, with which Jordan and its centrist approach and moderate leadership attempts to cope. Between mid-April and mid-May 1987 several such events took place which demonstrate the unpredictable situation in the region, for example the Palestinian National Council (PNC) meeting in Algiers and its unnecessary abrogation of the 11 February 1985 Jordanian–Palestinian Accord – unnecessary since it was already defunct. The closure of the PLO offices in Cairo, and the fence mending that ensued and still ensues, is another example. The unification of various PLO factions and its reflection on Syrian–PLO relations is also uncertain. Even more unpredictable is the outcome of the Kuwaiti request to have American flags raised on its ships along with the hiring of Soviet ships to transport some of its oil. This has also contributed significantly to the unfolding drama in the Gulf. Furthermore, the reported secret meeting between Presidents Saddam Hussein and Hafiz al-Assad in Jordan, the meeting between King Hassan and President Ben Jadid over the Polisario affair, and the call by Chairman Arafat for a binational Arab–Jewish state over all of Palestine, and his willingness to meet with any Israeli leader including Mr Yitzhak Shamir to negotiate the matter, were notable developments and are indicative of the fundamental concern Middle Eastern leaders have for finding a solution to some of the region's seemingly intractable problems.

If this sample of events reflects anything, it is the volatile and sometimes violent nature of Arab politics. Jordan, situated in the heart of the area, is particularly conscious of and vulnerable to the potential violence of the surrounding areas. To its west is a powerful Israel always ready to teach its neighbours a lesson. To the east lies Iran, inspired by a messianic zeal which it believes gives it licence to assert its will regardless of law or even morality. In both Israel and Iran the leaders speak and act like ancient biblical prophets, extremism being in their view conducive to the nature of prophecy. To Jordan's north and east are Syria and Iraq, both militarily and ideologically powerful states, whilst in the south lies Saudi Arabia, financially and ideologically strong, yet also with its own ambitions.

Thus the view from Amman is hardly a comforting one, what with the concomittant internal pressures for development and the ever-present superpower rivalry menacing the area. Jordan seems to live from one crisis to another, its moderate, centrist leadership perhaps its weakness, but also the greatest asset contributing to its survival.

The Palestine problem

With what date in history should one commence the saga of this internecine dispute between the two semitic cousins? With the descendents of Abraham, the Arabs and Jews; or with Theodore Herzl and the first Zionist Congress in Basle, Switzerland in 1897? Or perhaps the proper date is the Balfour Declaration of 1917 when those who did not own the land gave this land of others to those who did not belong to it? Possibly the 1947 UN Partition Plan would be a good beginning, or 15 May 1948, when the Zionist idea became reality. The wound inflicted on the Arabs in 1948 has been kept open not only by successive military defeats since, but also by the insults hurled at the Arabs on individual and national levels each day. The price to both Arabs and Jews has been a further insecurity, weakening and dependency on others. The security of the whole region is in jeopardy while genuine independence is but a slogan.

In the two major global conflicts of this century the Arabs sided with the West, only to be rewarded by betrayal of promises and dreams. The question of right and justice remains of momentous importance with the Arab peoples, who now sue for peace. Arab acceptance of UN Resolution 242 of 1967 and 338 of 1973 did not emanate from their belief in the justic of these resolutions, nor because they met Arab demands, but from a recognition of the world balance of power, the need to avoid nuclear confrontation, and the need to stop the terrific haemorrhage of human and material resources and to divert these resources towards development.

In the summer of 1986 Mr Yasser Arafat called for an international peace conference on the 'basis of international legality and Security Council resolutions related to the question of Palestine and the Middle East including Resolutions 242 and 338'. The Israeli response was both quick and negative; once again they shifted their ground and increased their price. Israeli officials were quoted as saying 'There is nothing new in this; . . . our stance towards the PLO has nothing to do with its acceptance of 242. We say the PLO is a terrorist organisation.' Early in May 1987, following the conclusion of the PNC meeting in Algiers, and touring the Gulf States explaining its results, Arafat again raised the question of convening an international conference. This time he went even further offering to meet with any Israeli leader, including Yitzhak Shamir, with the aim of bringing an end to the Palestine problem on the basis of a democratic bi-national state over all of Palestine. Arafat said he was responding to an offer by Ezer Weizman, conveyed to him by an unidentified journalist at the PNC meeting in Algiers, to discuss the idea of setting up a Palestinian state that would be confederated with Israel. Chairman Arafat's offer to meet with any Israeli leader and to discuss the possibility of even an integrated democratic Arab–Jewish state over all of Palestine was calculated to demonstrate the extent to which he was prepared to go in bringing an end to the internecine conflict.

Once again the Israeli response was negative. On the same day that Arafat made these statements (6 May 1987), a spokesman for Shamir said, 'We are ready to negotiate with Jordan, Syria, with every sovereign state [but] not with an organization whose aim is bloodshed and killing'. Shimon Peres responded angrily to a 'charge' by Shamir that the Israeli Labour Party was willing to negotiate with the PLO by saying, 'the Labour Party is not going to negotiate with the PLO and opposes inviting the PLO to an international conference'. It is interesting to note that Israel conducted at least fourteen air raids on Lebanon during the period between January and May 1987. On Wednesday, 6 May 1987, ten civilians were killed and on the previous Friday, eighteen. By Sunday, 10 May, the total killed was thirty-seven, those wounded numbered 119. The West Bank and Gaza Strip remains under military occupation, their inhabitants subjected daily to killings and degredations of various kinds.

By any civilized standard, acts of violence and terror are ugly and inhuman phenomena, especially when they are directed against innocent civilians. But in questioning the meaning of terrorism one must ask: is it legitimate for certain peoples and not for others? Were Menachem Begin or Yitzhak Shamir terrorists when they were fighting for what they considered a national cause? Israel, with its Zionist outreach throughout the Western world, has convinced the West that its terror activities against civilian towns and villages, raids on refugee camps and bombings and raids as far as Baghdad, Beirut and Entebbe are legitimate. Israel has succeeded also in diverting attention from the causes of terrorism to its results.

The daily terror under which the Arab world exists, particularly the Palestinians, Jordanians, Lebanese and Syrians on the individual and national levels, exacts too high a price. According to Arab culture in Islam, 'Peace is the master of all judgements'. Peace is the only answer but it has to be an honourable, just, comprehensive and permanent peace, not a peace reflecting the military realities of the present. The present leadership in the Arab world now is moderate and has been working towards peace. However it matters what form the peace is in; it should not be peace at any price, but a peace that this and future generations can live with. The present weakness and disarray of the Arab world cannot continue indefinitely.

A major ingredient of the peace that Jordan and the Arabs seek is for Israel to abandon its designs for further expansion along with its superior attitude towards the area and its peoples. Instead of viewing itself as an advanced outpost of Western civilization, it must learn to live with the people in the region on terms of mutual respect. It must define its identity, its limits, indeed its very geographical borders, otherwise it will continue to live in insecurity however far it may expand and conquer. Whenever it may expand, it will be surrounded by Arabs. While this may be the era of Zionist hegemony, we also recognize the weakness as well as the intrinsic and as yet unutilized strength in the Arab world itself. In defining itself Israel will not only settle down in the area in some modicum of normality, but it will also enhance the stability of the area and devote its resources to its own peaceful development. Defining Israel's borders is also by definition the delineation of the Lebanese,

Syrian, Jordanian, Palestinian and even Egyptian boundaries as well.

Peace as presently envisaged by Jordan is the answer, otherwise the moderation shown by Arab leaders today may one way or another degenerate into another cycle of violence. Israeli radicals, whether conscious of it or not, are the best allies of Arab radicalism now lurking in the background. Israeli intransigence since 1967 in reaching a meaningful resolution of the conflict is manifested in their policy of distorting facts on the ground in the occupied territories, in their outreach of violence in Lebanon and elsewhere, in their disdain of international law and order, and in their constant manoeuvrings, and manipulation of events to avoid a peaceful settlement. In the long run, it is they who invite Arab radicalism to come to the surface once again. Aware of these facts, King Hussein has worked tirelessly since 1967 to bring about a negotiated settlement.

Arab sovereignty over East Jerusalem, as well as the evacuation of the West Bank, the Gaza Strip and the establishment of the Palestinian state, are some of the ingredients of the peaceful settlement envisaged by Jordan. Such a vision was encompassed by the Fez Peace Plan of 1982 and pertinent United Nations resolutions. Other elements of this peaceful settlement include the evacuation of the Syrian Golan Heights, Lebanon and Taba. Peace is as simple or as difficult to achieve as people will make it. In looking over Israel's record in the past two decades and its euphoria of success particularly since 1967, the prospects for peace are grim.

There are many obstacles to peace and not least of them is the fragmentation and disarray of the Arab world. Arab lack of consensus, in addition to military weakness, is the major contributing factor to their present weightlessness in regional and international affairs. Such a condition has been encouraged and cleverly manipulated by Israel. The exclusion since 1967 of a meaningful European and Soviet input towards a peaceful resolution of the conflict has been another factor. Concomitant with this development has been the thus far negative influence of the United States whose support of Israel seems inexhaustible. Such US support led to King Hussein's refusal to visit the United States in 1987 in protest at the part played by the Reagan administration in the continuing stalemate.

The last major obstacle to peace has been Israeli reluctance to reach a peaceful settlement. A few remarks seem to be in order here. The Arabs and the Israelis have now swapped approaches, with the Arabs now suing for peace while Israel vacillates, uncertain what it wants. This latter situation has been exacerbated since the 1984

Israeli elections and the establishment of the two-headed coalition cabinet. The Arab–Israeli military imbalance has also been a contributory factor. Finally, in looking over the Arab–Israeli–American triangular factors since 1967, and in projecting these into the future, little hope seems to emerge for the prospects of peace in the area.

The Iran–Iraq war

In the southern combat zone along the borders of Iran and Iraq the heat of the summer may reach 50 degrees centigrade. With the stench of blood, festering wounds and gunpowder and the desolation wreaked on the terrain, the conflict often descends to barbaric depths. This is another illogical conflict. It seemed as if an irresistable force has met with an immovable object. No one knows the price even in material terms. Billions of dollars, the depletion of once healthy national treasuries, the destruction of villages, towns, cities and economic and military installations and a halt in development plans. The psychological damage and the rekindling of ancient animosities and hatreds, real and imagined, cannot be fathomed either. The grim statistics speak of as many as a million youths death on one side and about one-third that number on the other. Most families in both countries have dead to mourn.

Iran had the edge in human resources and in ideological commitment. By the tens of thousands, youths with bandanas around their heads squat on the ground pounding their chests with their fists, proclaiming 'At your command, Oh Lord, at your command' as they listen to their commanders in preparation for joining combat. Around their necks they carry the key to Heaven – (through) 'martyrdom'.

Opposing this fierce and primordial religious fervor is a country with a secular ideology and superior military hardware. With the ethnic and religious diversity of Iraq, the secularism of the Ba'ath Party constitutes a common ground, the lowest common denominator upon which the various ethnic and religious groups can agree. In the beginning as well as now, Iraq's aims were limited. It wanted to impress upon Iran the need for Iraqi territory, its objection to the occupation of the three islands of Abu Musa and Lesser and Greater Tunb, and Iranian claims on Kuwait and Bahrain.

The border dispute is a historical one. Iran's claim to supremacy over the Gulf area and to the annexation of certain parts of it, date back to the early sixteenth century. The rise of the Sunni Ottoman Empire (1516) in the West coincided with the assumption to power of the Safavid dynasty in Iran (1502) and its adoption of the *Ithna'ashari* from Shii Islam. Before the 1975 Algiers treaty became defunct, the immediate cause of the war in 1981, several treaties were concluded between the Ottomans and Iran in an attempt to delineate the common border. Major treaties were concluded in 1555, 1558, 1590, 1618, 1639, 1746, 1823, 1847, 1911, 1913, 1914, 1937 and 1975. Throughout the Ottoman period its sultans frequently mobilized to deter Iran from occupying Iraq.

Though modern Iran has been a largely independent, unified state with recognized borders for almost 500 years, Iraq's establishment followed the conclusion of the First World War. Yet, since the 1920s, in both countries nationalism has been thwarted and frustrated. Iran, with greater territory, resources and an ancient culture antedating Islam, began thinking of itself, especially since the advent of the Pahlavi dynasty, as a power that should have primacy, even hegemony, over the entire Gulf region. The term 'Pahlavi' adopted by Reza Shah, father of the late Shahanshah Mohammad Reza, refers to the rulers of ancient Parthia; the old name, Iran, was also adopted in 1935 to replace the more recent Hellenistic name Persia. Iran's distinguished and distinctive national character is of ancient origin. When Islam came to Iran, Iran had its own Aryan racial roots, its own distinctive language and its own distinctive Zoroastrian religion. That the Arab conquest did not break Iran's historical continuity and their adoption of Shiism is seen by some observers as a subconscious attempt at the maintenance of a separate distinctiveness and cultural identity. Ahmad Khasrawi (1890–1946), a modern Iranian historian, advocated a return to a form of Zoroastrianism while the Iranvij society, a group of intellectuals formed in Reza Shah's time, still argued that 'the Arabs never conquered Iran; according to them, Shiism is Zoroastrianism in Muslim clothing'. The territorial dispute is thus reinforced by religious, national and even personal rivalry. That the Shiah holy places of Najaf, Kerbala and Kazimein are within Iraqi territory compounds the issue.

The Iranian revolution with its transnational pan-Islamic ideology seeks a total war in which it will refashion the image of its adversary into a copy of its own. How dare Iraq with its secular ideology and its young leadership stand in its path: the path, or its version thereof, of Islamic resurgence and revival? The vision of the future held by the elderly Imam Ayatollah Ruhollah Khomeini was at drastic variance with that of the forty-six-year-old secular Saddam Hussein.

Both Iran and Iraq are developing countries undergoing the agonies of transition from one level of life to another. The discovery, by both, of their weakness *vis-à-vis* the Western intrusion in military, economic and cultural terms was indeed a shock. The initial response of the two countries was similar though more advanced in the Iranian case because of the determined, though with hindsight disastrous, efforts of the Shah to modernize the country. The Shah's own delusions of grandeur could not be absorbed by the average man who could not relate to the tremendous changes taking place which encroached upon every aspect of his life, even his very soul. Alienation and bewilderment were further intensified by a severely repressive regime that tolerated no adverse opinion and acted literally, though illigitimately, as the fountain of ultimate truth. The Shah paved the way for the Imam and this time the ruler speaks in the name of a truly ultimate truth; that it is his own version of the truth is another matter but to the average Iranian, especially in the villages, small towns and rural areas, he smoothly moved under its aegis. The religious charisma of the clergyman clashed violently with that of the secular leader.

Where do the two countries go from here? No one knows the extent of the damage already done: militarily, economically and psychologically. And while Jordan supported Iraq from the beginning, it also realized the tragic consequences of the continuation of hostilities and the threat to the security of the entire Middle East region.

The power struggle between the two neighbours has already created a power vacuum in the area. Under threat, the nations of the area have abandoned all pretence to non-alignment.

Although Jordan has supported Iraq from the outset, it always viewed the conflict as a lamentable affair that should never have taken place. Hence Jordan worked for and supported every effort to bring a negotiated settlement. Its support of Iraq is prompted by its commitment to the Joint Arab Defence Treaty under the Arab League Charter as well as its realization that should Islamic radicalism not be contained, the danger to the stability of the whole region would be immense.

Iraq's efforts to bring Iran to the negotiating table eventually prevailed, but just as the Arab–Israeli conflict and that of Lebanon has proven, it is easier to start a war in the Middle East than to bring it to a conclusion. These two conflicts, each with their own distinctive internal characteristics and external connections, deteriorated into wars of attrition. And while the bloodshed has ceased in one conflict, the other has developed its own eruptions, lulls and momentum, with rhetoric on the national, regional and international levels building its own momentum with no easy end in sight.

Suggested further reading

Abu Jaber, K. (1985), 'Jordan's view of the regional factors affecting peace in the Middle East', in S. Hunter (ed.) *Political and Economic Trends in the Middle East*, Westview Press, Boulder, Colo.

—— (1986), 'The Iran–Iraq war: regime security and regional security', in M. Ayoob (ed.) *Regional Security in the Third World*, Croom Helm, London.

Amin, H. (1981), *Shat al-Arab wa Wad'uh at-Tarikhi (The Historical Background of the Arabian Gulf)*, Dar al-Hurriyah, Baghdad.

Ayoob, M. (ed.) (1986), *Regional Security In The Third World*, Croom Helm, London.

Bill, J. (1983), 'The Arab world and the challenge of Iran', *Journal of Arab Affairs*, Vol. 2.

Bin Talal, Crown Prince Hassan of Jordan (1981), *Palestinian Self-Determination*, Quartet Books, London.

—— (1984), *Search For Peace*, Macmillan, London.

Binder, L. (1964), *The Ideological Revolution In The Middle East*, John Wiley, New York.

—— (1965), 'Iranian nationalism', in B. Rivlin and J. S. Szyliowicz (eds), *The Contemporary Middle East*, Random House, New York.

Brown, L. C. (1984), *International Politics and the Middle East*, Princeton University Press, Princeton.

Cottam, R. (1984), 'The Iran–Iraq war', *Current History*, January.

Day, A. R. (1986), *East Bank/West Bank*, Council on Foreign Relations, New York.

Dekmedjian, H. (1980), 'The anatomy of Islamic revival: legitimacy, crisis, ethnic conflict and the search for Islamic alternatives', *The Middle East Journal*.

Findley, P. (1985), *They Dare To Speak Out*, Lawrence Hill, Westport, Conn.

Ghareed, E. (1983), 'The forgotten war', *American–Arab Affairs Journal*, No. 5.

Green, S. (1984), *Taking Sides*, William Morrow, New York.

—— (1986), 'Sliding toward war', *The American Arab Affairs Journal*, No. 18.

Grummon, S. R. (1982), *The Iran–Iraq War: Islam Embattled*, Praeger, New York.

Harb, O. al-Ghazaly (1986), 'The Gulf Co-operation Council and regional security in the Gulf', in M. Ayoob (ed.) *Regional Security in the Third World*, Croom Helm, London.

Helms, C. M. (1983), 'The Iraqi dilemma: political objectives versus military strategy', *The American–Arab Affairs Journal*, Summer, No. 5.

Hudson, M. (1986), 'The conflicts of the Middle East: their importance for Americans', *American–Arab Affairs Journal*, No. 18.

Ismael, T. (1982), *Iraq and Iran: Roots of Conflict*, Syracuse University Press, Syracuse.

Jureidini, P. and McLauren, R. D. (1984), *Jordan*, Praeger, New York.

al-Mashat, A. (1986), 'The Arab–Israeli conflict: a view from Cairo', in M. Ayoob (ed.) *Regional Security in the Third World*, Croom Helm, London.

Miller, A. D. (1986), 'Jordan and the Arab–Israeli conflict: the Hashemite predicament', *ORBIS*, Winter.

Neuman, R. G. (1986), 'Disarray in the Middle East: is there any light at the end of the tunnel', The American–Arab Affairs Journal, No. 18.

al-Rawi, I. (1981), *Shat al-Arab Fi al-Manzur al-Qanuni Abr al-Tarikh (Shat al-Arab from the Legal Point of View Throughout History)*, Dar al-Hurriyah, Baghdad.

Saunders, H. H. (1986), 'US policy and Middle East peace: a critical view', *The American–Arab Affairs Journal*, No. 18.

Shikara, A. A. (1985), *al-Dawr al-Istratiji Li al-Wilayat al-Muttahidah al-Amrikiyyah Fi Mantiqat al-Khaleej al-Arabi Hatta Muntasaf al-Thamaninat (The Strategic Role of the United States until the Mid 1980s)*, Matba'at Kazim, Dubai.

Shipler, D. K. (1986), *Arab and Jew*, Times Books, New York.

Stempel, J. D. (1981), *Inside The Iranian Revolution*, Indiana University Press, Bloomington, Ind.

Chapter eleven

Jordan's foreign policy: regional and international implications
Saleh A. Al-Zu'bi

Introduction

Jordan is a small country of fascinating contrasts. Historically and politically it is very new, yet very old. The ruins of its empires of antiquity are linked with modern highways. Its physical climate ranges from arid desert to green mountainous and hilly areas. Its people are mostly Moslems, but many of its shrines are also sacred to Christian and Jewish pilgrims (see Copeland 1972, pp. 9–12).

Like many states in the Middle East, Jordan has been influenced by the social, economic, political and ideological problems which have dominated the region since the beginning of the century (see Vatikiotis 1972, pp. 77–89). Problems of social and political progress, modernization, ethnic and religious aspirations, the Arab–Israeli conflict and the clashing of individual state interests have left their mark on the internal and external policies of many countries in the Middle East, including Jordan (Vatikiotis 1972, pp. 89–115).

Located at the centre of the Arab world, Jordan's foreign policy is a function mainly of its response to the volatile circumstances surrounding the Middle East. This of course implies a special readiness and farsightedness of decision makers in Jordan to cope with the diversity and magnitude of these circumstances and currents in the region (see Al-Maranati et al. 1971, pp. 231–48).

Given the persistence of inter-Arab differences on the form and substance of any joint Arab cooperation, and given the scarcity of the domestic resources, Jordan is forced to steer a moderate and flexible policy which has to be carefully measured to ensure the stability, security and development of the country. Such a policy should be able to deal with the problems of the Arab–Israeli conflict, the plight of the Palestinian people and the resistance movements, the role of the major powers in the area, questions of inter-Arab rivalry, and the country's dependence on foreign assistance (Al-Maranati *et al.* 1971, p. 248).

The story of Jordan and the challenges it has been facing was nobly summarized in King Hussein's address to the European Parliament at Strasbourg in 1983 when he said:

> Jordan is the land of a courageous, dynamic and proud people who never bent before adversities. They have striven to display a positive example to others through clarity of vision, courage and dedication and built, despite huge obstacles and an uncertain future for our entire area and all who live in it, a modern stable oasis of peace and harmony along the longest cease fire line of any Arab State with Israel and the occupied territories.
>
> (Al-Hussein 1983, pp. 5–10)

The foreign policy of Jordan is broadly based on the following principles.

1 On a regional level, it is based on the principles of Arab and Islamic solidarity, and functions according to its commitments to the charter of the Arab League and the Arab summit decision. The restoration of Arab solidarity and the defence of the Arab common interests have been repeatedly emphasized by the King and translated by the Jordanian government into policies and practices. In his address to Parliament's fourth regular session on 2 November 1986, King Hussein stated:

> 'By the grace of God and the cooperation of the brotherly Arab leaders, we revived and developed bilateral relations with each Arab state individually. It is our hope that bilateral relations will develop in such a manner as to lead to a collective understanding which will restore Arab solidarity to its proper place. Bilateral relations, positive though they may be, cannot be, a substitute for collective Arab action.
>
> (Al-Hussein 1986).

2 On the international level, Jordan's foreign policy is based on the principles of non-alignment, the commitment to the charter of the United Nations, and fostering of the spirit of the Islamic solidarity and cooperation (see Al-Hussein 1985).

In addressing the fortieth session of the General Assembly, King Hussein also praised the role of the United Nations and strongly voiced Jordan's adherence to its charter. He said:

> During its forty years, the United Nations has achieved, through its specialized agencies which rendered invaluable services to the

international community at large, as well as through its General Assembly and its organs, a number of spectacular results. Wherever an armed conflict has broken out, it has been there to mediate between the warring factions, or to separate them. When millions of innocent people have been turned to refugees, it has been there to provide assistance.

(Al-Hussein 1985)

Referring to the Palestinian question, and the responsibility of the United Nations, he added: 'It is our hope that it will soon come to an end by arriving at a just, durable and comprehensive settlement of the Palestinian problem and related issues. This should be done in accordance with the United Nations Charter and in the implementation of is resolutions.'

To determine the scope and dynamics of the political process in Jordan one has to take the following topics into consideration (Abu Odeh 1986).

Factors influencing Jordanian foreign policy

Geopolitical or physical factors

If Egypt nowadays is the clearest example of the embodiment of the connection between foreign policy and economy in the Arab area, Jordan is the clearest example of the embodiment of the connection between foreign policy and geographical location. Naturally, this does not negate in either case the presence of other factors that influence the directions of their foreign policies but the economy in Egypt's case and the geography in Jordan's case are the two most important factors in influencing their respective policies.

Jordan is surrounded by five countries, each of which has at least one source of power which Jordan lacks. To the west there is Israel, which is superior to Jordan in military strength and is allied to one of the superpowers, the United States. To the north there is Syria, which has a military, demographic and psychological edge over Jordan and has a friendship treaty with another of the superpowers, the Soviet Union. To the east there is Iraq, known for its military, demographic and economic strength, which also has a friendship treaty with the Soviet Union. To the south-west there is Egypt, which enjoys demographic, cultural and military strength. Finally, to the south there is Saudi Arabia, which possesses financial strength (Abu Odeh 1986, p. 4). Moreover, Jordan is geographically the closest Arab country to Palestine and has the longest borderline with it, and thus it has been the most affected by the cause of its people.

Since the mid-1950s, Jordan's location has forced it to adopt a position of neutrality in its regional policy amidst the forces that surround it, and when the area witnessed disputes between some countries, Jordan's first priority was always to stay safely out of these disputes (Abu Odeh 1986, pp. 5–7).

If disputes couldn't be totally avoided, then Jordan would ally itself with another country to achieve an equal distribution of power. For instance, when the United Arab Republic was founded between Syria and Egypt in 1958, Jordan formed an alliance that same year with Iraq under the Hashemite Union. When the revolt of 14 July occurred in Iraq and the union was disrupted, Jordan turned to a foreign power, Britain, to contain the results of disruptions as a preliminary step to reestablishing a redistribution of power.

Jordan's Arab policy stems from a deep conviction that a stable and developing Jordan cannot continue without the existence of a healthy Arab atmosphere in which it can live and interact. Consequently any alliance with any country in the region would be a temporary one, with the intention of achieving a distribution of power, under which Jordan, along with other countries, can contribute to normalizing relations in the Arab world.

Perhaps the policy maintained by Jordan at the present time is a good example of that. When the Arabs boycotted Egypt following the Baghdad summit of 1978, Jordan was keen to maintain informal relations and avoid open hostility. Jordan renewed its diplomatic relations with Egypt in 1984, then in 1985 it renewed its ties with Syria, while at the same time it clearly and solidly supported Iraq in its war with Iran. Under this policy Jordan was able to have dialogues with all conflicting Arab factions and to contribute, along with other countries, to establishing a unified Arab view of the dangers threatening the Arab world. In other words, although Jordan boycotted Egypt along with the other Arab countries, it did not hesitate to reestablish relations with it when it sensed a growth of imbalance of power and a threat to the Arab world. Jordan also did not hesitate in responding to the Committee of Settling Differences in the autumn of 1985, and Jordan was the party that initiated relations with Syria, while Syria allied itself with Iran.

On the international level, Jordan is seeking to transform its geographical location from a liability – where regional forces are concerned – into an asset – where international forces are concerned. In other words, Jordan constantly tries to increase its strategic importance so as to remain in a powerful position. There are a number of political and economic factors that can help Jordan. These include:

1 the strategic importance of the region, and its oil wealth;
2 the competition among industrialized nations for the Arab consumer markets;
3 the importance of the Arab world as a transit route to the East from Europe;
4 the struggle between the two superpowers to consolidate their areas of influence while avoiding confrontation (Abu Odeh 1986).

At the first glance, Jordan might not seem to have much importance in the light of these facts. It does not have a large consumer market like Egypt, Saudi Arabia and Iraq, nor is it an oil-producing country, and its location does not affect international trade. Moreover, Jordan does not have any friendship or defence treaties and thus has no foreign military bases. Yet Jordan, by virtue of its location, can play a negative or positive influence on the interests of the major powers in the area through the enactment of its regional role. Jordan's self-ordained regional role can be manifested in shouldering the following responsibilities:

1 the role of mediator between the different stands and viewpoints of the Arab states in the Middle East to preserve harmony among them, and to protect and develop the concept of Arab regional order;
2 the role of the calming element in the region, and the unappointed official spokesman for the voice of moderation;
3 the role of assistance to the conservative Arab states, namely the states of the Gulf Cooperation Council (GCC), since the regional security of Jordan and these states is more or less integrated.

Jordan has in the past sent military delegations to a number of Gulf states to assist them in organizing and training their armies, and this assistance continues, though at a reduced level. It also sends civilians to aid these states in building up their administrative and educational networks. At the same time Jordan still receives delegations from different Arab Gulf states in its military academies for study and training, due to the confidence these states have in Jordan's military standards and in Jordan's commitment to the rules of professionalism in its military policy.

As for the superpowers, despite their competition, they are generally satisfied with Jordan's regional role as long as Jordan has a calming effect which, along with the other elements, prevents confrontation between states in the area. The superpowers have a tacit agreement to keep the conflict in the Middle East under control.

Perhaps the best example of the superpowers' desire to

avoid any confrontation with each other was in 1970. At that time Jordan was trying to restore law and order, and the Jordanian armed forces clashed with the fighters of the PLO. This prompted Syria, an ally of the PLO at that time, to invade Jordanian territory and clash with the Jordanian armed forces. When the armed forces settled the situation and rebuffed the Syrian invasion by utilizing the Jordanian Air Force alongside the army, the Soviet Union pressed Syria not to escalate its operations by sending in new troops, especially the Syrian Air Force. The Soviet stand stemmed from its fear of a major confrontation with the United States, which had placed its Sixth Fleet in the Mediterranean on alert.

The United States is as satisfied as the Soviet Union with Jordan's position of restraining Arab–Israeli tension. The United States is also satisfied with Jordan's role in assisting the Arab Gulf states and coordinating with them in matters of training and defence (Terrill 1985a). These states are important for the United States' oil strategy in the area. Jordan does not constitute a threat to these states – it is rather a source of support for them. The same logic applies to Western Europe's perception of Jordan's regional role.

As for the significance of Jordan's geographical location within the framework of the region, it has always been important for transit commerce from south to north and vice versa. In this perspective, Jordan is especially important for its neighbouring countries. Iraq recognized the importance of Jordan throughout its conflict with Iran, especially access to the port of Aqaba for strategic imports. Jordanian support to Iraq in the Gulf War has involved a number of different policies including the provision of a Jordanian supply corridor for war materials, diplomatic backing in the inter-Arab and global political arenas, and various forms of low-level military support. Jordanian diplomatic and political support for Iraq throughout the war was vital. Jordan has helped to bridge the political gap between Iraq and the Arab monarchies of the Arabian peninsula (Terril 1985b).

Where Syria is concerned, Jordan's importance to it rates as highly as Syria's importance to Jordan. But since the Iran–Iraq War, and as a result of the closing of the borders between Syria and Iraq, Jordan has become economically more important for Syria because it has become its only land passageway to the whole Arab peninsula and Africa. The same can be said, to a lesser degree, regarding Jordan's importance with respect to Saudi Arabia, Egypt and Turkey.

As for Israel, Jordan has the longest border with Israel. It is also the largest barrier standing between the Arab Gulf states and Israel's future ambitions for economic and financial control of the region.

Resources

One of Jordan's primary problems is the discrepancy existing between Jordan's meagre natural resources on the one hand, and the size and growing needs of its population on the other. The geographical location of Jordan imposed the heaviest burden of the Palestinian tragedy of 1948. Then the population of the country suddenly tripled. This imbalance between resources and population forced Jordan into a state of dependency on other states, from which Jordan is still struggling to get away.

The story of Jordan's dependency on others to close the gap between its resources and its needs has gone through many stages (Al-Maranati *et al.* 1971, pp. 236–8). Until 1965, Jordan's dependency was largely on Britain, but in 1966–7 this economic and financial dependency moved to the Arab countries who could not fulfil their commitments. This forced Jordan in 1967–8 to transfer its dependency to the United States. Since 1973 Jordan's dependency has been on the Arab Gulf states who provided significant aid and job opportunities that enabled Jordanians to earn much needed foreign exchange.

Now, one of the major concerns of Jordan is how to revive the economy and restore the high growth rate achieved prior to 1982. The recession which the Arab petroleum-exporting countries faced in 1984 reflected adversely on the Jordanian economy. Pursuant to the Bahgdad agreement, the Arab petroleum-exporting countries pledged themselves in 1978 to grant Jordan economic aid worth $1,250 billion to supplement the Jordanian budget for the completion of some economic projects. In 1984, however, this aid dwindled to $660 million, almost half of the original sum, and it has declined further since.

The situation in the neighbouring Arab countries is still no better, in fact in some aspects it is even worse. The oil prices have sharply fallen, jeopardizing the social and economic plans of Gulf States, the Iraq–Iran War drags on and the situation in Lebanon continues to be fraught with extreme uncertainty. In view of this, it is natural that Jordan should orient its regional policy toward the role of balance-keeper between the countries of the region, and to endeavour to maintain cordial relations with them all.

History

The historical dimension as a factor influencing political decisions is clear in Jordan's foreign policy. By history we mean the self-image that Jordan possesses in the consciousness of its leaders and population. The essence of this self-image is that Jordan cannot but be an Arab state in character and distinction. Its policy must be directed to the Arab cause and Arab solidarity for the following reasons (Abu Odeh 1986).

1 Jordan's royal family is an extension of the Hashemite family of Mecca, a family which has been chosen at the beginning of this century by Arabs to lead the great Arab Revolt.
2 The Hashemite family embodies two major dimensions in the Arab nationalistic character: the religious dimension and the historical dimension.
3 Jordan is the only remaining Arab land that still adopts the Hashemite rule. This makes Jordan the only remaining state that symbolizes the legitimacy of the Arab nationalistic character in both its religious dimension and the historical dimensions after the dissolution of the Hashemite rule from Syria, the Hijaz and Iraq respectively.
4 The Jordanian population who supported Emir Abdullah, founder of the Kingdom, shared the prince's ambition and expectations that Jordan should be the centre for the liberation of Greater Syria from its colonizers with the aim of unifying it, thus achieving one of the central goals of the great Arab revolt.
5 These ideals, matured and deeply rooted throughout the years in the education and cultural programmes, became psychologically, historically and politically the fundamental basis of the Jordanian Arab national consciousness.

In addressing the European Parliament in 1983, King Hussein emphasized these ideals, and the challenges he faces as a Hashemite leader:

> The country which I have had the honour to have served the greater part of my life, the Hashemite Kingdom of Jordan, is a part of the greater Arab Nation. The Arab and Hashemite struggle throughout history has been one and the same. I am a proud descendant of the prophet Mohammed, of the house of Hashem, of the tribe of *qureish*, the oldest and the most eminent family in Arabia. I am the grandson of Hussein Bin Ali, the chosen leader of the great Arab revolt often known as the great Arab revival, which started at the beginning of this century. I am the grandson of Abdullah the founder of the Hashemite Kingdom

of Jordan. Throughout my life I have felt, and continue to feel, humbled before the example of my forefathers for their total dedication and commitment to the honourable and just cause of the Arabs – to their sacred right to live in freedom, dignity and peace. My country has committed itself to the defence of Arab freedom, security, stability and the right to progress in the entire Arab World.

(Al-Hussein 1983, pp. 1–7)

This historical dimension, along with dependency and geographical location, have played a major role in reshaping the structure and direction of Jordan's national and regional policy. Such a policy was not fundamentally the result of selfish attitudes and reactions, but rather it stemmed from a deep faith in the Arab cause and a keen and deliberate policy.

Jordan is anxious to regain the vitality of the Arab solidarity which began to deteriorate in the second half of the 1970s, when a number of Arab states started unilaterally to deal with regional and international issues, instead of handling them within the framework of joint Arab action.

As we notice, dependency, geographic location and the historical dimension have all contributed in shaping and emphasizing the Arab nationalistic approach in Jordan's regional policy. Such an approach stems from Jordan's commitment to the Arab common interests, more than to state-centred interests, in dealing with regional matters. It also explains Jordan's need to create a healthy atmosphere in which it can interact and cooperate easily.

Jordan's adherence to the principles of Arab solidarity and its non-alignment with any of the two superpowers stems from its need to avoid political pressures in conducting its regional and international diplomacy. However, continuation and success of this policy under such delicate and complicated circumstances is rather miraculous.

Constraints on the formulation and operation of Jordanian foreign policy

Because of its geopolitical location, and because of the deteriorating economic, military and social situations in the region, Jordan is bound to face many challenges which must be taken into consideration in the course of the formulation and execution of its foreign policy. Some of these constraints are as follows.

There is a discrepancy between the available resources and the needs and expectations of the state. This pressing factor is apparent in Jordan's relations with the Arab Gulf states from whom Jordan receives aid. These states are also important markets for both agricultural and manufactured goods. The number of Jordanian citizens working in the Gulf states is estimated at 350,000. These workers remit considerable amounts of foreign currency. For this and other reasons Jordan is very careful to maintain cordial relations with these states, based on understanding, cooperation and mutual interest. This requires that Jordanian policy makers keep contacts with these states on the highest level through the signing of agreements in all fields of cooperation. In the light of the economic difficulties in the region, Jordan needs to restructure its economy and define its priorities, especially in the fields of energy and water utilization. There is a growing need in Jordan for water. This problem is getting more urgent in the light of the policies and practice of other neighbouring countries, especially Israel and Syria.

The demographic formula

By the demographic formula we mean the Jordanian Palestinian presence in Jordan. Jordan's internal politics and its foreign and regional relations have been increasingly determined by the Palestinian problem since 1948 (Peretz 1969, pp. 354–7).

This factor needs wise and delicate consideration because the slightest mistake in dealing with it would turn it into a dividing and weakening factor rather than one of strength for the country. The demographic factor has been playing an effective role in Jordan's foreign policy since 1948. Its influence ranged from negative to positive according to the developments of the Palestinian cause. Although it emerged when the PLO was established in 1964, it did not take on a serious dimension until June 1967, when along with other factors it influenced Jordan's decision to enter the war on the side of Egypt. It emerged clearly again in March 1972 through the United Arab Kingdom plan (Peretz, 1969, p. 355).

Under this plan, the Kingdom would federate a Jordanian regime with one in Palestine or the West Bank. Jerusalem would be the Palestinian capital; Amman would be capital of the Jordanian region, and the federal capital. Although the King would rule both regions, there would be autonomy for both, and a federal council of ministers. Again in 1974 it emerged in the Rabat Summit when Jordan and Arab States decided to recognize the PLO as the sole authorized representative of the Palestinian people. Since then the demographic factor has become strong enough to impose itself on the process of the formulation of Jordan's foreign policy on the regional and international levels.

In spite of the political importance of the Rabat decision, little has changed in the relation between the West Bank and Jordan since 1974. In fact Jordan's intention to preserve the traditional links with the West Bank has become more intense. The long-standing economic and family ties between the two banks of Jordan have continued under the open bridges policy, and these now also encompass Gaza. In November 1974, King Hussein stated that Jordan would continue to pay some 6,000 officials in the West Bank who worked for the government prior to 1967. Economic links have been strengthened by Jordan's increased imports from the West Bank and by its continued extension of development grants and loans to firms and industries in the West Bank. Private Jordanian loans to the West Bank municipalities are still guaranteed by the Jordanian Government.

Perhaps one of the most obvious manifestations of the Jordanian–Palestinian formula was Jordan's adoption of the comprehensive development plan for the West Bank. The Jordanian leadership perceived this formula and deal with it within the framework of the great Arab revolt 'in which the existence of social, religious, ethnic and regional pluralism is one of its basic assumptions'. The Hashemites looked at the demographic factor in its popularistic dimension as a strengthening factor, rather than a weakening one in Arab political and social life.

This wise and perceptive view stands behind the progress and development Jordan has undergone in spite of its scarce resources. Nowadays, social and political pluralism is not just a view, rather it has become a deliberate policy for the government since the establishment of the Hashemite Kingdom of Jordan. However, one cannot lose sight of the fact that pluralism might be very dangerous when it is merely dealt with as a political problem (Abu Odeh 1986).

Israel

Israel represents one of the major constraints on Jordan's regional and international policy. Jordan has always to be on the alert toward the vastly superior military strength of Israel. Technically speaking Jordan is in a state of war with Israel. Under the present circumstances, and because of Israel's military superiority and unpredictable expansionist policies, Jordan has to moderate its tactics, as follows, to avoid Israeli reactions.

1 It should not provoke Israel by letting Palestinian organizations

operate from Jordanian territory in a guerrilla war against Israel, or in any other military action in the absence of a comprehensive Arab military plan, because

- any Israeli military action against Jordan, especially along the border, could damage Jordan's economic resources such as the agricultural projects in the Ghor Valley, the potassium plant, and the port of Aqaba;
- an Israeli attack could destroy the water resources that are used in agriculture in the Ghor Valley;
- Israel might exploit any military tension as an excuse for deporting Palestinian people from the occupied territories;
- Jordan might be forced to use up all its limited financial resources.

In this perspective, any military confrontation between Jordan and Israel is out of the question unless it stems from a solid and unified Arab defensive stand; otherwise, the tragedy of the 1967 War will be repeated.

2 Jordan should not contribute to the change of status quo or the balance of power between Israel and the Arab countries without taking the necessary precaution and preparation. In Israel's view the imbalance of power might occur when Jordan and one of its Arab neighbours are united, or when there is a substantial Arab military force installed on Jordanian territory, or when Jordan acquires destructive weapons that might threaten Israeli residential areas, or when Jordan enters into an alliance which Israel might consider as a threat to Israeli security.

3 It should not provoke Israel by using water sources which Israel claims as her own on a *de facto* basis and in the absence of an agreement on water resources between Israel on one hand, and Jordan and Syria on the other.

Mechanisms of Jordanian foreign policy

The Jordanian political system has continued to revolve around His Majesty King Hussein since his accesssion to the throne in 1953. Foreign policy and decision making are in his domain. It is the King who outlines Jordan foreign policy and supervises its implementation. He is considered crucial for the execution of foreign policy through his global relations and the utilization of his personal relations with many world leaders. His political beliefs, his reason and his experience as a ruler mean he can establish strong, personal relations with leaders of the world, and establish good bilateral relations between Jordan and other states.

In the field of Arab politics, the King believes as a Hashemite in Arab nationalism and Arab unity. However, his interpretation of Arab nationalism is quite different from other Arab leaders in the area who advocated other variants of Arab nationalism. To him Arab nationalism means:

> . . . the ultimate loyalty of the individual to the Arab world as a whole; it demands that a Jordanian be an Arab first and a Jordanian second, an Iraqi an Arab first and an Iraqi second, loyalties to lesser concepts have seriously weakened our ability to pursue constructive policies.

With regard to Arab unity, King Hussein calls for a debate on the practical steps to be undertaken, as the principles of Arab unity have already been agreed upon. There are, he said, four natural units in the Arab-speaking world: the fertile crescent, the Arabian peninsula, the Nile Valley and the Maghreb. As to practical steps towards Arab unity he suggests:

> Let the countries in these natural units associate themselves in whatever way they choose, as a step towards the great goal of the Arab nation. Let their association be voluntary, and let it embrace only what the people of each country want to embrace, whether it be cultural, economics, or defence – let political alliance, if it is desirable at all, be the last step. To such a proposal Jordan pledges the full weight of its power and strength – it would subscribe immediately to any practical step designed to realise it. Our only plea is for well considered action.
>
> (Al-Hussein quoted in Khadduri 1981, pp. 106–7)

In regional politics the King believes and maintains a moderate and neutralistic policy towards rival neighbouring countries. 'If he found himself drawn into an alliance with one neighbour, or joining a coalition of one bloc against another, he very soon reverted to traditional neutrality' and normal relations (Abudiah 1985). The King's foreign policy consists of the principle of 'asserting Jordan's independence, pursuing a neutralistic policy with neighbours, and coming to an understanding (formal or informal) with a great power that would protect that independence.' (Khadduin 1981, p. 109.) In the global conflict between East and West the King did not hesitate to declare himself to be on the side of 'freedom' and the 'free world'. This policy was designed to protect Jordan's independence and to provide the economic and technical assistance

233

necessary for the development of the country (Abudiah 1985, p. 147). However, Jordan has managed to enjoy good and respectable relations with almost all major and influential powers in the world. King Hussein's many visits to most of the important capitals in the last decade have helped to establish new types of relations between Jordan and those capitals.

Jordan has made ties with cultural, scientific, economic and humanitarian regional and international institutions. His Royal Highness Crown Prince Hassan devotes himself to these matters, whose importance must not be underestimated in the formulation of foreign policy. Decision makers are undoubtedly influenced by the views, writings, researches and opinions of reliable authorities in the different realms of knowledge. The King employs a number of methods to execute and implement foreign policy. Among these are:

- the institutions of the state, especially the Foreign Ministry and the Ministry of Information which should operate within the framework of ensuring Arab solidarity and Arab unity of action on the regional level, as well as non-alliance and close cooperation with friendly states on the international level;
- the armed forces, which constitute an important means of implementing regional policy in Jordan on two levels:

  1 protecting the state by deterring enemies and preventing them from carrying out harmful and embarrassing acts against the country; and on the same level, preparing to act as an integral part of the military Arab force for the defence of the Arab national interests and the liberation of the Palestinian occupied land;
  2 preparing to pay a regional role by helping out Jordan's natural allies in the area, the Gulf states;

- regional and international organizations;
- the sharing of power on an equal basis by both Jordanians and Palestinians in the legislative and executive authorities, a method which saved the country some of the social and political pressures Jordan faced in the past, especially after the Rabat summit in 1976.

It is noteworthy that until the mid-1950s the Jordanian armed forces were an expression of foreign policy in its antagonistic sense. Since then they have become a means of executing foreign policy in its defensive sense. Moreover, the Jordanian armed forces constitute a reliable asset that serves the common purpose of the regional and international interests of the country (Vatikiotis 1972, pp. 149–51).

Current problems and implications

The problems that still exist on the agenda of Jordan's foreign policy include the following:

- the Palestinian question in all its dimensions and implications;
- the restoration of the Arab order and Arab solidarity (which explains Jordan's relentless efforts to reconcile relations between Syria and Iraq);
- the Iraq–Iran War;
- a constant search for financial and technical support for Jordan's development programmes;
- the control of water resources and the attempt to develop these resources;
- facing unemployment by creating new chances for the Jordanian labour force in the oil-producing Arab countries, and exploring new markets for Jordanian exports;
- restructuring the economy and relieving the burdens of foreign debt;
- expanding and developing sources of energy.

Conclusion

Assessment of Jordan's foreign policy clearly shows that Jordan faces two types of problem: one type of a permanent nature, such as cooperation for development on the Arab and regional levels; the other, at least theoretically, of a temporary nature, such as the Palestinian issue which is both an old and a new issue.

A glance at Jordan's foreign policy shows vividly its relative but commendable success, especially if viewed against the background of Jordan's sociopolitical conditions, needs and resources. We can evaluate the success of Jordan's foreign policy on the following grounds.

1 The Kingdom enjoys stability in the midst of a regional atmosphere inflamed with struggle, competition and conflict.
2 Jordan is the only Arab country which maintains good and normal relations with other Arab countries, some of whom have tense relations with each other.
3 Jordan is the Arab party which through its mediation, efforts and initiatives has been able to prevent the Arab–Israeli conflict from

becoming a permanent fact. King Hussein has personally been able to revitalize the idea of the international conference, which is currently under discussion on a regional and international level after a lapse that lasted for nearly ten years.

4 Through its successive development plans, Jordan has attained a high rate of growth, higher than that of many Third World countries. The average individual income in Jordan had risen to over $2,000 per annum.

5 Jordan still enjoys a good international reputation for paying its debts. Apart from Saudi Arabia, all of Jordan's neighbouring countries are undergoing financial and economic difficulties, while Jordan, the country with the least resources, has avoided a real crisis.

To understand further the scope of the success of Jordan's foreign policy, we must bear in mind that Jordan is a small country of limited resources surrounded by countries with regional ambitions. Jordan is situated in an area of international power struggles. It belongs to a nation which has been historically torn by struggles against internal as well as external enemies. A third of the Palestinian population lives in Jordan and belongs to it. The Palestinian problem drags on and on and constitutes a potential threat to the peace and security in the area. The mere consideration of these political realities illustrates the delicacy of Jordanian foreign policy and its limitations, as well as the complicated avenues Jordan needs to take in order to execute such a policy.

Finally, if foreign policy for developing nations represents a symbol of self-growth the development, and if for the industrialized nations it is a means for the promotion and protection of their interests for Jordan it is the most important means for its existence, stability and prosperity. This reason is enough for King Hussein to act as the initiator, the administrator and the supervisor of Jordan's foreign policy, using his experience, wisdom and excellent personal relations to make the best of it on the regional and international levels.

References

Abu Odeh, H. E. A., Minister of the Royal Court (1986), 'Foreign policy in Jordan', a lecture at the Centre for Strategic Studies, University of Jordan, November.

Abudiah, S. (1985), *The Process of Decision Making in Jordan's Foreign Policy*, Department of Culture and Art, Amman.

Copeland, P. W. (1972), *The Land and People of Jordan*, J. P. Lippincatt, New York.

Al-Hussein, His Majesty King Hussein (1983), Speech delivered at the European Parliament at Strasbourg, Ministry of Information, Department of Press and Publicity, Amman.
—— (1985), Address to the Fortieth Session of the United Nations General Assembly, Ministry of Information, Department of Press and Publicity, Amman.
—— (1986), Address to the Fourth Regular Session of the Jordan Parliament. Ministry of Information, Department of Press and Publicity, Amman.
Khadduri, M. (1981), *The Hashemite House: Arab Personalities in Politics*, Middle East Institute, Washington, DC.
Al-Maranati, A. *et al.* (1971), 'The Hashemite Kingdom of Jordan', *The Middle East: its Governments and Politics*, Wordworth, New York.
Peretz, D. (1969), 'The Hashemite Kingdom of Jordan', *The Middle East Today*, Praeger, New York, pp. 354–7.
Terrill, W. A. (1985a), 'Jordan and the Defence of the Gulf', *Middle East Insight*, Vol. 4, No. 1, April.
—— (1985b), 'Saddam's closest ally, Jordan and the Gulf War', *Journal of South Asia and the Middle East Studies*, Vol. IX, No. 2, Winter.
Vatikiotis, P. J. (1966), *Politics and the Military in Jordan*, Praeger, New York.
—— (1972), *Inter Arab Relations: Politics in the Middle East*, Prentice Hall, London.

Index